FRAGILE URBAN GOVERNANCE

Fragile Urban Governance

Evolution, Decline, and Empowerment of Local Self-Government in India

GANGADHAR JHA

MANOHAR
2018

First published 2018

ISBN 978-81-935609-3-8

Published by
Ajay Kumar Jain *for*
Manohar Publishers & Distributors
4753/23 Ansari Road, Daryaganj
New Delhi 110 002

Typeset by
Kohli Print
Delhi 110 051

Printed at
Shri Ganpati Enterprises
Delhi 110 052

Contents

Preface

Urban local self-government (ULSG) constitutes the grassroot level of government that, unlike the higher levels of government, has close interface with the local communities. It is a level of government at the local level in urban areas that is, in true sense of the term, a government by the communities, of the communities and for the communities. This specific feature of local government, therefore, makes it highly communitarian. Because of its close proximity with the citizenry, it is said to be under intense public gaze of the local communities that is supposed to ensure local government accountability. It also provides a forum to the local communities to deliberate on problems confronting them and devise appropriate solutions keeping in view local situation, preferences and priorities. In recent years, the role of urban local self-government has acquired larger perspective. It is called upon to make cities and towns livable, enhance the quality of life of the urban population and by providing urban civic services and urban infrastructure efficiently, it enables the cities in attracting investment that fosters economic growth. Moreover, it serves as a nursery for imparting political education to the local populace in practice of democracy that enables the local political leaders graduate to higher levels of governments.

Development of local government in India has a long and somewhat chequered history. However, after Independence, the urban local governments declined. The decline was brought about because of a number of reasons, the most important being higher priority given, after Independence, to other critically important sectors as compared to urban governance and management of urban service delivery. In such a scheme of priorities as also a subdued level of urbanization in the years following Independence, ways and means for strengthening urban development sector in general and urban local self-government in particular, took a back seat.

Making local governance part of the List II (the State List) in the Seventh Schedule of the Indian Constitution over which the state governments have unfettered authority to legislate and take initiative for their strengthening and empowerment further contributed to its decline. Local self-governments—both urban and rural—became creatures of state governments. Even though it became part of the State List, the state governments became quite indifferent to the need for empowerment and strengthening its organizational capabilities. This made the urban local self-governments institutionally weak and fiscally fragile. There was also encroachment on traditional local functions by creating specific purpose authorities. Encroachment extended even to the sources of revenue that led to weak fiscal capability. Weak governance and unsatisfactory service delivery led to alienation of local citizenry that has a direct stake in effective functioning of local government institutions. Urban local self-governments became subject to myriad types of control by the state governments that more often resulted in dissolution of elected Councils and supersession without holding fresh elections for their reconstitution for a number of years. In certain instances, even for a number of decades. As a result, there was hardly any element of 'self-government'; after supersession, they, by and large, acted like any apolitical state government department under bureaucratic control.

Indifferent attitude of state governments towards empowerment and strengthening of urban local self-governments impelled the central government in the late 1980s to intervene for empowering them both in rural and urban areas. This thinking was reinforced by a worldwide wave of decentralization in the 1980s that swept the globe across developed, developing and transitional economies in Central Asia and Eastern Europe. Virtues of decentralization, devolution of planning, development and governance to the local self-governments led to a long debate in the literature on fiscal federalism and decentralization that as well influenced the official thinking for strengthening decentralization. The first generation theory (FGT) of fiscal federalism propounded by Wallace Oates in the early 1970s envisages provision of local public goods whose benefits are limited to the local government jurisdiction, by the local government only. It disaproves provision of a single and uniform public output in all jurisdictions by the central government. Provision of local public goods according to the demand and preferences of local jurisdiction, according to this view, maximizes social welfare. More the heterogeneity of choices with respect to locally provided services, more will be the welfare gains.[1] In case of services having spillover of benefits beyond the local area, the Decentralization Theorem of Oates advocates giving matching grants to the decentralized governments that will enable them internalization of benefits. In such a scheme of things, the fiscal federalism theory believes that decentralized governments will be in a position to pursue local welfare maximization by providing local public goods upto the point where marginal social benefits for the society as a whole equal marginal costs. Provision of services by the local self-governments thus enhances efficiency of service provision. The motive of public agencies for maximization of social welfare forms cardinal assumption of the fiscal federalism theory.

This assumption has been recently questioned after the advent of the social choice theory.[2] This theory argues that in place of maximization of social welfare, the public decision makers are mostly engaged in maximization of their own objective by maximization of budgets, enhancement of power and influence, large staff and higher salaries. Also, subsequent to the first generation of fiscal federalism, newer ideas crystallized that are collectively called the second generation of fiscal federalism.[3] The second generation theory (SGT) of fiscal federalism pleads that in the developing countries the institutional context and hence the structure of incentives are quite different and weak from the industrially advanced countries. Accordingly, the public agencies are not that benevolent to maximize social welfare. On the contrary, in a social choice environment, the public officials (the local government elected representatives) are engaged generally in maximization of their own objective—winning local elections.

Weingast, therefore, suggests designing institutional mechanisms such as (i) putting in place an inter-government transfer system that helps in correction of vertical and horizontal fiscal equity, designing fiscal incentives for promoting local economic prosperity through a mechanism of non-linear transfer system, (ii) adopting fiscal interest approach showing how different tax system produces different fiscal incentives for the political officials to choose appropriate policies for design of market, creating hard budget constraints and dealing with corruption. He also suggests warding off the tendency towards centralization that provides policy benefits to the central governments even in subverting democracy. Bardhan, after recounting the positive gains of decentralized governance, points to the institutional context and structure of incentives and organization in developing and transitional economies that necessitate going beyond the ambit of traditional fiscal federalism literature. He as well emphasizes the virtues of encouraging 'market preserving federalism'. This, according to him, provides the local governments incentives for local economic development and designing situational and fiscal mechanisms for putting in place a hard budget constraint. He cites example from China, where the local governments developed Township and Village Enterprise (TVE) that became engines of economic growth. It also provides an example of 'market preserving federalism'. Besides promoting local economic growth, TVEs helped local governments in enhancing their revenues. China also provided negative incentive to the local governments by denying bailout to TVEs. This helped in putting in place hard budget constraint. On the contrary, absence of incentive mechanisms for local governments in Russia could not lead to development of vibrant local business enterprises. Thus, decentralization in the context of developing and transitional economies entails that the local governments need to be engaged in service delivery and also in development of 'market preserving federalism'. This requires devolving more powers to the local governments who should have more information for the provision of varieties of local service to the local communities and incentives for promoting local economic development.

In addition to the above, benefits of decentralization is ineluctably dependent on a strong system of accountability and participatory governance that provide local communities a space to participate. Local governments will need to be accountable for the decisions taken by them. This will also enhance transparency in the operations of local government. The existing power structure in developing countries, however, acts as hindrance to inclusive provision of local public services as there is often found to be a tendency amongst the local power elites to capture power and influence local government policies in favour of their own class. Effective decentralization, therefore, must also involve changing the existing power structure within the communities, improving opportunities for participation and voice and engaging the hitherto disadvantaged or disenfranchised in the local political process.[4] Questioning the basic assumption of FGT and development of SGT, it needs to be emphasized, has not discarded the virtues of decentralization. SGT simply complements the former by flagging newer dimensions involved in designing a scheme of decentralization. The case for decentralization got further boost from the Principle of Subsidiarity and the Local Government Charter adopted by the European Union in 1985.

Besides the above discussed benefits of decentralization, there is yet another aspect of it that provides strong motivation for decentralization, empowerment and strengthening of urban local self-governments in the country. The process of urbanization results in addition of substantial number of urban population. Increases in urban population create additional demand for urban services and infrastructure provided by the local self-governments. Since 1901, urban population has increased from about 25.86 million in 1901 to about 377.1 million in 2011. This indicates that the urban population has increased by about more than 14 times. The decadal growth rate of urban population has increased to 38.82 per cent in 2011 from 28.6 per cent in 2001. For the first time since Independence, the absolute increase in population is more in urban areas than in rural areas. According to the 2011 Census, the total urban population of about 377 million lives in as many as 7,935 towns. This increased from 5,161 towns in 2001. Of the total number of towns, the number of statutory towns increased from 3,799 in 2001 to 4041. In addition to the statutory towns there are 3,894 Census towns that do not have any form of urban local government. The number of these towns has increased from 1,362 in 2001 indicating an increase of 2,532 new Census Towns in

2011. The Census Towns require a modicum of basic urban services that are non-existent in these towns. Also, urban population in some of the states is close to 50 per cent of the total population that points to the traditional saying that 'India lives in villages' becoming a myth. The pace and scale of urbanization is also becoming a compelling reason for strengthening decentralization and organizational capacity of ULSGs.

A wave of decentralization that swept developed, developing and transitional economies across the globe after the 1980s as also the implications of rapid increase in urban population, led to thinking amongst the policy makers in the country to decentralize planning, development, and services provision to the sub-nationals—the local self-governments. As the states in the past could not take affirmative action in empowering and strengthening of local self-governments under the framework of the different municipal Acts in different states,—both rural and urban—the central government took a bold decision to provide for empowerment of local self-government in the Constitution of India itself by amending the Constitution. After a long drawn debate and generation of high voltage political heat in the Indian Parliament over the enactment of the original 65th Constitution Amendment Bill in 1989, finally the Parliament enacted the Constitution (74th Amendment) Act in 1992. This created a hype about its efficacy in empowerment and strengthening of urban and rural local self-governments. It was hailed as the harbinger of a new era of empowered and strengthened institutions of local self-government.

High expectations about the Constitution (74th Amendment) Act, 1992, however, could not be sustained over the years. Experience of its implementation (74 CAA) in more than a couple of decades of its enactment has led to disillusionment. No doubt, the 74th CAA has led to empowerment of weaker sections of the local communities for countering the issue of local elites capturing power in ULSGs—one of the concerns of the SFT. It has granted the ULSGs a constitutional right to exist by qualified withdrawal of provision for their dissolution and supersession. It has also rationalized the hitherto ad-hoc fiscal transfers by bringing local governments within the purview of the State Finance Comissions, and the central Finance Commission by amending the terms of reference of the latter—yet another concern of the SFT for designing inter-government transfers.

A close look at the 74th CAA and its aftermath, however, indicates striking gaps at three levels. At the first level, looking back at the constitutional provisions in Part IXA of the Constitution, two things come to mind. First, the provisions relating to building of institutions such as structures for intra-city decentralization, participation, urban planning, District Planning Committee, Metropolitan Planning, Municipal Functional Domain were diluted in the final enactment of the original 65th Constitution Amendment Bill that was qualitatively different from the finally enacted 74th Constitution Amendment Act. Second, the 74th Constitution Amendment Act itself has gaps, some of which are quite conspicuous. Examples are absence of provisions with respect to executive system in the urban local self-governments as is provided for in the higher levels of government; non-existence of provisions relating to the sources of revenue; constitution and composition of Wards or Ward Committees; clarity about local fiscal domain, and conceiving urban planning process in two water tight compartments of rural and urban local governments. Such an isolated planning process for rural and urban self-government is not in a position to address common planning issues transcending these two sets of local governments. It is also silent about what happens after the plans prepared by the Panchayats and the Municipalities are finally consolidated by the District Planning Committee. There are problems also with respect to the fate of District Planning Committee that is created within a jurisdiction of Metropolitan Planning Committee constituted in metropolitan areas. The metropolitan areas consist of urban and rural areas as well. Above all, the abolition of the Planning Commission by the new government that came to power at the centre in 2014, has led to uncertainties about planning itself.

These gaps in the 74th Constitution Amendment Act apart, the laws enacted in the different states that have an interface with urban governance, were required to be brought in conformity with the new constitutional provisions. At the second level, the conformity legislations enacted after the 74th CAA as well have several gaps. This second level of gaps in the state conformity legislations are exacerbated by gaps, at the third level, in implementation. It is curious that even some of the obligatory provisions of the Indian Constitution have not yet been implemented despite so much time has elapsed after enactment of the 74th CAA. The result is obvious. Empowerment and strengthening of urban local self-government remain elusive despite an amendment brought about in the Constitution. What could be the reasons for this? Is it because of gaps in the scheme of empowerment and strengthening that were put forth in the Constitution and in the conformity legislations in the various states? Or, is it because some of the constitutional provisions are not implementable? Or, is it because the state governments lack the will for empowerment of local government?

The issues for empowerment and strengthening local government have acquired critical importance because the traditional and popular saying that India lives in villages is proving to be a myth. A much more vibrant, literate, and even a volatile urban India is emerging that demands effective, efficient, inclusive and responsive urban local self-government. If the issues in empowerment and strengthening urban governance are not addressed suitably, lack of capability and empowerment is likely to undermine the very stability of cities that happen to be the engines of economic growth. It will adversely affect the national growth initiatives because the fate of national economy is now largely contingent on what happens to the cities that contributes to the extent of about 70 per cent of the GDP. The central government itself now has much more stake in effective urban governance because several urban sector programmes have been launched by it with huge budgetary allocation. Efficient use of these resources is ineluctably dependent on strong administrative capability of urban local self-governments. Development of 100 smart cities itself requires that both the urban local self-government and the citizens residing within local urban areas are 'smart'.

Empowerment, even if the initiative for this is made effective and sound, is unlikely to enable the urban local self-governments in effective, equitable and responsive delivery of urban services and provision of much needed urban infrastructure for economic growth. Besides empowerment, the urban local self-governments need a strategy for strengthening of their organizational capability which requires focused capacity development initiatives. The urban local self-governments are crumbling under the weight of a maze of urban sector programmes and missions launched by the central government and the state governments' own project largely because of weak organizational capability. Perennial fiscal stress, shortage of adequate number of staff that is qualified and skilled, freeze on recruitment of new staff in most of the states, absence of modernized recruitment rules, old and antiquated organizational structure that is not amenable to performance of emerging municipal functions, absence of performance management mechanisms, work culture, lack of need-based training and participatory approach to local governance do not permit them to be pro-active and capable of addressing the challenges emanating from the process of urbanization and urban growth.

The present volume is devoted to an analysis of development and subsequent decline of the institutions of urban local self-governments in India, the initiatives taken for their empowerment and strengthening especially the big-bang decentralization initiative through an amendment of the Constitution of India, gaps in these initiatives, and a fragile organizational capacity of the urban local self-governments that does not enable them in effective performance of the functions mandated to them. It also stresses to put in place a framework of action that must be taken for enabling them to function as an effective level of government in urban areas. It also raises issues in empowerment and strengthening of urban governance. Hopefully, it will prove useful for policy makers, practitioners and students of urban governance, public administration, and urban management.

GANGADHAR JHA

NOTES

1. Wallace E. Oates, 1972, *Fiscal Federalism*, New York: Harcourt Brace Jovanovich.
2. G. Brennan and J.M. Buchanan, 1980, *The Power to Tax: Analytical Foundations of a Fiscal Constitution*, Cambridge: Cambridge University Press.
3. Wallace E. Oates, 2005, 'Towards a Second-Generation Theory of Fiscal Federalism', *International Tax and Public Finance* 12, pp. 349-73; Pranab K. Bardhan, 2002, 'Decentralizatiion and Governance', *Journal of Economic Perspectives*, 16(4), pp. 185-205; Barry R. Weingast, 2014, 'Second Generation Fiscal Federalism: Implication for Decentralized Governance and Economic Development', *World Development*, 53, pp. 14-25.
4. Bardhan, op. cit.

Acknowledgements

This book, in a way, is an outcome of my long years of interest in urban sector and local self-government especially the urban local 'self-governments' that have been struggling to keep pace with the demand for urban services and urban infrastructure. Decline in the institutions of urban local self-government and enactment of the Constitution (74th Amendment) Act, 1992 for addressing this decline provided additional motivation to me for writing this book. The motivation was driven largely by a paper I wrote on this subject immediately after the enactment of this historic Constitution Amendment Act. The paper was a critique of this milestone decentralization initiative. Publication of this paper in a journal led to an interesting debate on the things I had written on this subject. In the last twenty-five years after publication of this paper, most of the stuff written in this paper, however, has been supported by the operational experience of this decentralization initiative. Therefore, for long, a lot of my friends, colleagues and well-wishers have been coaxing me to write on this subject expansively. I am grateful to all of them for motivating and even provoking me to write this book.

First of all, I am grateful to Professor Mohit Bhattacharya, initially my senior colleague at the Indian Institute of Public Administration (IIPA), New Delhi, subsequently a Centenary Professor of Political Science at the Calcutta University and later on the Vice-Chancellor of the Burdwan University for a decade who had been cajoling me on a continuous basis to write the book. I, therefore, owe to Mohit Babu my motivation to write this book. Professor Abhijit Datta, yet another senior colleague at the Centre for Urban Studies of the IIPA, was a storehouse of knowledge on local government and local government finance. I gained much of the insights into nuances of governance, its role, structure and working of local government in India and abroad from him. I am indebted to him for this that aroused in me an interest to write on urban local government and decentralization. I am also thankful to Ashwajit Singh, Vice-Chairman and Managing Director of IPE Global—an international consultancy organization. Upon his continued persistence I joined IPE by taking voluntary retirement from the National Institute of Urban Affairs, New Delhi where as a Professor I was engaged in urban sector training, research and consultancy. Working with IPE gave me an opportunity to closely look at local governance, decentralization and service delivery in action and learn about these by working with urban local self-governments in the various urban sector consultancy projects supported by inter-national donor agencies in India and in a number of countries abroad. I am appreciative of Ashwajit in giving me opportunity for consolidating my knowledge about local governments, impediments faced by them and the systems, procedures and mechanism devised by governments for local governance in some of the countries I worked.

The latent motivation for long to write on decentralization and urban local self-government that was aroused by Mohit Babu got a boost from Sunil Koul, my friend and colleague I was working with in a World Bank supported project for the Ministry of Urban Development now renamed as Ministry of Housing and Urban Affairs. I am thankful to him for repeated insistence to write on this subject. In fact, he made me start scribbling the first chapter of this book while working with him. I am extremely grateful to him for persistently motivating me to write on this subject. Serious analytical writing requires an appropriate and enabling ecology that provides an environment and opportunity to brainstorm on subtle aspects and nuances of decentralization and urban governance. I am thankful to Hitesh Vaidya, initially my associate in an Indo-USAID project and subsequently my close friend and colleague, now country Manager, UN-HABITAT, India. He, in a way provided the required ecology to debate the various issues in decentralization in general and the 74th Constitution Amendment in particular. He ungrudgingly engaged in brainstorming on important aspects of decentralization in the context of the 74th Constitution Amendment and its working or not working and the reasons thereof whenever I wanted to discuss these with him. Professor H.M. Mishra, the founding Director of the National Institute of Urban Governance and Management, Bhopal has been a source of unrestrained support. He has been instrumental in enabling me sharpen my insights about urban governance. I am thankful to him for the frequent long debates we had on various aspects of urban local governance when we were drafting the proposed new unified municipal law for the state of Madhya Pradesh from which I benefitted immensely.

My thanks are also due to M.P. Sharma, former Chief Commissioner of Income Tax and a practicing lawyer in the Delhi High Court who had a long stint with the erstwhile Municipal Corporation of Delhi as Financial Adviser. He proved to be a valuable source of knowledge on legal aspects of municipal governance and the 74th Constitution Amendment Act. At times I had to turn to him on constitutional history of local government especially during the colonial rule and clarifying contemporary issues in urban governance that have close interface with law. His advice and suggestions on municipal administration and legal aspects involved in it helped me in clarifying some of the legal issues and practices in decentralization.

Dr. Payel Sen, former Head of the Department of Political Science, the West Bengal State University, Kolkata, has been yet another source of strength with whom I not only discussed my thoughts on decentralization and urban governance but who also went through some of the preliminary draft chapters of this volume and offered useful suggestions. Her insights and suggestions on various aspects of urban local governance, operational experience of decentralization especially in the state of West Bengal, helped me in firming up my views while writing this book. I am immensely grateful to her for the valuable support and creative ideas she provided to me. I am also thankful to Nimisha, my daughter who has been working on climate change, resilient cities and impact of privatization and outsourcing on urban local governance, for her valuable support and ideas on urban governance. I depended on her to a great extent in surfing the internet and exploring the references on the subject. My thanks are also due to a large number of friends especially Chetan Vaidya, the former Director, School of Planning and Architecture, Delhi and many others for their valuable support, encouragement and inspiration to make the publication of this book a reality. Finally, I am extremely grateful to Mr. Ramesh Jain and Mr. Siddharth Chowdhury of Manohar Publishers & Distributors for their professional diligence in seeing the volume through to the press.

Valuable support and help provided by my friends and colleagues notwithstanding, I am alone responsible for deficiencies and gaps, if any, in this book.

GANGADHAR JHA

CHAPTER 1

Urban Local Self-Government: Its Role and Evolution

Cities in history have been centres of far-reaching economic innovations, productive activities, art, culture, trade and commerce. They have been cradles of many civilizations since the ancient times. The life and times of the Harappan cities in the middle of the third millennium BC and the ancient Greece are even now frequently referred to with nostalgia. Socio-economic and politico-cultural roles of cities have remained intact over time both in medieval and modern India. Though India is said to 'live in villages' with agriculture as the main support system, the cities and towns, it needs to be appreciated, contribute about 70 per cent of the Gross Domestic Product (GDP) of India.

Since time immemorial, large populations in absolute terms, high population density and sprawling physical areas have constituted some of the specific features of urban settlements. These specific characteristics of urban settlements became persuasive reasons to innovate institutional mechanism for governance and delivery of services that could be specific to the obtaining situation. Political theory gives evidence of this mechanism in terms of the Social Contract Theory that was conceptualized and developed by genius of the trinity of political thinkers Hobbes, Locke and Rousseau who in the eighteenth century questioned the relevance of the then prevailing Divine Origin Theory of state. The Social Contract Theory is credited with giving an explanation to the origin of the state and the civil society for governance with adequate checks and balances. Even before this, Kautilya's *Arthashastra* dating back to 300 BC as well contained ingeniously conceived tenets of statecraft and governance. Governance of urban settlements also found its expression in the European tradition of 'self-governing city' propounded in ancient Greece. This was revived in the Middle Ages by creation of chartered corporations and 'free cities' and was renewed subsequently by 'civic improvement' campaign in the nineteenth century. During the colonial rule in America, the Americans as well got an impetus from the colonists' campaign for 'municipio libre', i.e. the Home Rule. This has continued to be the guiding force for creating institutions of local self-government in towns and cities in the United States of America.

In our own country—India, institutional arrangement for urban governance evolved, crystallized, and was refined during the Mughal rule, the subsequent Company rule, the Colonial rule and in the independent India. However, for the first time, an organized system of urban government was introduced by Lord Ripon on 18 May 1882 through the famous Ripon Resolution. The basic objective of the Ripon Resolution was to promote the growth of responsible local government for imparting political education to the native Indians. Lord Ripon's efforts were subsequently reviewed, refined and strengthened by the Royal Commission on Decentralization in 1907, and the famous Montague-Chelmsford Reforms of 1919.

WHY LOCAL GOVERNMENT?

The Constitution of India already provides for a federal structure consisting of central and state governments for which it contains elaborate provisions that help the polity in the fulfilment of the aspirations of the people for social and economic growth and the quality of life. Why then should there be a need for local government? The virtue of local self-government and its institutions whether rural or urban, lies in its closest interface with the local citizenry. Importance of local self-government is best reflected in a dispatch sent by the British Secretary of State to the African Governors in as far back as 1947 (Her Majesty's Government 1947). It emphasized that the key to success lies in the development of an 'efficient and democratic system of local government'. It laid stress on expressions such as (i) local, (ii) efficient, and (iii) democratic.

The system of government has to be 'local' especially because it must be close to the common people and solve their problems. It should be 'efficient' because it must be capable of managing local services in a way that could help to raise the standard of living and the quality of life of the local citizenry. It must also need to be 'democratic' because it must find a place not only for the growing class of educated men, but should also command the respect and support of the mass of the people. Local government is the only level of government which is communitarian. Of the three levels of government—national, state, and local—the local self-governments and its institutions[1] are the only level of government that is not only closest to the local communities but also happens to be a level of government that is of the communities, for the communities and by the communities in true sense of the term. Being located closest to the local communities, as compared to the other levels of governments, it is better placed to have knowledge about the nature of local problems and formulate an appropriate strategy for resolution of these problems. It serves as a forum for the local communities to deliberate on their own problems and, through consensus, devise realistic solutions that is in conformity with the realities of the local situation.

PRINCIPLES OF LOCAL SELF-GOVERNMENT

A number of principles have guided the creation of local government since time immemorial. Principle of local self-government constitutes the cornerstone of the European Union. The Charter of Local Self-Government has been adopted by the member countries of the European Union especially for achieving a broader goal of unity between its members. Local self-government is deemed by the European Union as a mechanism for safeguarding and realizing ideals and principles which constitute the common heritage of the member countries of the European Union. The Charter of Local Self-Government has placed local self-government at the centre stage (European Union 1985). In its Preamble, the Charter of Local Self-Government (Annex 1) alludes to the principles some of which are mentioned below:

- Local governments as a foundation of democratic regime;
- Right of citizens to participate in the conduct of public affairs is one of the democratic principles that are shared by all member States of the Council of Europe and it is at the local level that this right can be most directly exercised;
- Safeguarding and reinforcement of local self-government in the different European countries is an important contribution to the construction of a Europe based on the principles of democracy and decentralization of power;
- Existence of local authorities with real responsibilities can provide an administration which is both effective and close to the citizen;
- Local self-government is best amenable for exercise of democratic principle of citizens' right to participate in the conduct of public affairs; and
- Local government as a means of effective public administration, decentralization and power.

These principles contained in the European Charter of Local Government have not only helped create local governments in Europe but is extremely important for constituting communitarian local self-government in any society. This communitarian character of local self-government and the close proximity between the governments and the citizens also brings it under an intense public gauge that is instrumental in improving local government accountability and transparency in governance. Principles of local government mentioned above and the virtues of local government contained extensively in the history of political thought, are primarily guided by its attribute of having the closest interface between the government and the citizens. It is obvious from the European Charter of Local Self-Government that the basic principles contained in its Preamble eulogizes citizens' right to participate in the conduct of public affairs. It constitutes the basic democratic principle and that this basic right can be directly exercised only in the local government. It observes that existence of local authorities with real responsibilities can provide an administration which is both effective and close to the citizen.

ROLE OF LOCAL GOVERNMENT

The role of local self-government institutions is so pervasive and the services provided by them is so close to the daily lives of the local communities that it is said to care for the local citizenry from the 'cradle to the grave'. The role of local government needs to be seen in the context of its proximity with local communities—an attribute not to be found with respect to higher levels of government. Being located closer to the local communities, it is better placed to adopt plans and programmes within the specific context of local realities and local aspirations. In South Africa, the new Constitution of 1996 in its chapter on local government (Chapter 7) embodies a system of cooperative federalism by designating local government as one of the three 'spheres' of government, it provides for functions of local government that include (i) providing democratic and accountable government for local communities, (ii) ensuring provision of services in sustainable manner, (iii) promoting social and economic development, (iv) promoting safe and healthy environment, and (v) encouraging involvement of communities and community based organizations in local government affairs.

The role of local government also needs to be viewed in the context of changing socio-economic and technological situations. Changes in technological, social and economic conditions require the local governments to create conditions for enhancing competiveness of urban centres. The urban local self-government plays varied role that can be grouped into (i) enhancing economic efficiency and economic growth of urban settlements through strategic planning and provision of urban infrastructure, (ii) promoting social development by integrating together various fabrics of social and cultural life, (iii) promoting a sound tradition of democratic way of life at the 'grass-root' level, and (iv) playing a stabilizing role in the economy through cautious fiscal management.

ECONOMIC EFFICIENCY

The institutions of local self-government help in enhancing economic efficiency by providing basic urban services according to local preferences. Being located closest to the local citizenry, local government is better placed to bring about adjustments in its budgets to provide a bundle of services that corresponds to the preference of the local communities. Conceptual perspectives on the local government jurisdiction entail economic efficiency gains emanating from nature and extent of local government jurisdiction. These include postulates of the social choice theory, principle of fiscal equivalence and voting with one's feet. Provision of local government services within the benefit area and its overlapping with the benefit area (fiscal equivalence) enables equation of marginal cost and marginal benefits which enhances economic efficiency and contributes to optimal provision of public services (Shah and Shah 2006; Olson 1969; Oates 2005). Principle of fiscal federalism also alludes to proximity of local government and users of its services and the devolved local fiscal tools for financing of services that encourages fiscal responsibility and efficiency (Oates 1972). Tiebout argued that larger the number of local government jurisdictions especially in a metro area and greater the variety in quality and quantity of service provision amongst them, the closer the consumer will come to fully realizing his preference (Tiebout 1956). In such a situation, consumer voter chooses a local government jurisdiction whose tax and public expenditure patterns are in accordance with preference function of the consumer of local government services. Thus 'voting with feet' contributes to formation of jurisdictions that create market like situation for service provision and hence enhances economic efficiency.

LOCAL ECONOMIC DEVELOPMENT

Cities and towns have been centres of economic activities. They are said to be engines of economic development and growth. As mentioned earlier, urban settlements in India already contribute about 70 per cent of the Gross Domestic Product (GDP). A World Bank strategy paper observes that in the low income countries, urban areas account for about 55 per cent of the Gross National Product (GNP), about 73 per cent in middle income countries, and about 85 per cent in high income countries (World Bank

1999). This is largely because of a high productivity brought about by urban agglomeration economies that create an economic environment of mutual support and synergy amongst a variety of economic activities and availability of urban infrastructure. These become instrumental in attracting a host of economic activities to the urban space. It contributes to creation of employment and generation of income for the city dwellers and hence for the national economy. Institutions of local self-government need to enhance the competitive ability of cities by augmenting urban infrastructure and services for making the cities livable and attractive for investments. The New Economic Policy adopted in the 1980s through its liberalization, globalization and a series of financial sector reforms led to a spurt in investments in industries and trade. Most of these have happened in the cities. Globalization in particular, has brought about an unprecedented growth in international financial flows that is uninhibited by national boundaries. It has contributed to international flows of ideas and knowledge, and closer economic integration of countries through increased flow of goods and services, capital and even labour. It is hoped that it will raise the level of living standards throughout the world, provide especially to the poor countries an access to overseas markets and allow foreign investments (Stiglitz 2006). In the wake of globalization, nations across the globe are compelled to go through structural adjustments for enhancing national competitive abilities, global trade and foreign direct investments (Rabinovitch 1999). Cities are now competing amongst themselves especially in western and southern parts of the country to attract private and foreign direct investments. This is primarily driven by rich urban infrastructure and the quality of life articulated by the institutions of local self-government. The urban local self-government institutions are required to create and enhance conditions for attracting investments and contributing to the economic development initiatives at local, state, and national levels. Effective urban governance thus enhances economic role of cities by augmenting the level of urban infrastructure, which in turn creates conducive conditions for attracting investments—both private and public. Added investments contribute to creation of opportunities for generation of employment and income that in turn feeds to revenue generating opportunities for local governments (buoyancy in local government revenue).

Thus, provision of urban services and urban infrastructure creates conditions in urban centres for attracting investments and supporting economic development activities. Obviously, urban sector performs a significant economic role in national economic development. It is because of remarkable productivity of cities that it contributes to national economic growth. It is, therefore, said that the future of national economies is crucially dependent on what happens to the cities. A noticeable feature of urbanisation the world over is that urban agglomerations have proved to be a pre-requisite for industrialization.[2] Urbanization brings about concentration of people and economic activities in cities that articulate high density of people and of firms in urban space. Such a process promotes economic efficiency through spillover of information amongst producers, efficient functioning of labour markets and savings in transportation costs (Henderson 2000). By virtue of such a catalytic process, cities are increasingly assuming a leadership role especially in a globalized regime by attracting investments and harnessing human and technical resources for achieving unprecedented growth in productivity and competitiveness (UN-HABITAT 2002). This is corroborated by global evidence of economic efficiency of cities.[3]

Effective urban governance by the urban local self-government thus plays a catalytic role in increasing the pace of national economic development. Special attention is, therefore, required for developing institutional capacity of urban local self-government especially in India's small and medium towns which are inadequately served with urban infrastructure and services. This is important also because when these urban settlements graduate to higher size categories of towns, they are physically not prepared to bear the strains of growth. This inevitably leads to coming up of slums, squalor, unauthorized colonies and new sub-standard growth that are devoid of the barest necessities of life. Mistake of unregulated growth and deficient service levels involve prohibitive financial, economic, and social cost later on.

SOCIAL DEVELOPMENT

'Social overhead' such as elementary education, public health, welfare services, community development, empowerment of weaker sections of the society and the facilities to enjoy leisure constitute functions being performed by the local government. Performance of these functions goes a long way in promoting social development. Rapid pace of urbanization and urban growth has its toll on the quality of local environment which the urban local governments are called upon to conserve and protect for ensuring better living. Efficiency and effectiveness of environmental services provided by local governments and the quality of these services positively contribute to improvement of urban environment. Being highly communitarian form of government, a people centred approach to resolve local problems by them promotes social justice. Endowed with bottom up approach and equally a bottom up structure makes local government better positioned to contain discontent and mobilize available local energy and skills for promoting grassroot level social and economic development (Kothari 1999).

An important dimension of urban local self-government especially in the context of exploding urbanization and urban growth brought about by migration is to create conditions for sociocultural adaptation of migrants flocking to the cities.

DEMOCRATIC IDEAL

Local self-governments are located at the cutting edge level as compared to the state and the central governments. Interaction of local self-governments with the local citizens and the users of local services is most intense. This close proximity with the users of services, nevertheless, enables them to have a better feel of local needs. This helps the local communities in solving their local problems according to their own priorities and programmers. Local action, initiative, and drive make local plans and schemes more realistic. It is because of these virtues characterizing the local self-governments that several political thinkers such as James Mill, J.S.

Mill, Bryce, Dicey, Montesquieu, Tocqueville, Laski and others have espoused its cause and advocated its usefulness. Located nearest to the local communities also makes local government subject to intense public gaze of the civil society. This goes a long way in promoting local government accountability and transparency. Local action, initiative, drive and enthusiasm make local plans more realistic and in proper relationship with local needs as well as circumstances. Involvement of local populace in the local government activities imparts them experience for participation in governance at higher levels. J.S. Mill, in particular, liked the local government as it develops the best citizenry. He thought it to be a readier method of education in public affairs (Chester 1951). Local self-governments happen to be valuable nurseries that impart political education in democracy to the local leaders. There are myriad examples of how this has helped local leaders in graduating to higher levels of governments for handling public affairs. Lord Bryce, having surveyed experiences of several countries, concluded that local self-government constitutes the best for education in democracy and the best guarantee for its success. It creates amongst citizens a sense of their common interest in common affairs and also common duty that these are efficiently and honestly administered.

Diffusion of political power and executive decision is an essential ingredient of a welfare state. Local governments are important instruments in this regard. A well organized system of local government is much likely to preserve and strengthen qualities of local initiative, civic pride, and public spirit. It also inculcates a sense of community on which a genuine democracy must rest (Robson 1966). Literature on virtue of local self-government also refers to local self-government as effective weapon for channelling local pressure, articulating and aggregating local interest that may not necessarily coincide with the ideas of central government (Meenakshisundaram 1999).

FISCAL AND ECONOMIC STABILIZATION ROLE

Though Musgrave's celebrated 'Multiple Theory of Public Household' envisages separate treatment of public want satisfaction under

'Allocation Branch', income redistribution through taxes and transfers under 'Distribution Branch', and stabilization of economy under 'Stabilization Branch' (Musgrave 1959), this normative concept, in certain conditions, holds good even for performance of stabilization goals at the local level by the local self-governments as well. Oates, for example, believes that there exists 'some modest scope for decentralized government to play a supportive role in redistributive and macroeconomic policy' (Oates 2005). This role, however, has to be seen in the context of constraints such as lack of power with the local government for creation of money, and limitations on borrowing. This precludes the local self-governments from incurring of expenditure during depression and vice versa. Also, recurring nature of municipal expenditures and spillover of benefits to other local government jurisdictions constrain the performance of this role. Even with these constraints, local governments have enough scope for manoeuvring their finances strictly in accordance with the avowed fiscal goals of the national government (Jha 1988). By contributing to reducing the overall public sector deficit, the local governments need to avoid soft budget constraints (Ebel and Vaillancourt 2001).

Fiscal policy entails accomplishment of national goals without too much of fluctuations. This is inevitably dependent on managing spending, taxation and borrowings such that it contributes to an expansion and stability of the national economy. During the great depression in the last century, local governments in the United States of America were found to be 'fiscally perverse' as they cut back expenditures and increased taxes in the down turn and behaving just in the opposite fashion during economic boom (Hansen and Perloff 1945). Revenues and expenditures of the local governments taken together constitute a sizeable financial resource at the national level which, if properly regulated according to national objective of macro-economic management, can re-enforce the impact of national monetary policy. It is worth quoting Hansen and Perloff in this regard: 'ideally, it would be desirable if the state and local governments could reinforce the federal government and follow a counter cyclical policy involving flexible spending, borrowing and tax programmers'.

Economic stabilization role of local governments seems even more striking as an anti-inflationary measure on the revenue side. Strains of rapid development generate inflationary trends especially in developing economies because of bottlenecks and inelasticities. Local self-governments could take out additional resources through levy of taxes especially on the wealthier sections of service users. Likewise, they can generate expansionary movements through scaling up public works during deflation. Thus, by appropriately regulating and integrating their fiscal operations with national policy objectives, local governments have enough space for contributing to macroeconomic management initiatives of the central government.

The foregoing analysis of the role of local self-government thus brings out their varied role into sharp focus. Global experience of devolution of authority to the sub-national governments as well reveals that the wave of decentralization that ensued in the 1980s, swept several economies across the globe due to a variety of motivations. These included improved economic efficiency and accountability, increased resource mobilization (Campbell and Brakarz 1991), more equitable and efficient service delivery through better use of local knowledge, improved governance driven by local responsiveness and political participation, allocation efficiency in terms of improved welfare, political stability, stable finances, and reduced strain on finances of the higher levels of governments (Bird and Vaillancourt 1998). Decentralization of decision-making for planning and development of local government areas, however, is critically contingent on the extent and the nature of fiscal decentralization. Whereas deepening of democracy at the local level due to decentralization promotes transparency and accountability in the local decision-making process, fiscal decentralization prevents 'tax exporting' and facilitates funding at the margin through fiscal transfers from the higher levels of government. It also promotes accountability of the decision makers to fully bear the cost of decisions taken by them.

Countries across the globe—developed, developing and transitional—have been swept by decentralization in the recent decades. Developed countries are taking fresh looks in re-designing intergovernment fiscal relations in the wake of globalization and decentralization to the markets. Developing countries as well are engaged in decentralising governance and tax authority for enhancing national economic development and improving the quality of life of their citizens (Owens and Panella 1991). The transitional economies, in particular, constitute an interesting example of decentralization in varying forms and degree after the demise of centrally planned economies (Hovrath 2000; Peteri 2002; Martinez-Vazaquez and McNab 1997).

However, analysis of development of urban local self-government after Independence has revealed both a decline in their institutional capacity as also weakening of the bold initiative taken towards closing years of the last century. The analysis has also revealed far-reaching role that the local self-governments have to play. They are presently not in a position to perform these roles as they lack in institutional capacity to do so (discussed in Chapter 8 in detail). Urban local self-government, therefore, needs to be strengthened and empowered as the third tier of government at the local level. Although the 74th CAA was especially enacted to this end in view, it has not yielded the desired results especially, among other things, for three reasons. First, the 74th CAA itself has certain gaps that minimized its efficacy in strengthening of urban local self-government. Second, enactment of the 74th CAA required putting in place basic instrumentalities of governance in terms of functions, funds, staffing, organizational structure, performance management system, human resource development initiatives, and institutional incentives. These have been conspicuously lacking. Third, the state governments, by and large, seems to be lukewarm in effectively implementing the 74th CAA and strengthening of local self-government. These issues are specifically dealt with in the subsequent chapters.

EVOLUTION OF URBAN LOCAL SELF-GOVERNMENT IN INDIA

Urban local self-government in India has evolved since ancient times with a chequered history of occasional glory, decline and refurbishment. Glancing over the history of development of local government in India imparts valuable knowledge and insights into varying roles assigned to the urban local self-government over the centuries that kept on changing with changes in the obtaining socio-economic nd political situations over different times. An interesting feature development of local government especially during the colonial was that the role to be performed by the local government was ed on a sustained basis with frequent changes in the role to gned to them. It also shows that the initiatives taken for nent of local government during the colonial rule were also accompanied by important thinking on the role to be played by local government. History of development of local government during the British rule, therefore, depicts a sustained debate on the role of local government. The thinking during this debate primarily oscillated around two pivotal roles to be played by the local government such as (i) promoting administrative efficiency, and (ii) acting as a nursery of democracy for imparting training to the local politicians in managing public affairs. Public policy during the British rule depicts that the choice for adopting one of these two roles for the local governments depended on political ideology and administrative insights of the then policy makers.

The type of urban local government to be constituted in ancient India was not very different from the existing typology of urban local self-government in different size categories of cities and towns. In ancient India as well, different types of local government were created in different types of urban settlements that were largely guided by the variation in the scale of functions to be performed by the urban settlements of different size categories. State capitals and larger towns had a differentiated type of local government as compared to smaller towns. By and large, governance of urban areas was vested in a state appointed official called the 'City Superintendent' (Venkatarangaiya and Pattabhiraman 1969). Kautilya in his magnum opus—*Arthashastra,* that contains tenets of statecraft and political economy—gives an account of governance of urban areas in ancient India, though it does not describe the structure of urban local government prevailing in those days. The *Arthashastra,* nevertheless, enumerates functions and responsibilities of City Superintendent that were different from the contemporary general municipal functions that is centred around the provision of basic civic services and urban infrastructure. The functions that were performed under the aegis of the City Superintendent were mostly in the nature of regulatory functions including performance of functions relating to law and order (Kautilya's *Arthashastra* as translated by Shastri 1967). A glimpse of urban local government structure is also found in the writings of Megasthenese, an ambassador sent by the Greek emperor Seleucus to the court of the Mauryan emperor, Chandra Gupta, around the year 300 BC. Writing about the local government structure then obtaining in the city of Patliputra (contemporary Patna), he describes the city having divided into bodies that were looking after industrial arts, entertainment of foreigners, births and deaths, trade and commerce, and manufacture of articles as well as its sale through government notice (Venkatarangaiya and Pattabhiraman op. cit.). The observations of Megasthenese on local government in Patliputra are quoted below:

> . . . the city is divided into six bodies of five each. The members of the first look after everything relating to the industrial arts. Those of the second attend to the entertainment of foreigners. The third body consists of those who inquire when and how births and deaths occur, with the view not only of levying a tax, but also in order that births and deaths among both high and low may not escape the cognizance of government. The fourth class superintends trade and commerce. The fifth class supervises manufactured articles, which they sell by public notice. The sixth and last class consists of those who collect the tenths of the prices of the articles sold.

During the Mughal rule as well, the urban local government functionary was appointed by the state—a practice that has continued all these centuries and persists even now.[4] Responsibilities for administration of cities were vested in a bureaucratic functionary called the *kotwal*. He had a very high status and he used to overview every aspect of the city life including law and order. He used to appoint 'Mir Mohalla' or the Headman for every Ward of the city. His functions also included maintenance of an inventory of houses and roads. He directed the location of cemeteries, slaughter houses and development of colonies for sweepers. His jurisdiction also included regulation of markets, weights and measures, local prices and imposition of local taxes, tolls and transit duties. Even though it was a 'centralised autocratic regime', it was nevertheless 'responsive if not responsible to local opinion' (Tinker 1967).

LOCAL GOVERNMENT DURING THE COMPANY RULE

The Mughal rule crumbled in the wake of inroads made by the East India Company. After the advent of the Company rule, the country witnessed an all-round decline in the then existing socio-economic conditions. With the demise of the Mughal rule, the institution of local government not only declined but it disappeared also. After the Company usurped power and consolidated its position in India, it established Presidencies towards the fag end of the seventeenth century. The Presidencies consisted of a central town and its suburban outgrowth and were governed by the President and the Council that was created especially for the purpose of effective rule of the Company. It was at this point that the concept of local governance started taking roots. The credit of becoming the first Presidency to have a semblance of municipal government went to the Madras Presidency. The urban settlement of Madras came into being after the local chieftain granted a small site of land to the Company in 1639. The site, to begin with, was used by the Company to transact their business of trade and commerce. Trade and commerce undertaken by the Company from this site resulted in growth and expansion of this small site in the form of an urban settlement. This led to the coming up of the city of Madras. Acquisition of urban attributes of this site and in its neighbourhood started posing problems for its regulation and civic administration especially for sanitation.

Further growth of this urban settlement soon contributed to problems of civic administration in the spheres of justice, sanitation, public health, education and other services. With a view to address these diverse civic problems, the Directors of the Company wanted to constitute a municipal corporation for this urban settlement. This acquired the name of the city of Madras (Venkatarangaiya and Pattabhiraman 1969). However, this required putting in place local finance system for financing the solution to the burgeoning civic problems. It was thought that the natives of Madras would happily agree to pay local tax for financing of services especially because under a system of local government, they would be taxing themselves rather than be taxed by a despotic power. Finally, Sir Josiah Child, the then Governor of the Company, became instrumental in creation of the first municipal government in the country—the Madras Municipal Corporation in September 1688.

The Madras Municipal Corporation was created under a Charter Act passed by James II, the then British Monarch. It was largely modeled on the local government system then obtaining in Britain. It was not an elected local government. Representation on the Madras Municipal Corporation was given based on racial considerations. Even amongst the bureaucrats, the key positions of Town Clerk and Recorder (Judicial) went to the Englishman (Tinker op. cit.). It consisted of a Mayor, 12 Alderman and 60 Burgesses, who were appointed from amongst the Europeans living in India. It was constituted to pass on a part of the financial burden of administration to the local people and, therefore, it was equipped with taxation powers. However, contrary to the wishful thinking of the Company rule, creation of this municipal corporation could not motivate the natives to pay for civic improvements. Resistance to pay taxes was encountered soon after the setting up of the corporation. Ultimately in 1726, the Corporation was replaced by a Mayor's Court, which had some judicial rather than civic functions.

As the Madras Municipal Corporation was created by the East India Company, it had British moorings especially in so far as the functions of the municipality were concerned. The functions entrusted to it were largely influenced by the then practice of the English Boroughs that had to perform judicial functions as well. Functional domain of the Madras municipality, therefore, tilted towards performance of judicial functions; it had a Board of Record (Judicial) in Civil and Criminal Causes. Also the rosy hopes of its promoters that the natives residing within the new municipality would pay municipal taxes, could not actualize. As mentioned above, there was vehement opposition by the natives to the imposition of local taxes.

Following the creation of Municipal authority in Madras in 1688, for another about 38 years hardly any initiative was taken either for resurrecting the newly created municipal authority in Madras or for creation of newer ones. In 1726, there was a second Municipal Charter for setting up municipal authorities in the Presidency towns of Bombay and Calcutta and for reconstitution of the Municipal Corporation of Madras. The new Charter provided for a Mayor and nine Aldermen. Creation of Municipal Corporations was once again largely governed by racial considerations of the Company; as many as seven of the nine Aldermen were Englishmen. Process of municipalization in the three Presidencies, however, could not address the emerging municipal problems in these growing Presidency towns.

A new initiative towards creation of local government in urban settlements was, therefore, taken in 1793. The Charter of the East India Company was renewed that led to further expansion in trading activities undertaken by the Company. Sporadic attempts were made to enable the Municipal Corporations to address at least the problem of conservancy so that a system of public health could be put in place. The Justices of Peace were, therefore, created and they were required to appoint scavengers for collection of garbage and repair the streets. Also, another initiative was taken again to assess the possibilities of payment of rates (Property Tax) by the households. But judicial bias that continued and got engrained in the creation of municipal bodies did not allow them to perform hardcore municipal functions. Mixing of judicial and municipal functions led to strong judicial bias in the functioning of the municipal authorities at the neglect of performance of civic functions. There was a realization about it in the 1840s and, therefore, Justices of Peace in Bombay were compelled to hand over direct responsibility for municipal service to altogether a new variation of municipal authority. A Board of Conservancy was created in Bombay that consisted of seven members. The new added concern for addressing municipal functions led to giving attention to creation of municipal authorities in the emerging small and distantly located towns also. As a result of this new thinking in the Company, an entirely new step was taken in 1842 by enacting the Bengal Act of 1842 that had leanings towards creation of municipal authorities through a system of Charter to be submitted by the citizens of an emerging urban area. This Act provided that in case the people of any town desired to create a municipal government, they could submit an application that was required to be signed by two-thirds of the households residing in such towns (GoI 1951). Although municipal authority was set up only in one town, it soon became defunct as the inhabitants of the town not only refused to pay the local tax but also prosecuted the Collector for trespass when the latter attempted to levy the local tax. Another attempt was made again in 1850, this time on an all India basis by enacting a new Act. This Act as well contained principle of volunteering for creation of local governments mentioned before.

Thus, till the first half of the nineteenth century, attempts for setting up of municipal government were, by and large, limited to the three Presidency towns of Madras, Bombay and Calcutta. Despite this, the municipal authorities were more or less quasi-judicial bodies and, therefore, could not show any substantial concern in addressing burgeoning municipal problems. Problems of sewage disposal, water supply, and sanitation continued to be unattended by these newly created municipal authorities.

LOCAL GOVERNMENT UNDER THE BRITISH RULE

The Company rule in India came to an end in 1858 after the suppression of the mutiny of 1857 that is said to be the First War of Independence. Consequently, power was transferred to the Crown and India witnessed the advent of the British rule. The Mutiny had severe repercussion on the finances of the imperial rulers. The British rule in India was, therefore, seized with finding ways of reducing increasing fiscal burden on the exchequer. Pruning fiscal burden on the exchequer, therefore, became the motivating force for creation of local government in urban settlements so that a part of the fiscal burden could be shifted to the municipal authorities. This became an important reason for Britain to have a fresh look at local government system and design it afresh. To quote from an authentic study of local government foundations in India: 'The first British apprenticeship in administration was served in provinces where the most typical indigenous institutions had already been submerged by a super-imposed system, whose sole purpose was the collection of revenue. Continuity between the new forms of government and the local institutions of old was, therefore, almost impossible' (Tinker op. cit.).

Obviously, behind the ostensible motivation and considerate leanings towards creation of local government was the endemic financial problem that was worrying the Imperial Government. The British Rule in India, therefore, introduced an Income Tax as a temporary measure to get over the recurring financial problem. It was, however, abolished in 1863. A fresh impetus to the growth of local government came in 1863. This time, the government's attention was especially drawn by the Royal Army Sanitation Commission to the appalling, unhealthy and fast deteriorating sanitary conditions of towns all over the country. As a result of the serious situation presented in the Report of the Royal Sanitation Commission, the colonial government enacted several Municipal Acts for various provinces. These Acts authorized governors to order for formation of a municipality in urban areas of different provinces. Also, in order to provide a financial cushion to the imperial finance, the expenditures to be incurred on town police was suggested to be met by funds to be mobilized locally.

The initiative taken in 1863 mentioned above, was soon followed by a new Resolution, this time by Lord Lawrence's government in 1864. This Resolution urged the Provinces to create local government in urban areas along with introduction of local taxation. The Resolution makes interesting reading for combining the philosophy and importance of local government and the need for making it financially viable: 'The Governor-General-in-Council is of the opinion that in this question is involved a matter of higher import than mere financial convenience. Local taxation should as far as possible be accompanied by local administration and local responsibility. His Excellency is most sincerely desirous that every opportunity should be given to the people to participate in the management of their local affairs' (ibid.).

This Resolution was well received by the Provinces which enacted legislations in this direction. As a result, municipal governments were created in almost all important towns in the country (ibid.). However, they were still not in conformity with the concept of 'local self-government'. This was primarily because of bringing the District Magistrate at the centre stage of urban governance (GoI 1951). He was given overwhelming powers of control over municipal governments.

The Resolution of 1864 was soon followed by yet another Resolution that became an important precursor for establishing local government in India. Lord Mayo's Resolution of 1870 on Policy of Financial Decentralization stressed the need for associating Indians in administration. Through this, it decentralized certain responsibilities to the provinces. The Resolution required strengthening of municipal government for this purpose. The purpose of this Resolution was to delineate certain administrative duties for the provincial governments by the supreme imperial authority. By means of this resolution, Lord Mayo bestowed the responsibility of allocation of funds in the sphere of public works, medical facilities and education to the local or provincial governments who in their turn were expected to rely on local taxation. It was thought that the resolution would promote local interest, supervision and care that were necessary for success in the management of funds devoted to education, sanitation, medical relief and local public works. Such localization of funds, he believed, would help in the growth of self-government and at the same time facilitate association between the citizens of the Indian provinces and the British.

Despite subtle nuances of local self-government in this Resolution, it was once again pushed through largely with an objective of relieving imperial finances from additional fiscal stress as the mutiny of 1857 that led to the advent of British rule in India had quite adverse repercussions on the finances of the colonial government. Decentralization from centre to provinces was, therefore, primarily conceived for resource generation by the provinces. It also stressed the need to develop local self-government institutions 'for strengthening municipal institutions and for association of Natives and Europeans to a greater extent heretofore in the administration of affairs'. Lord Mayo's Resolution, nevertheless, resulted in considerable increase in the number of municipal bodies in urban areas with fairly well demarcated spheres of local government functions and constitution of elected Councils. Various regions like those in the north-west, Punjab, undivided Bengal and Madras introduced municipal taxes to implement this policy.

In the wake of Lord Mayo's Resolution, Municipal Acts were enacted in almost all provinces. Such an upsurge in enacting a legal framework for local governance notwithstanding, the concept of 'self-government' was still eluding. It did not encourage the principle of election largely because the District Magistrates abhorred the idea of extending elective principle in local government and granting representative character and status to local government. The Indian middle class liberals had been opposing the practice of non-representative local government and arguing for introducing electoral practice in creation of local government so that a system of representative local 'self-government' could be heralded in India. Notwithstanding bureaucratic disposition of the District Magistrates, the North-Western provinces and the Central Province adopted elective principle and for the first time, tried to promote the concept of local 'self-government' in India. As a result, Municipal Corporations in the Presidency towns of Calcutta, Bombay and Madras got a system of partial election chiefly owing to the pressing demand of the Indian middle class liberals.

LORD RIPON'S RESOLUTION: A LANDMARK IN THE INTRODUCTION OF LOCAL SELF-GOVERNMENT

After Lord Mayo's Resolution of 1870, educated Indians cherishing the ideals of democracy and liberty started striving seriously for attaining freedom from the colonial rule. Lord Ripon, the then Viceroy and also a liberal, wanted to provide for an outlet to this upsurge for freedom. He thought that handling of national and provincial administration by Indians themselves would require an apprenticeship in local administration. He, therefore, issued a Resolution on 18 May 1882 on local government primarily to provide for a forum for imparting political education to the Indians. This Resolution, in particular, is said to be the forerunner of local government institutions and Lord Ripon as the father of an organized local self-government in India. Lord Ripon's Resolution brought about a perceptible shift in the objective behind creation of local self-government institutions. He was of strong opinion that local self-government institutions were needed primarily as 'an instrument of political and popular education' (quoted from Venkatarangaiya and Pattabhiraman op. cit.). Till the 1870s, the objective for creation of local government was promotion of administrative efficiency in public administration. This, for the first time, shifted to providing political education to the citizens. To quote from Lord Ripon's Resolution, 'It is not primarily with a view to improvement in administration that this measure is put forward and supported. It is chiefly designed as an instrument of political and popular education.'

Lord Ripon's resolution, in a way, propounded new principles that were supposed to guide creation of local self-governance institutions in future in India. These principles included the following:

1. Political and popular education, rather than promotion of administrative efficiency, was to be the primary objective for creation of local governments;
2. Municipal Boards were to contain two-thirds majority of non-officials and these were to be elected wherever possible;
3. Local bodies needed to have mostly elected non-governmental Members and Chairmen;
4. Local governments needed to be constituted only by holding local elections; Chairmen of all local Boards to be non-officials wherever possible;
5. Control on the local bodies would need to be only indirect rather than direct;
6. These bodies must be endowed with adequate financial resources to carry-out their functions. To this end, certain sources

of local revenue should be made available to the local bodies which should also receive suitable grants from the provincial budget;
7. Local government personnel should operate under administrative control of the local bodies. The government personnel who are deputed to local government must be treated as employees of the local government and subject to its control; and
8. The resolution of 1882 should be interpreted by the provincial governments according to the local conditions prevalent in the provinces.

The broader contours of Lord Ripon's Resolution on local government, for the first time, depicted nuances of representative 'self-government' as far back as in 1882 and that too during the colonial rule. This specific feature and liberal thinking attributed to Lord Ripon an epithet as the 'father' of local government in India. The Resolution also solicited cooperation of officers for promoting growth of responsible local government in India. It also envisaged transfer of sufficient resources for meeting required expenditures if new functions were to be transferred to the local government. External control was envisaged to be limited to approval of raising of loans, imposition of new taxes, interference in the event of negligence in discharge of duties, and temporary suspension of the Municipal Board (GoI 1951). Power of absolute supersession required approval of the Supreme Government. It is worth mentioning that these aspects of local government are operating even now since the days of Ripon.

Lord Ripon's Resolution was followed by enactment of new legislations for incorporating provisions of the new Resolution. The Punjab Government was the first to have accepted the liberal ideals of Lord Ripon and enacted the Punjab Act XIII of 1884. New legislations were enacted in the Presidency towns—in 1884 in Madras, and in 1888 in Bombay and Calcutta. The 1888 Bombay Act soon became a model for enactment of similar laws in other provinces though this Act, much against the 'principles' enunciated by Lord Ripon, handed over the responsibility of urban governance in the hands of an appointed bureaucrat—the Municipal

Commissioner—who is more accountable to his cadre rather than to the urban local self-government. This model of executive system in local self-government is essentially an epitome of a weak Mayor system that travelled far and wide to other provinces as well for creating and regulating municipal governance especially in large cities. Basic feature of the 1888 model is that it bifurcates deliberative and executive powers and functions. Council of the Corporation happens to be the supreme deliberative body that is assisted in its day-to-day functioning by the Standing Committee. The Commissioner, who is appointed by the State Government, enjoys all the executive powers and functions and is responsible for carrying out decisions of the council and the Standing Committee. The Mayor's position is reduced to a mere figurative head. This Act, in particular, sowed the seeds of a weak Mayor system in India that has been replicated in several states.

In the wake of Lord Ripon's Resolution, non-official Chairmen were installed in a large number of municipal authorities which had two-thirds majority of non-officials. However, even though Chairmen were non-officials in certain Provinces, the District Magistrate still had a dominating position with the result that officials were installed as the Chairman through open invitation. On a positive side, attempts were also made to increase financial responsibilities and generate municipal financial resources. Maintenance of town police at the expense of municipal revenues was also discontinued in most of the Provinces; the funds so released were supposed to be spent on augmentation of services such as education, medical relief, and local public works.

DECENTRALIZATION COMMISSION AND LOCAL GOVERNMENT

After Lord Ripon, although much headway was made in moving towards establishment of representative local self-government, the post-Ripon regime, however, witnessed the advent of a system of centralized decentralization to a very large extent. Towards the dawn of the new century, the system of local government once again came under scrutiny, this time by the Royal Commission on

Decentralization that was appointed in 1907. The Decentralization Commission had the mandate to enquire into financial and administrative relations of the Government of India and the provincial governments and also the authorities subordinate to them. The Commission in its Report submitted in 1909, once again laid emphasis on administrative efficiency as the prime objective for local government rather than on political education—a philosophy that was so dear to Lord Ripon. Following the footsteps of Lord Ripon's ideals, the Decentralization Commission as well suggested minimizing official control over local government and stressed the need for non-officials as the Chairmen and Members in local government. When the Decentralization Commission was deliberating on local government, hardly any local government management system had evolved in India. The Commission, therefore, suggested emulating the English practice of involving elected representatives in the day-to-day functioning of local administration by replicating the popular British practice of Committee system. It recommended for election of the Presidents of the local government by the municipalities themselves. It did not, however, favour installing elected Presidents in the District Local Boards; the Collector was suggested to continue as the President of these Boards. It also suggested that Municipalities should be given the necessary authority to determine the taxes to be levied and they should prepare their own budgets after keeping a minimum reserve fund. It favoured a system of grants for local governments and, therefore, recommended that the government should give grants for public works like water-supply, drainage schemes, etc.

Outside control over the local bodies was suggested to be restricted to giving advice, suggestions and audit. Nevertheless, it suggested that the government control over the municipal powers of raising local loans should continue and prior sanction of the government should be obtained for lease or sale of municipal properties. These practices of control, it is worth mentioning, continues till today.

Primary education was suggested by the Commission to be the municipal responsibility. It also suggested that if the resources of the municipalities permit, they should spend also on providing secondary education. Financial control on budget and taxation was also suggested to be minimized. Local government was suggested to be given autonomy in increasing any tax within the limits set out in the statutes—a practice that is in vogue in different states even now. An important suggestion was to withdraw such functions that were not in the nature of local functions such as famine relief, town police, maintenance of district hospitals, etc. In order to improve management capabilities at the local level, it recommended appointing an Executive Officer similar to the Commissioner as in the Bombay Municipal Corporation in all the towns with a population of one lakh and more. A Medical Officer and an Engineer were also suggested to be appointed in towns of more than 20,000 population.

These suggestions were accepted by the colonial Government of India. However, the working out of details was left to the provincial governments, which did not do anything substantial to give operational form to these useful suggestions. Soon there was an outbreak of the First World War. Attempts to strengthen local government weakened considerably in the wake of this war. A careful reading of suggestions of the Decentralization Commission reveals that most of the suggestions given by the Commission are practiced even now in different states.

After the Report of the Decentralization Commission, another milestone in declaration of the ostensible role of the local government came in 1918 in the shape of a Government of India Resolution. This Resolution reaffirmed political education as the basic role to be played by the local government institutions. It declared that 'The object of local self-government is to train the people in the management of their own local affairs and the political education of this sort must in the main take precedence on consideration of departmental efficiency.' It also reaffirmed the need for extending franchise in the local bodies and stressed the need for elected rather than nominated Presidents for manning municipal affairs and governance.

MONTAGU-CHELMSFORD REFORM OF 1919

The year 1914 witnessed an outbreak of World War I (1914-18). This became a compelling reason for the British Government to solicit support and cooperation of Indians. After the war was over, a policy statement was made in the British House of Commons on 20 August 1917 by the Secretary of State for India Edwin Montagu for setting up of responsible government in India. Reacting to this, the then Viceroy of India Lord Chelmsford while addressing the imperial legislature declared: 'The domain of urban and rural local government is the great training ground from which political progress and sense of a responsibility have taken their start . . . it is time . . . to accelerate the rate of progress and thus to stimulate the sense of responsibility in the average citizen and to enlarge his experience' (Tinker op. cit.).

Thus, the objective of promoting political education again came to the fore taking precedence over administrative efficiency. The Secretary of State and the Viceroy, Lord Chelmsford jointly submitted a Report in July 1918 that is popularly known as the Montagu-Chelmsford Report. Concurrently with this, the Government of India applied its own mind on the subject of local government. In August 1918, the colonial Government of India came out with a Declaration and announced a package of policies on local government in the form of a Resolution in May 1918—about a couple of months before the Montague-Chelmsford Report. The Montagu-Chelmsford Report and the May Declaration almost reiterated the views expressed by the Decentralization Commission. One of the most important recommendations of the Montagu-Chelmsford Report was that the provincial legislatures had to be given more autonomy with respect to nation building subjects including local self-government. With this observation began the process of shifting local government from the central to the provincial domain that persists even today. It meant to make local government a provincial (now a state) subject to be dealt with more autonomously by the Provinces by implementing various policy recommendations on this subject. Among other things, it also recommended to provide for complete popular control in the local bodies for making them representative local government and the largest possible independence for them from outside control. The Resolution of May also expressed the same opinion. It was maintained that in order to give effect to the new policy, local bodies should be as representative of the people as possible primarily because they are called upon to administer public affairs at the local level. Their authority in the local functional domain should be real and not nominal and they should not be subject to unnecessary controls rather they should be allowed to learn by making mistakes (GoI 1951).

Consequent upon the Montagu-Chelmsford Report, a major constitutional reform was pushed through by enacting the Government of India Act of 1919. This Act gave a large measure of autonomy to provincial legislatures and local government was made a transferred subject; local government, for the first time, became 'creatures' of Provincial Government. All policy statements and resolutions issued in the past were now to be implemented by the Provincial Governments. For the first time the autocratic façade of a seemingly democratic institution of local self-government was done away with by removing the District Officers from the helm of local government affairs. Control mechanism of local government was put under the popular Minister in-charge of local self-government in the Provinces. Franchise of elections was widened substantially and the local government was given powers to vary their tax rates within the statutory limits thereby enhancing the local fiscal choice to a very large extent. This aspect of the 1919 Reforms even now constitutes a specific feature of municipal governance in some of the states. Municipal laws in some of the states provide autonomy to the urban local self-governments in increasing the tax rates within the minimum and the maximum rates provided for in these Acts. The Reform of 1919 thus democratized local governments and also widened their powers and functions. One of the most important reforms under the Government of India Act of 1919 was demarcation of local list of fiscal tools that were reserved for exclusive use of the local government. This Act, in fact, added a Local List of sources of revenue that was sanctified by the law of the land. The Scheduled Taxes Rules framed under Section 80A(3) and Section 129A of the Government of India Act, 1919 unequivocally provided that 'Nothing in these rules shall affect the right of a local authority to impose a tax without previous sanction or with the previous sanction of the local government when such right is conferred upon it by any law for the time being in force'.[5]

TABLE 1.1: TAXES AND RATES PROVIDED FOR IN THE LIST OF LOCAL TAXES IN GOVERNMENT OF INDIA ACT OF 1919

A: Taxes

1. Toll
2. Tax on land or land value and land and buildings
3. Tax on vehicles and boats
4. Tax on animals
5. Octroi
6. Terminal Tax on goods imported into local area in which an Octroi was levied on or before 6 July 1917
7. Water Tax
8. Drainage Tax

B: Rates in the Nature of Contemporary User Charges

9. Water rate
10. Lighting rate
11. Scavenging, sanitary or sewage rate
12. Fee for the use of markets and other public conveniences

Source: Schedule II of the Government of India Act, 1919.

Thus the Reform of 1919 largely replaced the decentralized type of government of the continental variety that was subject to elaborate control.

The democratic spirit of Reform, however, could not survive for long; it soon started waning. Indian leaders engaged in intense freedom struggle under the leadership of Mahatma Gandhi soon realized that the limited autonomy emanating from the 1919 Reforms was a mere attempt to divert the attention of the freedom fighters and weaken the struggle for Independence. The Indian National Congress soon started agitation for attaining complete independence from the colonial rule. This culminated in appointment of yet another Commission called the Indian Statutory Commission in 1920 to enquire into the steps to be taken for further reform in the system of responsible government that was introduced in the 1919. The Commission, presided over by Simon, also conducted intensive study of changes introduced in local government and reviewed these changes. Reviewing the actual functioning of local government, the Simon Commission did not feel very happy about the efficacy of the changes made in the wake of the 1919 Reforms. Diagnosing the causes, the Commission observed that the new elected executive system went a long way in democratizing local government; nevertheless, it also created an important administrative void. The elected executive system was seen to have 'a tendency to misapprehend what are the duties and functions of elected members' (Her Majesty's Government 1930). The Commission saw a tendency amongst the elected executive to meddle in the spheres of local administration that were legitimate domain of the appointed official. The Commission, therefore, wanted the local government in India to have counterpart of the Town Clerk in England.[6]

The Commission also found unnecessary laxity in the system of control by the provincial governments. In order to enhance the efficiency of local government, it thought desirable to have a large measure of control by the higher level of government. Even though a separate list of taxes was reserved for local government, it found them inadequate to meet their needs. This, to a large extent, was due to reluctance of elected members to impose local taxes. It also favoured the then English system of grants to be made conditional upon imposition of adequate taxation and acceptance of a considerable measure of central government control.

It is interesting to note that even after more than almost a century ago, observations of the Simon Commission still hold the ground; the tendency of elected officials to encroach upon the legitimate domain of appointed functionaries as also general reluctance of elected members to charge and impose new taxes devolved to the local government continue to be as knotty as these were about a century ago!

The Simon Commission was distressed to find a decline in the management and functioning of local government in India. This decline continued unabated and was at times exacerbated by mounting arrears in tax collection, embezzlement of municipal funds and communal and caste dissentions amongst the elected Councilors. Such a state of affairs continued till 1947 when India attained Independence from the colonial rule. Before this, in 1935, enactment of Government of India Act provided autonomy to the Provinces. Provincial legislatures enacted several new legislations on local self-government for widening powers and functions of local government. But at the same time, it also did a great damage to development and functioning of local self-government in years to come. The Local List of taxes earmarked in the Government of India Act of 1919 was abolished in the Government of India Act, 1935. This Act provided for only three lists, viz., Federal List, Provincial List, and Concurrent List. Such a retrograde step is even now being suggested to be retracted by reviving the Local List of taxes. The National Commission to Review the Working of the Constitution (discussed in detail in Chapter 5), however, did not favour its restoration as it thought that the time is not yet ripe for this (India 2002). The framework of local government conceived and implemented according to the Government of India Act, 1935 continued till India achieved Independence in 1947.

History of local government from ancient India till the advent of Indian Independence as analysed in this chapter provides interesting insights into the impulses that led to creation of local government and its gradual development into local self-government in more than three hundred years. It also, nevertheless, reveals several upheavals the institutions of local government have gone through during this period. It is worth mentioning that limited devolution to the local government during the British rule notwithstanding, all through the British regime, objectives of (i) administrative efficiency and (ii) political education constituted the guiding principle for setting up of local government in India. Since 1688 when India got the first municipal government in Madras to 1882—the year of the famous Lord Ripon's Resolution on local government—the guiding principle for creation of local government in urban areas was largely centred on promoting administrative efficiency. Lord Ripon, with a liberal disposition, wanted the local government to play the role as nurseries of democracy for imparting to the Indians basic education in democracy and handling of public affairs. The Decentralization Commission in 1909, once again altered the role of local government from imparting political and popular education to enhancing administrative efficiency. The attention of the then policy makers again shifted to imparting political education as the dominant role to be played by the local government in 1918. This was done through a Resolution of the Government in India in 1918 that reaffirmed political education to be the prime objective of creation of local government. The Montagu-Chelmsford Reform of 1919 as well accepted this objective. It is worth mentioning that the role of local government as a nursery of democracy paid rich dividend: a galaxy of eminent freedom fighters that emerged at the national scene for spearheading the struggle for freedom emerged from the arena of local government only. This included leaders like Bal Gangadhar Tilak, G.K. Gokhale, Jawaharlal Nehru, Subhas Chandra Bose and Sardar Patel among others.

This debate about the role to be played by the local government, however, could not continue in Independent India. This is said to be one of the reasons that clouded the institutions of urban local self-government and weakened them

NOTES

1. The term 'institution' connotes formal and informal rules operating within or across organizations (Ostrom 1990) that shape human interactions. Institutions have, within its ambit, both formal rules such as formal powers of office and also informal norms, roles and operating practices that are so stable, structured, and accepted that they can be said to be 'institutionalized'. Constraints and incentives derived from institutions influence participation, choices and performance of local governments (Clingermayer and Feiock 2001).
2. A recent study reports that simple correlation co-efficient between the level of urbanisation and per capita GDP across countries is about 0.85. See K.M. Murphy, 1989; J. Eton, and Z. Eckstien, 1994.
3. In South Africa, six major cities contribute about 53 per cent of GDP though they account for only 31 per cent of the total population of South Africa; Johannesburg alone contributes 14.98 per cent of GDP; Mexico city with only 14 per cent of the national population of Mexico, accounts for 34 per cent of national income; Shanghai with only 1.2 per cent of the total population of China, generated 12.5 per cent of its GNP and Bangkok and Sao Paulo account for about 10 per cent of the total population of their

respective countries' but produce 40 per cent of GDP of their countries (UN-HABITAT 2002).

4. Municipal Commissioner in Municipal Corporations and the Chief Executive Officer in other varieties of urban local self-governments are even now appointed by the state governments.
5. Government of India Act, 1919 used the expression 'local government' to denote the provincial governments; the term 'local authority' was the expression used to denote the Urban Local Governments.
6. The Town Clerk of London is an important position that has existed since the thirteenth century. Initially introduced in the City of London, it is an elected position that was originally to take the minutes of London council meetings, but over the years the Town Clerk has gathered responsibilities which include staff and executive powers.

REFERENCES

Bird, Richard and Francois Vaillancourt, 1998, *Fiscal Decentralization in Developing Countries*, Cambridge: Cambridge University Press.

Campbell, Tim, George Peterson and J. Brakarz, 1991, *Decentralization to Local Government in LAC.* Washington DC: World Bank.

Chester, D.N., 1951, *Central and Local Government, Financial and Administrative Relations*, London: Macmillan.

Clingermayer, James C. and Richard C. Feiock, 2001, *Institutional Constraints and Policy Choice*, Albany: State University of New York Press.

Ebel, Robert D. and Francois Vaillancourt, 2001, 'Fiscal Decentralization and Financing Urban Governments: Framing the Problem', in Mila Freire and Richard Streneds (eds), *The Challenge of Urban Governance*, Washington, D.C.: The World Bank Institute, pp. 155-71.

Eton, J. and Z. Eckstien, 1994, 'Cities and Growth: Theory and Evidence from France and Japan', Working Paper, no. 4612, Cambodia: NBER.

European Union, 1985, *European Charter of Local Self-Government,* European Treaty Series, no. 122, Strasbourg: European Union.

Government of India (Ministry of Health), 1951, *Report of the Local Finance Enquiry Committee.* Delhi: Manager of Publications.

Government of India, National Commission, 2002, *Report of the National Commission to Review the Working of the Constitution*, vol. l, New Delhi: Government of India Press.

Hansen, A.H. and H.S.Perloff, 1945, *State and Local Finance in the National Economy*, London: George Allen and Unwin.

Henderson, J.V., 2000, 'How Urban Concentration Affects Economic Growth', Working Paper, Infrastructure and Environment, Development Research Group, World Bank, Washington, DC: The World Bank.

Her Majesty's Government, 1947, *Dispatch by the British Secretary of State to African Governors*, London: Her Majesty's Stationery Office (HMSO).

Her Majesty's Government, 1930, *Report of the Indian Statutory Commission* (Simon Commission), vol. l, Command 3568, London: HMSO.

Horvath, Tamas M. (ed.), 2000, *Decentralization: Experiments.* Budapest: Public Service Reform Initiative, Open Society Institute.

Jha, Gangadhar, 1988, *Local Finance in Metropolitan Cities: A Study of Delhi*, Delhi: Mittal Publications.

Kautilya's Arthashastra, 1967, tr. R. Sharma Sastry, 8th edn., Mysore: Mysore Printing and Publishing House.

Kothari, Rajni, 1999, 'Issues in Decentralized Governance', in S.N. Jha and P.C. Mathur (eds.), *Decentralization and Local Politics*, New Delhi: Sage, pp. 9-16.

Martinez-Vazaquez, Jorge and Robert McNab, 1997, 'Tax Reform in Transition Economies: Experience and Lessons', *International Studies Program Working Paper* 97-6, Andrew Young School of Policy Studies, Atlanta: Georgia State University.

Meenakshisundaram, S.S. 1999, 'Decentralisation in Developing Countries', in S.N. Jha and P.C. Mathur (eds.), *Decentralization and Local Politics*, New Delhi: Sage, pp. 35-42.

Murphy, K.M., A. Shleifer and R. Vishny, 1989, 'Industrialization and the Big Push', *Journal of Political Economy*, 97 (2): 1003-26.

Musgrave, Richard A., 1959, *The Theory of Public Finance*, New York: Mcgraw-Hill.

Oates, Wallace E., 1972, *Fiscal Federalism*, New York: Harcourt Brace Jovanovich.

——, 2005, 'Toward a Second-Generation Theory of Fiscal Federalism, *International Tax and Public Finance*, 12: 349-73.

Olson, Mancur, 1969, 'The Principal of Fiscal Equivalence: The Division of Responsibilities Among Different Levels of Government', *American Economic Review*, 59 (2): 479-87.

Ostrom, Elinor, 1990, *Governing the Commons*, Cambridge: Cambridge University Press.

Owens, J. and G. Panella, 1991, *Local Government: An International Perspective.* Amsterdam: North Holland.

Peteri, Gabor, 2002, *Mastering Decentralization and Public Administration Reforms in Central and Eastern Europe.* Budapest: Local Government and Public Service Reform Initiative.

Rabinovitch, Jonas, 1999, 'From Urban Management to Urban Governance: Towards a Strategy for the New Millenium', *City Development Strategies*, no. 1, October.

Robson, 1966, *Local Government in Crisis*, London: George Allen & Unwin.

Shah, Anwar and Sana Shah, 2006, 'New Vision of Local Governance and the Evolving Roles of Local Governments', in Anwar Shah (ed.), *Local Governance in Developing Countries*, Washington, DC: The World Bank, pp. 1-44.

Stiglitz, Joseph, 2006, *Making Globalisation Work*. London: Allen Lane.

Tinker, Hugh, 1967, *The Foundation of Local Government in India, Pakistan and Burma*, Bombay: Lalvani Publishing House.

UN-HABITAT. 2002,'The Role of Cities in National and International Development', Discussion Paper, World Urban Forum, Nairobi: World Bank Forum.

Venkatarangaiya, M. and M. Pattabhiraman (eds), 1969, *Local Government in India: Selected Reading*, Bombay: Allied Publishers.

World Bank, 1999, *Elements for a New Strategy on Urban Development and Municipal Issues*, Washington, DC: World Bank.

CHAPTER 2

Urban Local Self-Government in Post-Independent Period

DECLINE AND WEAKENING OF URBAN LOCAL SELF-GOVERNMENT

After attaining Independence on 15 August 1947, the advent of self-rule provided an opportunity to have a fresh look at the system and structure of governance at the centre, in the states and at the local level. The process of drafting of its own Constitution began soon after and finally India was proclaimed as a Republic on 26 January 1950 under its own new Constitution. But urban local self-government did not find any place in the Constitution, much less giving it status of an autonomous and independent entity as a level of self-government at the local level in urban areas. The Constitution, in its Directive Principles, laid primary emphasis on organization of village Panchayats as a unique local self-government institution in the rural areas. Article 40 of the Constitution provided that 'The State shall take steps to organize village Panchayats and endow them with such powers and authority as may be necessary to enable them to function as units of self-government'. Even for the local government in rural areas, the Constitution did not lay down details of form, structure, functions and finances of the Panchayati Raj institutions. The Second Administrative Reforms Commission, looking back at the conditions prevailing at the time of framing of India's Constitution, ascribes this gap to the 'first and foremost requirement of the country' that 'was to consolidate itself as a nation. Over 400 princely states had been integrated with a more homogeneous federation of larger States. The next few years were, therefore, spent in reorganizing and strengthening the

States. The Constitution did not give prominence to the local bodies. . . .' (GoI 2007).

Leanings towards centralized decentralization that persisted during the colonial rule, therefore, continued even after India ushered in an era of self-rule in 1947. Institutions of urban local self-government that in the wake of the Montagu-Chelmsford Reform were for the first time made a transferred subject under the Government of India Act of 1919 and brought within the fold of provinces (now state governments) continued to be an appendage to the constitutionally autonomous state governments as before. Moreover, when India became independent from the colonial rule, the Government of India Act was still in force. This colonial Act impacted the Indian thinking on local government a great deal even after Independence. Following the pattern of allocation of functional domain between the centre and the states in the Government of India Act of 1935 into three Lists—Federal List, Provincial List, and Concurrent List—the Indian Constitution adopted the same pattern of allocation of subjects between the Centre and the States by changing the nomenclature of the first two Lists as the Union List and the State List respectively. Local government—both rural and urban—continued to be under the domain of the state governments as this was put under List II (State List) of the Constitution. Item 5 in List II of the Seventh Schedule of the Constitution became the responsibility of the states as mentioned below: 'Local government, that is to say, the constitution and powers of municipal corporations, improvement trusts, district boards, mining settlement authorities and other local authorities for the purpose of local self-government or village administration.'

Thus, under the new scheme of allocation of subjects between the Central and the State governments, local self-government institutions were made creatures of the state governments. As a result, only such powers and functions as also the sources of local revenue were devolved to the local self-government that were delegated to them by the state governments through specific legislations enacted by the state legislatures. Devolving of functions to the urban local self-governments came under the purview of the principle of *ultra vires.* Constitutionally, therefore, the ULBs became creatures of the state governments that created them by delegating to them some of their own powers and tax authority. Unfettered powers and authority of states over local self-government and constitutional limitations on the actions of the latter because of the principle of *ultra vires*, finds its subtle expression in what is called Dillon's Rule. Arising in the United States of America where as well, local governments happen to be the creatures of states and subject to the same principle of *ultra vires,* the presiding judge in a law suit in Iowa which is known as *City of Clinton* v. *Ceddar Rapids and Missouri Railroad Company*, and *Merriam* v. *Moody's Executors* in 1868 ruled thus (Wright 1988):

1. There is no common-law right of local self-government;
2. Local entities are creatures of the state, subject to creation and abolition at the unfettered discretion of the state (barring constitutional limitations);
3. Localities may exercise only such powers as are granted to them; and
4. Localities are 'mere tenants' at the will of the legislature.

As mentioned earlier, of the three Lists, local government as a subject appears in the State List that contains subjects which constitute the constitutional domain of the state governments and the local governments enjoy only such powers that are delegated to them under legislations enacted by the state legislatures. Hence, even though the structure of urban local government is invariably the same, provisions relating to the details of functions, executive system, sources of revenue, etc., in various state enactments are different. Constitutional position of local self-government also explains the advisory nature of the Central Government in matters relating to local government. The role of the Central Government is limited to giving guidelines, suggestions, and advisory to the state governments indicating standards of performance and launching of centre sector schemes from time to time for the states that are implemented by states through fiscal incentives offered by the Central Government. Since Independence, the Central Government has constituted Committees, Commissions, Task Forces and expert bodies for undertaking in-depth study of the problem confronting urban local government (GoI 1951; 1953; 1963; 1966; 1974; 1983; 1988a; and 1998b).

After Independence, initiatives were taken in different states for enactment of new laws for the urban local self-governments. Municipal laws were enacted by the state governments separately for different types of municipal governments such as (i) Municipal Corporations, (ii) Municipal Councils, (iii) Town Area Committees, and (iv) Notified Area Committees. After the Constitutional provision of 1992 for creation of only the Municipal Corporation, Municipal Council and Nagar Panchayats, the State of Tamil Nadu was the first to enact a single unified law for all the three types of urban local self-government. Following the tradition created by the much acclaimed Bombay Municipal Corporation Act enacted in 1888 during the British rule, the executive system in the Municipal Corporations, which constitute relatively larger form of city government created especially in big cities, became not only fragmented but also led to a weak Mayor system. The basic façade of the Bombay Act is that the elected Mayor happens to be a mere ceremonial head. The Municipal Commissioner—an appointed bureaucrat—enjoys all the executive powers. This has continued as an anathema to the concept of local 'self-government'. This bureaucratic executive system in the institutions of self-government travelled far and wide across the country and installing a weak political executive system became the fashion in different states and Union Territories. This came to be replicated even in smaller cities and towns having a Municipal Council form of urban local self-government. However, the states located north of the Vindhya Mountains (north India) especially in the eastern states, the elected Chairmen in Municipal Councils were exceptions to this style of executive system as they were vested with executive powers. As a result, they chaired both the Council and the executive wing and acting as a political executive. This healthy practice continues even now.

The laws enacted in some of the states after India became independent, were meant for rationalization of some of the laws enacted earlier during the colonial rule and also for setting up of municipal government of various types. Initiatives were taken for installing executive officers in municipal governments that did not have it and also for strengthening the chief executive—generally the appointed ones. Several state governments separately constituted study teams and committees for suggesting ways and means of improving the functioning of urban local self-government in their respective states. In 1966, much before the enactment of the 74th Constitution Amendment Act (CAA), an official Committee appointed by the Central Government in the late 1960s (GoI 1966), suggested appointment of a State Finance Commission by the state governments once in every five years before constituting of Central Finance Commission by the President of India under Article 280 of the Constitution. Similar views were reiterated by the Central Council of Local Self-Government and the All India Council of Mayors in 1972. Several state governments, therefore, appointed State Finance Commissions for rationalization of fiscal transfers to the local bodies. Following this the states of Andhra Pradesh, Orissa, Maharashtra, Karnataka, Tamil Nadu and West Bengal appointed State Finance Commissions even before enactment of the Constitution (74th Amendment) Act, 1992 (Jha and Mishra 1984). It is worth mentioning even at the cost of repeatation that such an initiative was taken much before the enactment of the 74th CAA. A similar mandatory provision was subsequently incorporated in the Constitution of India through an amendment of the Constitution by enacting the 74th CAA in 1992 (discussed in greater detail in Chapter 3). The state governments also created Directorates of Municipal Administration largely for supervision and control of the urban local self-governments rather the much required hand holding and strengthening of their institutional capacity. Setting up of State Finance Commissions by some of the states also could not positively impact transfer system primarily because there was hardly any will amongst the state governments concerned for implementing the recommendations given by these Commissions.

An important initiative was taken by the State Government of West Bengal in 1980. This State took the lead in introducing a strong Mayor system by drafting the Calcutta Municipal Corporation Act, 1980. This Act provides for the Mayor as the political executive and also a cabinet form of local self-government. The elected Mayor enjoys all the executive powers and he constitutes a Mayor-in-Council that is a semblance of a mini cabinet headed by him. The Members of the Mayor-in-Council have delegated portfolios to be looked after and managed by them. The appointed Commissioner performs executive functions and he is accountable to the Mayor-in-Council just as the Chief Secretary in a State Government is accountable to the cabinet. In 1997, the State of Madhya Pradesh as well adopted a similar system of Mayor-in-Council by amending the Madhya Pradesh Municipal Corporation Act, 1956 and introduced the Mayor-in-Council form of city government. The conspicuous difference between the two states, however, is that whereas in the State of West Bengal, the Mayor is elected indirectly following the tradition of Parliamentary Democracy prevalent in the country at the centre and in the states, the Mayor in Madhya Pradesh is elected directly by the electorate. Direct election of Mayor in Madhya Pradesh belongs to the practice adopted in the countries with presidential form of government as in the USA. The system of direct election of Mayor was followed also by some of other states such as Tamil Nadu, Chhattisgarh, Uttar Pradesh, Rajasthan (till the enactment of the Rajasthan Municipal Act, 2009) and Uttarakhand. An aberration in a system of directly elected Mayor especially in a cabinet form of local government is that if the Mayor and the political party in majority in the Council belong to two different political parties, the Mayor finds it difficult to function and even constitute his mayor-in-Council. This has happened in several towns in Madhya Pradesh and Rajasthan. Vexed up with this perennial problem of persistent conflict, Rajasthan finally abolished the direct election of Mayor. Yet, the State Government of Bihar is presently deliberating on direct election of Mayors in the state.

In 2003, through an initiative taken under a then on-going Indo-USAID collaborative programme called as FIRE-D (Financial Institutions Reform and Expansion—Debt market Development) for developing a market-based urban infrastructure finance system, a unified (single law for all the three varieties of urban local self-government) specimen law with political executive (strong Mayor) was drafted under this project. This was finally adopted by the

Government of India as a model law. This unified model municipal law as well has provisions for installing a political executive system in urban governance. Adoption/enactment of this model municipal law by the state governments also became part of the mission of the Ministry of Urban Development (MoUD). The State Government of Bihar became the first state to enact a new municipal law based largely on the model municipal law.

A significant step was taken after Independence in 1970 when through a Presidential Order, the Central Council of Local Self-Government was created consisting of the Union Minister of Health (now Minister of Housing and Urban Affairs) as the Chairperson and the State Ministers of Local Self-Government as its members. It was renamed as Central Council of Local Government and Urban Development in 1980. It is an advisory body for considering and recommending policy measures to the Central Government for allocation of funds and devolving of powers and functions to the urban local self-governments. The Council used to hold meeting on an annual basis for deliberating on the various aspects of local self-government. This used to provide valuable opportunity to review the progress made in empowerment of urban local self-governments and identification of policy initiatives for resolution of bottlenecks, if any. In 1962, the Mayors of the Municipal Corporations formed the All India Council of Mayors, which primarily flags issues in effective governance particularly of the Municipal Corporations and advises the Government on the related matters. Lately, however, the activities of the Central Council of Local Government and Urban Development has been tapering off; it no longer holds its periodical meeting as in the past for reviewing the local government performance, addressing the bottlenecks, and for flagging issues in strengthening of urban local bodies for effective service provision and urban governance. The last meeting of the Council was held during the tenure of the Atal Behari Vajpayee government (1998-2004) when the meeting was chaired by Ram Jethmalani, the then Minister of this Ministry. The Ministry of Panchayati Raj, on the other hand, has been doing this on a regular and sustained basis. This enables this Ministry in better stewardship of the Panchayati Raj institutions.

PROJECT-DRIVEN REFORM OF URBAN LOCAL SELF-GOVERNMENT

Strengthening of urban local self-government once again came to the fore in 2005. The Central Government (Ministry of Urban Development and Ministry of Housing and Urban Poverty Alleviation) launched a mega project called the Jawaharlal Nehru National Urban Renewal Mission (Jn-NURM) in December 2005. The project was implemented in 65 mission cities and in several non-mission cities and towns spread into 31 states and union territories. Though this project was named Urban Renewal Mission, basically it was a project focused on reform driven augmentation of urban infrastructure, not an urban renewal project *per se* which conceptually means renewal of traditional housing areas located especially in the core of the cities that have become derelict over decades of neglect (Jha 2009). To begin with, it was a seven-year project with an outlay of Rs. 66,085 crore. Though the project's lifetime was to end in 2012-13, couple of years' extension was given to this project for enabling completion of on-going projects. An important aspect of Jn-NURM was that besides being focused on strengthening and augmentation of urban infrastructure in the project cities, it was also configured for leveraging urban sector reforms. The reforms to be leveraged under this project included initiatives for strengthening and empowerment of the urban local self-governments. It contained (i) a wide list of areas for financial assistance, (ii) a number of project components that are eligible for financial assistance, (iii) substantial areas of mandatory reforms at the state and local levels and (iv) areas of optional reforms. Areas of assistance included capacity building of city governments, preparation of city development plan (CDP) and detailed project reports, development of urban infrastructure, community participation, information, education and communication (IEC). Financial assistance was given subject to preparation of CDP that was required to include, *inter alia,* strategy to implement reforms, city-level improvements and an investment plan to address the infrastructure needs in a sustainable manner.

Accessing of funds by the cities (and the states) was made contingent upon adopting a set of reforms at the state and local levels. State level reforms included:

(a) Implementation of decentralization measures as envisaged in the 74th Constitution Amendment Act. The states were expected to ensure meaningful association and engagement of urban local self-governments (ULSGs) in planning the function of parastatal agencies as well as delivery of services to the citizens;
(b) Repeal of Urban Land (Ceiling and Regulation) Act, 1976;
(c) Reform of Rent Control Laws for balancing the interests of landlords and tenants;
(d) Rationalization of Stamp Duty to bring it down to no more than 5 per cent;
(e) Enactment of the model Public Disclosure Law prepared by the Ministry of Urban Development to ensure preparation of medium-term fiscal plan of all ULSGs and release of quarterly performance information to all stakeholders;
(f) Enactment of the model Community Participation Law also prepared by the Ministry of Urban Development to institutionalize participation of civil society and introduce the concept of Area Sabha in the ULSGs; and
(g) Assigning or associating elected ULSGs with 'city planning function' and transfer of all specific purpose agencies that deliver civic services in urban areas to ULSGs within a period of seven years and creating accountability platforms for all urban civic service providers in transition.

Thus (i) Implementation of provisions of the 74th CAA by the state governments, enactment of (ii) Public Disclosure Law for imparting transparency and accountability and (iii) the Community Participation Law for putting in place the required structure and process for participation of civil society, (iv) assigning of urban planning functions, and (v) transfer of all special purpose authorities engaged in delivery of civic services to the urban local self-governments were, quite revolutionary areas of reform for empowerment and strengthening of local self-government in urban areas.

Areas of mandatory reforms at the city level that have important implications for strengthening institutional capacity of the ULSGs included:

(a) Adoption of modern accrual-based double entry accounting system in urban local self-governments and parastatal agencies;
(b) Introduction of a system of e-governance using IT applications such as GIS and MIS for various services provided by the city governments and parastatal agencies;
(c) GIS based property tax reform;
(d) Levy of reasonable user charges by the city governments and parastatals for full cost recovery of operations and maintenance or recurring cost within the next seven years;
(e) Internal earmarking of budgets within ULSGs for basic services to the urban poor; and
(f) Provision of basic services to the urban poor including security of tenure at affordable prices, improved housing, water supply and sanitation.

On the face of it, mandatory reforms conceived at state and local levels seemingly appear quite impressive for strengthening the urban local self-governments. This, however, is ineluctably dependent on the extent and nature of implementation of these reforms in actual practice. This is discussed in Chapter 6 in greater detail.

Development of local self-governments in the post-Independence period discussed above reveals that local government being a state subject, they have to be dependent on the will of the state governments for their strengthening through devolving of functions, funds, and functionaries. Concern for reconstruction of the country after the end of prolonged colonial rule, initiatives for economic and social development, governance, and the need for addressing problems of other high priority sectors, however, led to assigning of low priority to urban local governance in the initial decades of independent India. This was further reinforced by a low level of urbanization in the country that led the policy makers to give less attention to the need for strengthening them. Indifferent attitude of the state governments towards consolidating local self-governments and their strengthening gradually led to decline of urban local self-government in the country.

DECLINE OF URBAN LOCAL SELF-GOVERNMENT

The expectation that self-rule in post-Independent India would attract attention of policy makers for further consolidation, development and strengthening of urban local self-governments, however, could not actualize. Institutions of urban local self-governments declined. The decline was brought about by an indifferent attitude of the state governments, erosion in municipal functional domain, depletion of fiscal health of the urban local self-governments, and elaborate supervision and control over them by the state governments.

EROSION OF MUNICIPAL FUNCTIONAL DOMAIN

The state governments gradually started encroaching upon legitimate traditional municipal functions by creating para-statals and urban development authorities. Functions taken over by these include urban planning, zoning regulations and development of urban areas, water supply, sewerage, slum clearance and development in all states and even primary education in some of the states. Withdrawing of these functions was done on the plea that urban local self-governments lacked institutional capacity in terms of expertize, financial resources, institutional capacity and organizational culture. Advent of the World Bank funding of urban development projects in the 1970s further exacerbated the process of functional encroachment. The Bank insisted in creating altogether new organizations for getting funding from the Bank. Yet another de-facto reason was the vested interest of the state bureaucracy in building their own empire by creating para-statals and special purpose authorities which, unlike the municipal governments, are apolitical organizations and are, therefore, more amenable to direction and control of the state government departments to which the para-statals belong. There was hardly any appreciation of the fact that if the resources—human and financial—which were used to create the special purpose authorities, could be diverted to municipal entities the urban local self-governments would have been strengthened substantially.

Encroachment on municipal functional domain gave rise to newer problems, which adversely affected the process of urban planning, development and maintenance. First, the planning process became apolitical in complete disregard to the priorities and preferences of the local communities. The projects developed and implemented by the urban development authorities and the para-statals were thrust upon the municipal government in the maintenance phase for their operations and maintenance. Second, the urban local self-governments, not being involved and even associated in the planning of these projects, deemed it as something imposed on them. These projects, therefore lacked the much needed municipal ownership. Third, it had been creating the problem of financing of maintenance, as the maintenance of completed projects became additional liabilities of the urban local self-governments. The dichotomous compartmentalization of urban development into development and maintenance led to a situation where the urban local self-governments started refusing to take over the completed projects implemented by the para-statals and specific purpose authorities for operations and maintenance. This was witnessed in Calcutta, Kanpur, Delhi and elsewhere in a big way. In view of these, the Planning Commission's Task Force on Housing and Urban Development reporting in the mid-1980s, strongly recommended to give a halt to the on-going encroachment on the municipal functions and to restore the functions withdrawn from the municipal bodies (GoI, 1988a). Quite a few State Finance Commissions as well suggested the same. But this went on unabated even in the post-74th Constitution Amendment regime (discussed in greater detail in Chapter 3) despite addition of altogether a new Schedule of municipal functions in the Indian Constitution. However, this new Schedule of the Indian Constitution was reduced to a mere illustrative list of municipal functions. This hardly has any constitutionality. The Constitution has made it discretionary for the state governments.

Weak Executive System

Following enactment of the colonial Bombay Municipal Corporation Act, 1888 and its swift replication in other states, executive system, especially in the municipal corporations which are the largest and the most autonomous forms of municipal authorities became highly fragmented as it is based on the principle of separation of executive powers and functions. Under this model that spread to other states as well, whereas executive powers vested in the Council and its executive committees, executive functions are performed by the appointed Commissioner. Substantive executive powers enjoyed by an appointed executive, rather than by an elected Mayor, has led to bureaucratic control and hence erosion in local democracy and self-governance. This is in complete contradiction to conceptual groundings of the institutions of self-government.

Barring the states of West Bengal, Rajasthan and the municipal councils in Uttar Pradesh, Bihar and Orissa, the executive system in the urban local self-governments was and is still highly fragmented (for details of the nature of executive system, see Chapter 4 and Annex VII). Municipal Corporations in other states and municipal councils in the southern states have had a system of appointed chief executives and yet they are called the units of 'self-government'. In the remaining states, the Bombay Municipal Corporation Act of 1888 enacted during the colonial rule just after three years of the famous Ripon's liberal Resolution on local government, implanted a weak political executive, system, making the office of elected head merely a ceremonial head, an appointed executive enjoying all the executive authority!

The Executive system in urban local self-governments is thus highly centralized, fragmented and amenable to state control. In the southern states, municipalities as well have a fragmented bureaucratic executive system as is prevalent in municipal corporations. Thus in a majority of municipal governments, the prevalent executive system does not conform to the concept of 'self-government'.

Inadequate Resource Base

On the resources front, however, despite an increasing demand for services due to increase in the level of urbanization and urban growth, the local resource base started shrinking. The share of municipal authorities in the total public sector expenditure declined from about 8 per cent in 1960-1 to about 4.5 per cent in 1977-8. It further declined to approximately 2 per cent in 1991-2 (GoI 2007). This has adversely constrained institutional capacity of the urban local self-government in provision of services and their operational upkeep. Their weak fiscal strength has been a great constraining factor in enabling them to perform their role. Fragile resource base of the ULSGs is documented by almost all the official Committees and Commission in recent years. The High Powered Expert Committee for Estimating the Investment Requirements for Urban Infrastructure and Services (HPEC) has observed that: 'Urban local governments in India are among the weakest in the world both in terms of capacity to raise resources and financial autonomy. . . . ULBs' tax bases are narrow, and inflexible and lack buoyancy, and they have also not been able to levy user charges for the services they deliver to cover O&M and depreciation costs' (GoI 2011).

This Committee further noted that the share of urban local self-governments' own revenue in the total revenue has declined from 63 per cent in 2002-3 to 53 per cent in 2007-8. The end result of such a grim fiscal situation has been obvious. It has contributed to huge under-spending in relation to what is needed to build urban infrastructure and deliver public services within the overall framework of an inclusive society.

Reacting to an intense fiscal stress of the urban local self-governments, the Standing Committee of the 14th Lok Sabha expressed:

> . . . its deep anguish to note that most of the Municipalities, which are statutorily responsible for provisioning and maintenance of basic infrastructure and services in cities and towns, are under fiscal stress. They are given to understand that many of the Municipalities have not been able to carry out their assigned civic functions and pay salaries and wages to their employees, although, the financial conditions of bigger municipal corporations had not been as bad as of smaller municipalities. (quoted from GoI 2007)

The views expressed by the Second Administrative Reform Commission as well are not very different. It has also expressed the view that even after the 74th Constitution Amendment the financial position of the municipal institutions has not improved commensurate with their functions and responsibilities. It further observed that the position of the smaller municipal institutions is much worse and at times they find it difficult to even meet their establishment costs (ibid.). The Twelfth Finance Commission noted that the size of the municipal sector, measured in terms of resources raised and spent by the municipalities, was just one per cent of the GDP. The World Bank, while reviewing municipal finance in different developing countries observed that a comparison of per capita local revenue and expenditure in Poland, Russia, Brazil, Mexico or South Africa shows that Indian urban local self-governments spend and collect considerably less expenditure and revenue per capita than all of the comparison countries except Mexico. Citing examples, the Bank noted that Municipal Corporations in Maharashtra spend an average of $ 58 per capita that is well below Russia's average local expenditure of $ 349 or Poland's average local expenditure of $ 358.

Crippling Supervision and Control

An elaborate state control on the day-to-day functioning of municipal authorities was crippling the urban local self-governments. These powers were frequently exercised through inspection, calling of records and giving directions for performing civic functions. Besides these, the state governments also possessed and retain even now overwhelming powers of supervision and control in matters of appointment, approval of contracts and estimates above a predetermined amount, sanctioning of new posts, and framing of byelaws and rules. In fiscal matters, control pertains to deciding of tax rates and expenditures incurred. Despite being the units of self-government, it is inconceivable that the municipal authorities did not have powers to approve their own budgets and decide the tax rates. In many states the law provided for submission of municipal budgets to the state governments for approval before the budgets become operational. Such a practice exists even now in many states. As far as financial control on municipal governments is concerned, even the municipal corporations were required to obtain state approval of expenditures beyond certain limits that were ridiculously low. This in Kerala was Rs. 1 lakh, Rs. 50,000 in Andhra Pradesh, and Rs. 20,000 in Himachal Pradesh. In municipalities, the limit was even much lower. In Tamil Nadu, for example, it was Rs. 8,000 only. Obviously, with these controls, the municipal authorities could hardly be treated as embodiments of self-government.

The most drastic mechanism of control was applied by the state governments through an act of supersession of the urban local self-governments without reconstituting the Council through fresh election for years together. This resulted in prolonged supersession of a large number of municipal councils. The historical Madras Municipal Corporation which is the first municipal body to be constituted in this country, also became the first municipal authority in the country to have the longest spell of supersession, i.e. from 1974 to 1993. As of 1989, as many as 39 out of 71 Municipal Corporations then existing in the country were superseded in different states. Such elaborate and comprehensive control system smacked of the French system of administrative tutelage which the French themselves abandoned under the wave of decentralization under President Mitterrand. An expert of the World Bank, after surveying inter-government relations in various countries, put India under the category of 'perversely controlled' system of local government (Dillinger 1993). It needs to be mentioned that by virtue of being the 'creatures' of state governments, the institutions of self-government will have to live with supervision and control within a framework of master and agent syndrome.

THE BIG-BANG DECENTRALIZATION: THE CONSTITUTION (74TH AMENDMENT ACT)

The factors discussed above led to considerable weakening of the institutional capability of urban local self-governments. Decline in the institutions of self-government was so pervasive that it acquired a connotation which was identified with everything that is second grade and inferior. Observation of the then Prime Minister Rajiv Gandhi about tremendous leakage in funds allocated for rural development and poverty alleviation further buttressed the need for strengthening of local government. Something had to be done to strengthen and empower the urban local self-governments. Dithering of state governments on strengthening of urban local self-governments provided support to the liberal view of providing necessary elements for their empowerment in the Constitution itself. The outcome was a big bang decentralization by amending the Indian Constitution in 1992. It was thought that improving the lives of Indians requires decentralization of planning, development, financing, and taking of decisions to the local governments so that the local communities could have a greater say in devising of local plans and programmes for their own development and well being. It also became obvious that the state governments did not take the required steps for strengthening the local government institutions under the framework of the three Lists in the Indian Constitution. As the practice of devolving of power and authority to the local governments through enactments of laws by the state governments proved to be futile in strengthening and empowerment of the local governments—both rural and urban, it was thought prudent to provide for these in the Indian Constitution itself. With this end in view, a process of creating consensus amongst the state governments ensued in 1989 at the initiative of PM Rajiv Gandhi by holding a series of state and regional level conferences—Nagarpalika Sammelans. Finally 64th Amendment Bill for the Panchayati Raj institutions and the 65th Amendment Bill for the urban local self-governments were placed in the Parliament in 1989. The Bills became quite controversial. Two main arguments were advanced against the passage of the Bill. First, it was averred that the Parliament had no *locus standi* for enacting on local government that forms part of the State List on which the Parliament hardly has a jurisdiction. Second, it amounted to altering the basic structure of the Constitution which, according to a Supreme Court's ruling in 1973, cannot be obliterated (AIR 1973). These arguments not only delayed the process of amending the Constitution but also thwarted the enactment of the 64th (now 73rd) and 65th (now 74th) Amendment Acts. Subsequently, it was asserted that the spirit of the 74th Constitution Amendment was to bring about a change in urban local self-governance. The Bills were referred to a Joint Parliamentary Committee. Finally the Lok Sabha passed the Bill on 22nd December 1992 and the Rajya Sabha acted similarly on 23 December 1992. It received assent of the President of India on 20 April 1993. It was published in the Government Gazette on 20 April 1993 as the 'Constitution (Seventy Forth Amendment) Act, 1992' (74th CAA). This milestone amendment under Article 243ZF required the state governments to bring their existing Municipal Laws or enact a new law for bringing the then existing municipal laws in conformity with the provisions of the Constitution (74th Amendment) Act, 1992 within one year of the enactment of the CAA. All the state governments complied with this constitutional requirement and the 74th CAA became operational in 1993.

Tracing the evolution of local government in India thus reveals that decentralization has travelled a long journey over several millenniums with a chequered history of centralization of several forms. Centralized system of urban governance in ancient India was epitomized in City Superintendent and in *kotwal* during the Mughal Rule. With the advent of Company rule in India, the indigenous institutions of local governance gave way to a superimposed system that was created solely for collection of revenue, promoting administrative efficiency and performance of quasi-judicial functions during the Company Rule. With transfer of power from the East India Company to the British Government in 1858, centralized system of urban governance entered a new phase with feeble overtures of devolution to the local citizenry. Lord Ripon's historical Resolution of 1882 represented a forerunner of seemingly liberal approach to urban governance by introducing for the first time limited representation of non-officials especially for imparting them 'political and popular education'. The post-independent period, strangely witnessed a trend towards decline of urban local self-government due to a host of reasons, the most important of them being an indifferent attitude of the states in doing substantially enough to empower and strengthen them. Only towards the fag end of the last century, a step of far reaching importance was taken for this by enacting the 74th CAA. Implementation processes of new provisions in the Constitution got reinforced by launching a big urban infrastructure project that also had components for driving reforms for strengthening and empowerment of the urban local self-governments.

REFERENCES

AIR, 1973, *His Holiness Kesvananda Bharti Sripadgalvaru & Others v. State of Kerala and Another*, AIR, SC: p. 1461.

Dillinger, William, 1993, *Decentralization and its Implications for Urban Service Delivery*, Washington, D.C.: World Bank.

Government of India (GoI), 1951, *Report of the Local Finance Enquiry Committee*, Delhi: Manager Printing Press.

——, 1953, *Report of the Taxation Enquiry Commission*, Delhi: Manager Printing Press.

——, 1963, *Report of the Committee of Ministers Constituted by the Central Council of Local Self-Government*, Delhi: Manager Printing Press.

——, 1966, *Report of the Rural-Urban Relationship Committee*, vol. I, Delhi: Manager Prining Press.

——, 1974, *Report of the Committee on Budgetary Reform in Municipal Administration*, Delhi: Ministry of Works and Housing.

——, 1983, *Report of the Study Group on Constitution, Powers and Laws of Urban Local Bodies and Municipal Corporations*, Delhi: Ministry of Works and Housing.

——, 1988a, *Reports of the Task Forces on Housing and Urban Development*, Delhi: Planning Commission.

——, 1988b, *Report of the National Commission on Urbanisation*, Delhi: Ministry of Works and Housing.

——, 2007, *Sixth Report of the Second Administrative Reform Commission, Local*

Govenance: An Inspiring Journey into the Future, Delhi: Ministry of Personnel, Public Grievances and Pensions, Department of Administrative Reform and Public Grievances.

——, 2011, High Powered Expert Committee for Estimating the Investment Requirements for Urban Infrastructure and Services, *Report on Indian Infrastructure and Services*, Delhi: Ministry of Urban Development.

Jha, Gangadhar and S.N. Mishra, 1984, 'Development and Functioning of Urban Local Self-Government and Rural Local Self-Government in India', in Eastern Regional Organisation of Public Administration (ed.), *Comparative Study on Local Public Administration in Asian and Pacific Countries*, Tokyo: EUROPA, pp. 56-97.

Jha, Gangadhar 2009, 'Jawaharlal Nehru National Urban Renewal Mission: Bridging the Missing Gap', *Urban World*, 2 (2): 23-31.

Wright, Deil, 1988, *Understanding Intergovernmental Relations*, California: Brooks/Cole Publishing Company.

CHAPTER 3

Decentralization and Empowerment of Urban Local Self-Government: The Constitution Amendment

Decline of urban local self-government (ULSG) and diminution in its institutional capacity after India achieved Independence led to thinking for its strengthening and for bringing about improvement in the performance of ULSG institutions through decentralization. Steps were taken to strengthen them by taking appropriate steps. In this regard, four important initiatives taken at the national level in the post-Independence era for decentralization and strengthening of municipal governance are worth mentioning. These are (i) Creation of Central Council of Local Government and Urban Development, (ii) Enactment of Constitution (74th Amendment) Act, 1992 (74th CAA), (iii) Constitution of the National Commission to Review the Working of the Constitution in 2000 and (iv) Constitution of the Second Administrative Reforms Commission (SARC) in 2005. Whereas the Central Council of Local Government and Urban Development was created for deliberating on strengthening of ULSGs, the 74th CAA was enacted as a major initiative for empowerment and strengthening of municipal governments through decentralization of functions, finances and planning for local socio-economic development that could contribute to the national economic growth as well. The measures for strengthening of urban local self-government through decentralization were put in the Constitution of India itself so that these could be effectively implemented by the state governments. The National Commission to Review the Working of the Constitution was constituted to 'examine, in the light of the experience of the past 50 years, as to how best the Constitution can respond to the changing needs of efficient, smooth and effective system of governance and socio-economic development of modern India. . . .' As the urban local self-governments became constitutional entities through an amendment of the Constitution in 1992, the Constitution Review Commission also examined and reviewed constitutional provisions for them. SARC was given a broad Terms of Reference (ToR) to 'suggest measures to achieve a proactive, responsive, accountable, sustainable and efficient administration for the country at all levels of the government'. The ToR also required the Commission to consider Local Self-Government/Panchayati Raj institutions in addressing its broader ToR mentioned above. SARC, therefore, took a fresh look at local self-government both rural and urban after about fifteen years of enactment of the Constitution (74th Amendment) Act, 1992.

The first two initiatives are discussed below; views and suggestions of Constitution Review Commission and SARC are discussed in Chapter 5. However, discussion on the first two initiatives are preceded by looking into the conceptual overtures of decentralization in terms of concept, forms, and even risks and imperatives of decentralization as it is understood in the literature on this subject.

DECENTRALIZATION: THE CONCEPT

In simple terms, decentralization is the obverse of centralization. It is perhaps because of this attribute that very often this term is used to mean so many things, some of which are quite diverse. Shifting of administrative machinery from the centre to the periphery, granting some power to the functionary down below the top level in the administrative hierarchy, dispersal of branches from the headquarter to the region are quite frequently expressed to connote decentralization. Decentralization actually means that sub-national (or sub-state) units of government are given discretion to engage in effective (as opposed to illusory) decision-making process that affects the lives of the people who are residing within sub-national or sub-state jurisdictions (Wolman and McCormick

1994). A seminal report on Community Projects and National Extension Service in India submitted in the late 1950s defined it as 'a process whereby the Government divests itself completely of certain duties and responsibilities and devolves them on to some other authority' (GoI 1957). Decentralization thus connotes divesting of certain responsibilities and its devolving to sub-nationals in varying forms and degrees as has been observed in the recent past after the demise of the erstwhile centrally planned economies in central Asia and eastern Europe (Horvath 200; Peteri 2002; Martinez-Vazaquez and McNab 1997).

FORMS OF DECENTRALIZATION

Decentralization has several forms such as administrative decentralization, political decentralization, delegation and de-concentration (Cheema and Rondinelli 1983). Administrative decentralization entails transfer of civil servants and public functions to the local level. De-concentration has a more spatial connotation. It implies shifting of functions and resources, including personnel, by a level of government to other locations. It also involves shifting some of the functions of a department down below not to any other level of government but to the subordinate office of the same department. The interesting aspect of de-concentration is that often decisions can be made on the spot, under the principle of subsidiarity, without reference to Headquarters but ultimately authority is retained by the level of government which has effected de-concentration in the first instance. Principle of subsidiarity means that functions must be assigned to the lowest level at which they can be effectively executed. Hence, there are obvious benefits of de-concentration, both in terms of Principle of Subsidiarity and creating employment in less prosperous and low cost regions without ceding central control and authority. Delegation involves transfer of functions and duties to semi-autonomous bodies or public enterprises, usually without specifying the period of the transfer. This is done especially for the purpose of bypassing the central bureaucracy and avoiding the day to day controls in running the new enterprise. Delegation also means entrusting by an official some of his powers to his subordinate for speedy discharge of functions. Under delegation as well, ultimate authority is vested in the centre and the board or the executive of the agency.

Political decentralization involves devolution of power to the sub-national governments to take decision on their own. It provides autonomy to the sub-nationals for decision-making. In the context of local government, it means devolving of power and authority for planning and development to the local governments so that it has autonomy in making its own decisions in discharge of the mandated functions. It also means that the local governments need to take decisions in a transparent manner and must be accountable for the consequences of any decision taken by them. Fiscal decentralization, in a way, is part of political decentralization and involves devolution of powers and authority for raising resources and revenue generation. Devolution of functions, power and authority for decision-making, in order to be effective, needs to be accompanied by fiscal decentralization especially because devolution of functions does not carry any meaning unless it is accompanied by matching sources of revenue and the authority to use them in financing of the devolved functions.

Of the several forms of decentralization mentioned above, it is devolution of responsibility to the sub-national or local government for taking decisions for planning, development and services delivery that characterizes decentralization in true sense of the term. But this raises a valid question about the meaning of 'devolution of responsibility'. What actually is meant by devolving of responsibility? Rondinelli specifies 'responsibilities' to be devolved as 'authority to plan, make decisions (finance), or manage public functions' and these, under decentralization, have to be transferred to the lower levels of government (Rondinelli 1981). Decentralization thus connotes dispersion of political decision-making from the centre to the periphery, from the national to the sub-national levels of government. Political decisions contain within its fold, decisions to pursue policy of a particular type relating to development and welfare of the constituents, levels of expenditures to be incurred, its allocation to various functions and to raise revenue according to the revenue implication of expenditure decisions. Conceptual groundings of decentralization makes it obvious that there are important ingredients of decentralization. These are (i) extent of delegation of powers; (ii) formal legal responsibilities; and (iii) political resources. These, however, constitute only one of the two inter-linked themes of decentralization in the contemporary literature on the subject. The second relates to decentralization from governments to market, quasi-market and non-governmental organizations (Bennett 1994). Thus decentralization has come to acquire quite a broader connotation that includes devolving of responsibility not only to the sub-national levels of governments but also to multiple actors such as market, quasi-market and even the non-government organizations involved in development and enhancing the lives of the communities.

Decentralization also involves certain important considerations for its success that need to be taken into account. Three prime considerations in decentralization of authority relating to planning and development are (i) autonomy to the local communities in deciding what do they need for themselves, (ii) efficiency in provision of services in terms of (a) lower costs, and (b) quick response in addressing the concerns of the communities with respect to service delivery, and (iii) accountability of the decentralized units in (a) the use of resources, and (b) to the local communities in its day-to-day functioning and in provision of public services that are needed by the local communities. However, decentralization of power and authority to take decisions if not accompanied by devolution of tax authority to the sub-national governments (local self-governments) is unlikely to meet the objectives of decentralization. Political decentralization, therefore, needs to be accompanied by fiscal decentralization especially because fiscal decentralization ensures that local government is financially stable and strong and is, at the same time, also accountable for the decisions (financial and others) taken by it. It also imparts transparency and accountability in local governance. Financial accountability is achieved through adherence to (i) the regulations related especially to prevent preparation of deficit budgets, (ii) prescribed accounting standards, and (iii) effective tax administration systems and procedures. Transparency entails making decisions in public and in full disclosure of information used in making decisions. Public economics suggests two ways to put in place a scheme of fiscal decentralization. First is revenue assignment that needs to be in consonance with expenditure assignment (assignment of functions), and second is an appropriately designed fiscal transfer system to compensate the subnationals (local governments in this case) for the loss of efficiency in performance of local functions largely due to externalities arising out of spillover of costs and benefits. As regards the first, the matching principle has three important aspects that acquires the centre-stage: expenditure responsibilities must be matched with tax authority (revenue sources), revenue capacities should be matched with political accountability, and the local areas benefiting from local government services should be matched with financing of such services (Bird 1994; Shah 2004).

Decentralization of decision-making for planning and development of local government areas is, therefore, critically contingent on fiscal decentralization. Whereas deepening of democracy at the local level through decentralization promotes transparency and accountability in local decision-making process, fiscal decentralization prevents 'tax exporting' and facilitates funding at the margin through fiscal transfers from the higher level(s) of government. It also promotes accountability for the decision makers to fully bear the cost of decisions taken by them.

BENEFITS OF DECENTRALIZATION

The wave of decentralization that ensued in the 1980s swept several economies across the globe due to a variety of motivations emanating from decentralization. These include improved economic efficiency and accountability, increased resource mobilization (Campbell and Brakarz 1991), more equitable and efficient service delivery through better use of local knowledge, improved governance driven by local responsiveness and political participation, allocation efficiency in terms of improved welfare, political stability and stable finances, and reduced strain on central finances (Bird and Vaillancourt 1998).

These motivations of decentralization impelled countries across the globe—developed, developing, and transitional—to opt for decentralization in recent decades. Developed countries started taking fresh looks in re-designing inter-government fiscal relations in the wake of globalization and decentralization to the markets. Developing countries and the transitional economies as well got engaged in decentralizing governance and tax authority for enhancing national economic development and improving quality of life of their citizens (Owens and Panella 1991). The transitional economies constitute interesting examples of decentralization in varying forms and degree after the demise of the centrally planned economies.

RISKS OF FISCAL DECENTRALIZATION

Fiscal decentralization—an important adjunct to political decentralization—if not properly designed, involves serious pitfalls. Risks include fiscal inequities and inefficiencies especially if the net fiscal benefits vary across different local government areas largely due to varying local fiscal capacities and undercutting of local government services on activities involving externalities (Shah 2004). Local governments may not have incentives to provide services that involve externalities primarily because such services benefit not only the communities residing within the local areas but also those that reside outside the local areas but do not pay for the provision of such services. The cost of provision of such services involving externalities is thus not met by the users of such services. This provides disincentive to the local governments for undercutting provision of such services. Fiscal decentralization is likely to increase costs of service provision and reduce efficiency in service delivery, and contribute to greater inequality and macroeconomic instability (Prud'homme 1991). Another risk emanates in situations when revenue decentralization is not matched by revenue mobilization (Bird and Vaillancourt 1998) due to reasons of fiscal profligacy or lack of institutional capacity for resource mobilization as is the case in most of the urban local self-governments in India across various states. Such risks are mitigated by suitably designing transfer system that imposes restrictions on local government borrowings, addresses spillovers of cots and benefits of municipal service delivery and strengthens local government institutional capacity.

IMPERATIVES OF DECENTRALIZATION

Accomplishment of objectives of decentralization is dependent on a number of imperatives and instrumentalities. These include (i) fiscal decentralization (revenue assignment in conformity with expenditure assignments and local government autonomy to set the rates), (ii) institutional capacity not only for effective tax administration, but for effective, efficient, inclusive and responsive discharge of mandated functions (iii) rational inter-government fiscal relations based on appropriately designed transfer system, (iv) system of local government accountability, (v) participatory structures and processes at the local level for enhancing accountability and transparency, and (vi) institutional incentives. Successful functioning of local government under a decentralized regime is largely contingent on addressing these imperatives.

STEPS TAKEN AFTER INDEPENDENCE FOR EMPOWERING URBAN LOCAL SELF-GOVERNMENT

As mentioned in the beginning of this chapter, steps were taken towards strengthening of urban local self-government in the post-independent India. The first of the couple of initiatives taken in this regard are discussed below.

Creation of the Central Council of Local Government and Urban Development

A significant step was taken after Independence in 1970 when through a Presidential Order, the Central Council of Local Self-Government was created consisting of the Union Minister of Health (now Minister of Housing and Urban Affairs) in the chair and the State Ministers of Local Self-Government. It was renamed as Central Council of Local Government and Urban Development in

1980. It was created as an advisory body for considering and recommending policy measures to the Central Government for allocation of funds and devolving of powers and functions to the municipal bodies. It served as a forum for discussing bottlenecks in strengthening local government capacity and its resolution through a deliberative process. The Council used to meet on an annual basis for deliberating on the various aspects of urban local self-government. Lately, however, the activities of the Central Council of Local Government and Urban Development has been waning out, it has almost become defunct and no longer holds its meeting as was the practice in the past for reviewing the local government performance, addressing the bottlenecks, and for flagging issues in strengthening of urban local bodies for effective service provision. This also indicates central government's lack of appetite for engaging in urban governance and its intense preoccupation with augmentation of urban infrastructure, development of new towns and 'smart cities' by adopting a project approach to urban development without caring for consolidation of urban governance and resolution of catalytic issues in this regard. The Ministry of Panchayati Raj, on the other hand, has been doing this on a regular and sustained basis. This enables this Ministry in proper stewardship of the Panchayati Raj institutions. The Ministry of Housing and Urban Affairs would, therefore, need to revive the Central Council for reviewing the functioning of ULSGs and focus on the required policy initiatives for strengthening urban governance and municipal management.

DEVOLUTION TO THE URBAN LOCAL SELF-GOVERNMENT: THE CONSTITUTION (74TH AMENDMENT) ACT, 1992

The 74 CAA happens to be a milestone for introducing decentralized urban governance in the country. As this was a step taken in a declining environment of urban local self-governance, it created much of hype as well. With a view to comprehend the 74th Amendment Act it would be advisable to analyse its contents and understand the motivation for its enactment as it was said to be a big bang decentralization initiative. The motivation for amending the Constitution is contained in unambiguous terms in the Statement of Object and Reasons for the amendment. It says: 'In many States local bodies have become weak and ineffective on account of a variety of reasons, including the failure to hold regular elections, prolonged supersessions and inadequate devolution of powers and functions. As a result, Urban Local Bodies are not able to perform effectively as vibrant democratic units of self-government.'

In order to address the 'reasons' for weak institutional capacity of urban local self-governments, it was thought necessary to provide in the Constitution itself the measures needed to empower them. Motivation for this came from the Report of the Singhvi Committee which was submitted in 1986 for revitalization of the Panchayati Raj Institutions (PRI), not for the urban local self-governments. The Committee had suggested to treat Gram Sabha as the base of a decentralized PRIs and stressed to treat the PRIs as institutions of self-governance which would actually facilitate participation of people in the process of planning and development. It also recommended giving constitutional recognition to rural local self-government and inclusion of a new Chapter in the Constitution for this purpose (GoI 1986). The process for decentralization, therefore, began for empowering the PRIs by giving them a constitutional status. Though giving constitutional status to the PRIs was not favoured by the Sarkaria Commission (GoI 1988), the central government accepted the recommendations of the Singhvi Committee. This was followed by series of consultation process with officials and elected representatives of PRIs. These consultation events prompted a similar thinking in the Ministry of Urban Development as well. Motivation to go for similar process for the urban local self-governments took shape in 1989 and similar consultation process followed in the form of what was then called—the Nagarpalika Sammelans for conceptualization of decentralization of urban governance as also for creating broad consensus around the concept of decentralization. It was viewed as an 'attempt to force the pace of change' and as an initiative in search of responsive administration (Sivaramakrishnan 2000).[1]

As in the case of PRIs, the Nagarpalikas (the Municipalities) as well had to be given constitutional recognition through an amendment to the Indian Constitution. It was thought that once the provisions are incorporated in the Constitution itself, these would become sacrosanct and the state governments will be obliged to implement the constitutional provisions. The two Bills drafted for decentralization, however, were subjected to high voltage political drama when introduced in the Parliament. Despite the best effort of the Congress party, which had a majority in the Lok Sabha, in floor management in the two houses of the Parliament, the Bill fell through in the Rajya Sabha by a margin of just three votes though the Lok Sabha had passed it earlier. Though the rejection of the Bill in the Rajya Sabha did not constitutionally oblige the Congress government to resign from office, the then Prime Ministser (Rajiv Gandhi) decided to resign and hold fresh elections for formation of a new government. After the general elections in 1989 that led to defeat of the Congress party, the two successive governments that came in power could not enact the two Bills for decentralization. Finally, the Bills were placed in the Lok Sabha by the new government that came in power after the general elections held again in 1991. The new government in power tried to project the two Bills as 'serious endeavour for empowerment of the people and the local bodies' (Sivaramakrishnan 2000).This time when the two Bills were placed in the Lok Sabha, these were referred to a Joint Committee of both the houses. Finally, the two Constitution Amendment Bills were passed by the Parliament in December 1992 after renumbering them as 73rd (for PRIs) and 74th (for ULSGs). The Constitution was thus amended in 1992 by enactment of the Constitution (74th Amendment) Act, 1992 by the Parliament. In compliance with constitutional provisions, after ratification of the Bills by half the states, it received the assent of the President of India in April 1993 and the provisions of this enactment came into force on 1 June 1993. The state governments had to bring the laws relating to PRIs and ULSGs in conformity with the constitutional provisions by 1 June 1994. In specific terms, the inadequacies mentioned in the Object and Reasons of the 74th CAA also envisaged to put, on a firmer footing, 'the relationship between the State Government and the Urban Local Bodies' especially with respect to (i) their functional domain, (ii) tax powers, (iii) arrangement for revenue sharing, (iv) ensuring conduct of local elections on a regular basis, (v) timely election in the event of supersession, and (vi) providing representation to the weaker sections such as Scheduled Castes and Schedules Tribes. Through the 74th CAA, a new part—Part IXA was added to the Indian Constitution.

The 74th Amendment to the Constitution of India is thus the culmination of a prolonged debate in post-Independent India for devising a democratic and empowered system of municipal government. It generated high expectations for emergence of a new structure of urban local government with additional devolution of functions, planning responsibilities, new system of fiscal transfers and strengthening of institutional capabilities. It raised high hopes and was viewed as a harbinger of a new era of empowered and vigorous system of urban local self-government. It also provided new opportunity for the urban local self-governments to derive their very existence from the Constitution itself. The expectations ran high that it will refurbish the whole system of urban local self-governance by implanting a new structure of municipal government with additional devolution of functions, planning responsibilities, new system of fiscal transfers and empowerment of women and weaker sections of the society. It was thought to provide much needed institutional capabilities to the otherwise fragile system of urban government in dealing with the impulses of urbanization and urban growth. In order to comprehend this decentralization initiative as also its efficacy in empowering of urban local self-government, one needs to look at the prime provisions relating to (i) constitution of the urban local self-governments, (ii) their structure and composition, (iii) empowerment of weaker sections (iv) powers and functions, (v) finances, and (vi) planning.

Constitution of Municipalities

The 74th Constitution Amendment Act uses the expression 'municipalities' for the urban local self-government. The municipalities are to be created by the Governor. Before the enactment of the 74th CAA, urban settlements had five types of local government, viz. (i) Municipal Corporation, (ii) Municipal Council, (iii) Town Area Committee, (iv) Notified Area Committee, and (v) Cantonment Board. The latter was and is even now constituted in cantonments by including its civilian urban outgrowth. The 74th CAA provides for creation of only three types of ULSGs such as (i) Municipal Corporation in 'larger urban area', (ii) Municipal Councils in 'smaller urban area', and (iii) Nagar Panchayats in 'transitional areas'. Interpretation of larger, smaller and transitional areas has been left to the discretion of the state governments. Nevertheless, the Constitution provides a cue to the Governors of various states for doing so by taking into account (i) population of the area, (ii) density of population, (iii) revenue generated for local administration, (iv) percentage of employment in non-agricultural activities, (v) economic importance of the area and 'such other factors as he may deem fit'. For amorphous 'transitional area' as well, the Constitution alludes to the areas that are in the process of transition from rural to urban. It, therefore, means such rural areas that are in the process of losing their rural attributes and acquiring attributes that are urban in nature. For these three different areas, the 74th CAA (Article 243Q) provides to create three types of ULSGs as mentioned below:

1. Municipal Corporation in 'a larger urban area';
2. Municipal Council in 'a smaller urban area'; and
3. Nagar Panchayat in 'a transitional area'.

Local government structure enshrined in the Constitution, as mentioned above, envisages three types of local government in urban areas such as Municipal Corporations, Municipal Council and Nagar Panchayats in larger, smaller and transitional areas respectively. The discretion given to the states in interpreting larger urban area, smaller urban area and transitional urban has led to creation of these varieties of urban local government in the different size categories of urban settlements according to the perception of the various state governments. Therefore, the size categories of the three types of local government vary a great deal across the various states. The discretionary power given to the state governments has possibilities of treating even a smaller area as a 'transitional area' and even a larger urban area as a smaller urban area. The 65th Amendment Bill which could not be adopted by the Parliament, did not leave any room for any interpretation or discretion as it had specified that a Nagar Panchayat was to be constituted in a transitional area with a population of 10,000 to less than 20,000, Municipal Councils in the town with a population of 20,000 to less than 3 lakh and Municipal Corporations in the cities with a population of 3 lakh and more. As discussed in greater detail in Chapter 5, the Second Administrative Reforms Commission has extensively commented on the local government structure enshrined in the 74th CAA and suggested alternative size categories of urban areas for constituting the three types of urban local self-government (GoI 2007).

An issue in the context of urban governance is governance of the Census Towns that despite being large in number are not yet brought within the fold of urban governance. The last Census of 2011 has shown that there are as many as 3,894 Census Towns that comply with the definition of urban settlement of the Census, but are not yet statutory towns. Despite being urban according to the Census definition, the residents in these towns do not get the much needed urban services and an opportunity to participate in governance even indirectly. The constitutional provisions would, therefore, need to address this existing void. Prime consideration for not converting a Census town into a statutory town is the benefit of transfer of substantial funds from the higher levels of government to these settlements that are still under the Panchayati Raj and get substantial transfer in the form of backward regional grant fund, and grants for rural development and central and state sector schemes.

Duration of Municipalities

The 74th CAA provides for duration of municipalities for a period of five years from the date of the first meeting of the municipality. One of the important and welcome provisions of the 74th CAA is that the municipalities are not to be dissolved and superseded *ad infinitum.* It provides that in case a municipality needs to be dissolved, the state governments have to follow the principle of natural justice; the municipality is required to be given a reasonable opportunity by the state government for being heard before its dissolution. If, even after this opportunity is given to a municipality for explaining the reasons for not dissolving it, a municipality is dissolved by the state government, the 74th CAA provides that, unlike the practice in the past when a municipality was kept under prolonged supersession, fresh election is now required to be held within a period of six months from the date of dissolution of the elected council. But after fresh election is held, the duration of the reconstituted municipality will be limited to only its remaining period of the initial five years. However, in case the remaining period of a dissolved municipality happens to be less than six months, fresh election is not required to be held after its dissolution.

Composition of Local Self-Governments

The 74th CAA provides that the urban local self-governments are to be constituted of (i) the elected representatives who are to be elected from different electoral wards of a municipality (ii) the Members of the House of the People (Lok Sabha) and the Legislative Assembly of the States representing constituencies which are wholly or partly under the municipal area, (iii) the Members of the Council of States (Rajya Sabha) and the Legislative Council of the States who are registered as electors within the municipal area; (iv) Chairpersons of Committees of the municipal authorities that are created by the state government under section (5) of Article 243S; and (v) persons having special knowledge or experience in municipal administration. The latter do not have the right to vote in the meetings of the Council.

Article 243R provides for inducting the Members of Parliament and the Members of the State Legislature as members of the municipality. Making the members of Parliament and the State Legislatures as the members of the local elected Councils is against the spirit of local self-government. They have also been given powers to vote in the meetings of the self-government institution. Their presence in the Council debates is unlikely to promote a free and frank debate by the locally elected Councilors. They are also likely to act as the 'Big Brother' described so cogently by George Orwell in his celebrated dystopian novel *1984* published in 1949.

The provision for making Chairpersons of the Committee to be created by the State Government under Section 5 of Article 243S mentioned above as well seems to be out of place. Municipal Act in different states has provisions for creation of various Committees other than the Wards or Ward Committees. Such Committees include Subject Committees, Ad-hoc Committees, Joint Committees, Public Accounts Committee, etc. These Committees are constituted of the elected Councilors only, one of whom is made Chairperson of the Committee. Chairpersons of these Committees already happen to be members of the municipality. The provision for inducting the Chairpersons of the Committees to be constituted under Section (5) of Article 243S is thus unwarranted. It also gives an impression that the State Governments, by constituting Committees in addition to the Committees already provided for in the Municipal Acts, are further empowered to interfere with the self-government institutions. Inducting Chairpersons of such unwarranted Committees as members of the elected council with a right to vote will be even more obnoxious and unwarranted. Such a provision to interfere in the affairs of self-government needs to be removed from the Constitution.

Empowerment of Weaker Sections of the Society

The 74th CAA also provides for empowerment of the weaker sections of the society by way of reservation of seats in every municipality. Every municipality is mandatorily required to reserve seats for scheduled caste and scheduled tribes. The number of seats to be reserved for them is to be decided on the basis of the proportion of population of each of these castes to the total population of the municipal area. For example, in case the population of scheduled castes is 15 per cent of the total population of the municipal areas, 15 per cent of the total number of seats to be filled through direct election is required to be reserved for this caste. The number of seats for the scheduled tribes is to be reserved in the similar manner.

The constitutional provisions also provide for rotation of such reserved seats in different constituencies. Of the total number of seats reserved for these castes individually, one-third of the seats so reserved is required to be reserved for women belonging to each of these castes. Seats are also required to be reserved for women belonging to other castes. One-third of the total number of seats including the seats reserved for women belonging to the two caste mentioned above, is required to be reserved for women. The seats reserved for women are as well required to be rotated in different constituencies of a municipality. The reservation of seats is extended to the offices of Chairpersons of the municipality as well. The 74th CAA provides that offices of the Chairpersons also are required to be reserved for scheduled castes, scheduled tribes and also for the women. The state legislatures have been given the discretion to decide the manner of reservation of seats for offices of the Chairpersons. It also gives authority to them for enactment of laws to provide for reservation of seats in offices of the Chairpersons in a municipality for even the backward castes.

Such an elaborate scheme of reservation especially for the offices of Chairpersons requires the municipalities to prepare a roster for reservation for scheduled castes, scheduled tribes, women and backward castes. Extending reservation even to the office of Chairpersons already has negative repercussions for effective urban governance. As the seats of Chairpersons are required to be reserved for different castes and also for the women, the Chairperson elected in the first instance is deprived of an opportunity to contest election for this office once again. This becomes instrumental in killing his/her motivation to be pro-active in improving urban governance. Such a system of depriving him/her of the second opportunity to contest for this office also makes the Chairperson prone to unethical practices.

Local Government Structure for Intra-City Decentralization

Urban local self-government institutions, as discussed in Chapter 1, happen to be located closest to the citizens as compared to the higher levels of government such as the state and the central governments. The intention of the Constitution Amendment Act is to put in place a system of intra-city decentralization for bringing local government even more nearer to the door steps of the citizens especially in large cities. It is a typical characteristic of the morphology of a city that as it grows in the wake of a high rate of demographic growth and the consequent swift physical sprawl, the nexus between the local self-government and the citizens gets disrupted. The citizens get alienated from the local government in this process; they do not get to know where to go for the redress of their grievances relating to delivery of municipal services. Intra-city decentralization, therefore, is an important mechanism to bring back local government nearer the citizens by creating appropriate decentralized structures and by developing an equally appropriate process so that the decentralized local government structures could interact with the citizenry in a responsive manner. The 74th CAA, therefore, provides for this structure by requiring the state governments to create Wards or Ward Committees in cities with more than 3 lakh population. Article 243S of the Constitution has provision for creation of Wards Committees 'consisting of one or more wards within territorial area of a Municipality having a population of 3 lakhs or more'. Thus, it provides for a two-tier structure of urban local self-government especially in the cities that have more than 3 lakh population. The first tier comprises the Town Hall—the main municipal office. The second tier is the Wards or Ward Committees. The provision in this regard as quoted above makes it obvious that Wards or Ward Committees have to be created either by pooling more than one ward together or in every Ward.

The Constitution has provision also for election of Chairpersons of the Wards/Ward Committees. Accordingly, in case of multiple Wards Committees, the councilors elected from the wards that are included to form the Wards Committee become its ex-officio members and they elect one from amongst themselves as Chairman. In case of Ward Committee created in each ward, the Councilor representing that ward becomes the ex-officio member and also the Chairperson as well. But in addition to the elected representatives, the Wards/Ward Committees are to have even nominated members. The 74th CAA gives discretion to the state governments to decide the composition, territorial area of a Wards Committee and the manner in which the seats in the Wards Committees are to be filled. Obviously, the type of persons who are to be nominated to the Wards/Ward Committee is not specified in the constitutional provisions. Constitutional provision with respect to composition of Wards/Ward Committees has given this onus to the state governments. Article 243S (2) (a) and (b) lays down that the 'Legislature of a State may, by law, make provision with respect to—(a) the composition and the territorial area of a Wards Committee' and '(b) the manner in which the seats in a Wards Committee shall be filled'. The 74th CAA thus provides the state governments discretion to nominate any one on the Wards/Ward Committees.

Article 243S gives option to the states for creating Wards Committees either by pooling a number of Wards together or a Ward Committee in each Ward within the territorial area of the urban local government. This has led to the creation of this Committee for multiple Wards only. Constitutional provisions also give discretion to the state governments for deciding the composition of Wards/Ward Committees. Discretion given to the state governments has led to nomination of additional members on this Committee besides the elected Councillors from the Wards pooled together. The enabling constitutional provision in this regard has thus (i) created a confusion and (ii) given discretion to the state governments for making provision for (a) the composition and the territorial area of a Wards Committee, and (b) the manner in which the seats in a Wards Committee are to be filled up.

Composition of Wards Committee as provided for in the Constitution happens to be yet another grey area. It provides prerogative to the state governments to nominate anybody on the Wards Committees. Such a provision is not amenable to much needed deepening of democracy at the Ward level. Specific types of persons to be nominated to this Committee especially from the civil society should have been specified in the Constitution rather than leaving it to State discretion. Presence of civil society representatives on the Wards Committee and for that matter on any

Committee of the Municipality contributes to transparency and accountability of the Municipality. The existing discretionary provisions to nominate the members do not go with the ethos of transparent and accountable self-government. Nominated members on the Wards/Ward Committees, by and large, happen to be the favourites of the political class; they hardly represent the civil society for enabling participatory governance in the true sense of the term.

Besides dilution in the composition of Wards Committees, this Committee has also lost its relevance in the wake of the Community Participation Bill (also called Nagar Raj Bill) that formed part of Central Government's agenda for its enactment in the states under the Jn-NURM project. Composition of Ward Committees under the Nagar Raj Bill is broad-based and its constitution requires bringing on it members from the civil society groups. The Bill also defines civil society in unambiguous terms. The basic intent of this Bill is to make the ward a basic unit for budgeting, planning and development. This Bill also has provisions for promoting semblance of direct democracy by constituting Area Sabha at the polling station level to be composed of all the adult members residing within the territorial jurisdiction of an Area Sabha. The Second Administrative Reforms Commission has as well suggested creation of a three-tier local government structure consisting of (i) Town Hall, (ii) Ward Committee in each ward, and (iii) Area Sabha.

Obviously, multiple Wards Committees have become largely irrelevant in a scheme of participatory local government structure with a Ward Committee in each ward as a forum for participation of civil society groups. It needs to be emphasized that existence of Wards Committees for more than one Ward along with a Ward Committee in each ward and Area Sabha, down below is prone to bureaucratization of local governance, overlapping and conflict. It would be advisable, therefore, to remove the provision for constituting of Wards Committee from the Constitution of India.

Municipal Functional Domain

The 74th CAA contains provisions with respect to municipal functional domain. It has added altogether a new Schedule in the

Indian Constitution—the Twelfth Schedule. It contains altogether 18 functions that should form part of the municipal functional domain. The functions mentioned in the Twelfth Schedule are contained in Annex II. The functions listed in the Twelfth Schedule allude to some of quite unconventional functions to be performed by the urban local self-governments. Article 243W that contains provisions relating to functions, on the face of it, makes quite an interesting reading of powers and functions of the urban local self-governments. It provides that the Legislature of a State:

> may, by law, endow the Municipalities with such powers and authority to *enable them to function as institutions of self-government* and such powers may contain provisions for the devolution of powers and responsibilities upon Municipalities, subject to such conditions as may be specified therein, with respect to—(i) the preparation of plans for economic development and social justice; (ii) the performance of functions and the implementation of schemes as may be entrusted to them including those in relation to the matters listed in the Twelfth Schedule (emphasis added).

The Constitution thus gives a message to make the municipalities vibrant institutions of 'self-government'. This is by far the core provision of Part IX A of the Indian Constitution as its prime objective is 'putting on a firmer footing the relationship between the State Government and the Urban Local Bodies'. Effectuation of such a provision for empowerment of urban local self-governments is, therefore, of paramount importance. Such laudable intention of the Constitution notwithstanding, the Constitution provides discretion to the state governments for devolving powers and the functions contained in the Twelfth Schedule to the urban local self-governments.

By making the Twelfth Schedule discretionary, functional domain of the urban local self-governments is still in a flux. Presence of parastatals in provision of urban services further contributes to fragmentation of functional domain of urban local self-government. Functions to be devolved to urban local self-government must take a holistic view of urban functions and all the civic services that are required to be provided in an urban area. All such functions need to be under the single umbrella of urban local self-governments. Fragmented local functional domain is primarily because of the discretion which the 74th CAA has given to the state governments with respect to devolving of functions to the urban local self-government. Left to the state governments, the devolution of functions may not be as complete as is supposed to be in the Twelfth Schedule. Drawing from the experience of indifferent attitude of the state governments in the past, the 74th CAA should not have left actual devolving of functions on the will of the state governments. A couple of developments in this regard all the more make one to believe that the functions listed in the Twelfth Schedule are going to be confined within the Twelfth Schedule itself; they are not going to be actually devolved to the municipal bodies. Amendments introduced in the Bombay Provincial Municipal Corporation Act in Gujarat and in most of other states in the garb of 'new enactment' for incorporating the spirit of the 74th CAA is at most a patchwork rather than altogether a new enactment. The inevitable result is that the local functional domain continues to be what it has been in the past.

Inclusion of 18 functions in the functional domain of the urban local self-governments gave an impression that an era of constituting specific purpose authorities by entrusting such functions to the specific purpose authorities will come to an end with the enactment of the 74th CAA. It also gave an impression that henceforth state encroachment on municipal functional domain will stop all together as these have been specified in the new schedule of functions. However, parastatal organizations and specific purpose authorities like the Slum Clearance and Improvement Board, Water Authorities, Urban Development Authorities and the like still thrive in the states and the traditional municipal functions are as fragmented as before. Second, the Indian Parliament, within a few days of enacting the 74th Constitution Amendment Act, also enacted a new law for the National Capital Territory of Delhi that provided for taking away from the then unified Municipal Corporation of Delhi (MCD) the functions relating to water supply, electricity and urban transport. Subsequently, the MCD was also divested of slum improvement functions. It is worth recapitulating that all such functions are listed in the Twelfth Schedule and are to be devolved to the municipal authorities! This, in a way, also betrays a negative attitude of the state governments as also the

Parliament in devolving of functions to the urban local self-governments.

Another issue relating to devolution of functions pertains to the nature of some of the functions which seem to be quite ambitious and even redundant and irrelevant for municipal authorities especially in the existing context of fragile institutional capacity of ULSGs located especially in small and medium cities and towns in the country. Planning for economic and social development, protection of environment and promotion of ecological aspects, urban poverty alleviation are functions which belong to this category. It is not that these are not important functions. Performance of such functions requires a much strong financial capability and entirely different type of human resources which the Municipalities are lacking miserably. The existing weak fiscal base of the ULSGs does not permit them to provide even the basic municipal functions. Performing unconventional functions mentioned above seems quite daunting for them. To expect them to discharge these functions efficiently, and effectively, therefore, seems to be a tall order indeed. As discussed in Chapter 5, the Constitution Review Commission and also the Second Administrative Reforms Commission have expressed altogether different views on nature and contents of the Twelfth Schedule.

A pertinent issue with respect to municipal functional domain is about the number and the type of functions listed in the Twelfth Schedule. Sivaramakrishnan, besides referring to the legal apprehensions about making the Twelfth Schedule mandatory, also alludes to general opposition to creation of a mandatory list of functions on the ground that it would bypass the state governments. He also refers to how the functions contained in the Twelfth Schedule was pruned from as many as 37 functions in the first Bill to just 18 functions by taking out functions such as welfare of the weaker sections, women and child development, family welfare, urban electrification, non-conventional energy, public distribution system. Subsequently, the Constitution Review Commission and also the Second Administrative Reforms Commission have expressed their views on municipal functions contained in the Twelfth Schedule. These are discussed in Chapter 5.

In view of the above what was, therefore, required was to provide for a local list of functions in the Constitution of India keeping in view the existing weak organizational capacity of a large number of municipalities. The Twelfth Schedule was made discretionary possibly because the drafting team of the 74th CAA was conscious of the landmark judgement delivered by the Supreme Court's constitution bench in the *Kesavanand Bharti Case* in 1973 that stipulates that the Parliament cannot alter the basic structure of the Constitution such as secularism, democracy, federalism, separation of power (AIR 1973). Making the Twelfth Schedule mandatory was apprehended to alter the basic structure of the Constitution. It was apprehended that providing for a local list of functions, most of which would have to be carved out from the State List of the Constitution would alter the basic structure of the Constitution. This Schedule was, therefore, made discretionary and contains only illustrative list of functions to be performed by the ULSGs (Sivaramakrishnan 2000).

Functions of Wards Committees

The Constitution also gives discretion to the state governments with respect to functions to be performed by the Wards Committees. It provides for devolving to the Wards Committees such functions by the state governments which may be necessary to enable them to carry out responsibilities conferred upon them. It could be surmised that such a provision is impelled because of two reasons. First, it was perhaps thought by the drafting team of the 74th CAA that constitutional provisions should not contain even the minutest details about everything associated with decentralization and intra-city decentralization. Second, giving discretion to the state governments would enable the states to customize functions of the Wards Committee according to obtaining situations in the different states. Thus the constitutional provisions though provide for creation of urban local self-governments and grant them constitutional right to exist, the functions to be performed by them are not yet specified in concrete terms. No wonder, therefore, that the functional domain of the ULSGs vary a great deal across the various states.

Municipal Fiscal Domain

The 74th CAA does not contain provisions for devolving specific sources of revenue to the urban local self-governments. This has been left to the State Finance Commissions as part of their Terms of Reference. Before the 74th CAA, transfers from the state governments to the ULSGs were ad-hoc. It was also not based on any rational basis. The 74th CAA, through Articles 243I and 243Y of the India Constitution, has provided for constitution of State Finance Commissions (SFCs) for rationalizing fiscal transfers to the local government—both rural and urban—on some rational basis for strengthening their finances. Creation of SFCs once in five years by the state governments is a mandatory provision of the Indian Constitution. The Constitution requires SFCs to review financial position of the ULBs and recommend to the Governor of the states on the following:

Principles for:

- distribution of net proceeds of taxes, duties, tolls and fees leviable by the states and distribution of the proceeds from these between the states and the ULBs and also amongst the ULSGs.
- Determination of taxes, duties, tolls, and fees that may be assigned to, or appropriated by the ULSGs.
- Grants-in-aid to the ULSGs from the consolidated fund of the states.
- Measures needed to improve financial position of the ULSGs.

The terms of reference of the State Finance Commissions mentioned above are thus much broader than those of the central Finance Commission (FC) that is constituted every five years by the President of India under Article 280 of the Constitution. FC does not have the mandate to suggest measures needed to improve financial position of state governments or the ULSGs. Also, the terms of reference of the FC does not include determination of taxes, duties, tolls, and fees that may be assigned to, or appropriated by the ULSGs After the SFC reports are submitted to the respective Governors of states, the Governor has the constitutional obligation to ensure that the recommendations of the SFCs along with an explanatory memorandum relating to the action taken on these recommendations are laid before the state legislature. Another provision of the 74th CAA having important ramifications for strengthening financial capabilities of municipalities is the amendment of Article 280 of the Constitution by amending the Terms of Reference (ToR) of the FC. The amended ToR requires the FC to also recommend 'the measures needed to augment the Consolidated Fund of a State to supplement the resources of the Municipalities in the State on the basis of the recommendations made by the Finance Commission of the State'.

For any level of government, effective discharge of functions requires devolving of fiscal authority that must be in consonance with the range of functions to be performed by it. However, strengthening of municipal finance and the local resource base, under the 74th CAA, is left to the state governments to decide. The Constitution does not provide local list of revenue. It has very conveniently ignored this critical area (fiscal decentralization) of municipal governance. Taxes, duties, tolls and fees to be levied by them and assigned to them as also the grants-in-aid to be given to them have been left to the discretion of the state governments. The experience in the past suggests that in a large number of states, the state governments have not only been indifferent to the need of revamping of municipal finance but have also encroached upon the legitimate sources of local revenue. Profession Tax, for example, has been taken over by the state governments in Karnataka, Haryana, Madhya Pradesh, Meghalaya, Nagaland, Tripura and West Bengal. In Andhra Pradesh, Entry Tax is being used by the state government. In Madhya Pradesh, even Property Tax was taken over in the past by the state government. In the states of Rajasthan, Punjab and Himachal Pradesh, Property Tax—the prime source of local revenue—is not levied on all the properties. Left to the discretion of state governments, the prospects of refurbishing municipal finance system do not seem very bright. It was, therefore, required to specify the sources of local revenue in the Constitution of India itself so that there could be constitutional protection and guarantee about it. After all, the Government of India Act, 1919 had a local list of sources of revenue that was abolished at the time of enactment of the Government of India Act, 1935.

The only redeeming feature of the 74th Amendment in financial sphere is the mandatory constitution of Finance Commission by the state governments once in every five years. State Finance Commissions are to make recommendations regarding principles to govern the sharing of state taxes, duties, tolls, and fees between the state governments and the municipalities and also its distribution between the municipalities. The State Finance Commissions (SFCs) are also required to suggest the principles for determination of taxes, duties, tolls and fees to be assigned to them and the grants-in-aid to be given to the municipal authorities out of the Consolidated Fund of the state. It also has the mandate to suggest ways and means of improving financial position of municipal authorities. A silent feature of the 74th CCA relating to constitution of SFCs is the forthright and explicit provision about the recommendations of the SFCs which in the past were generally filed. Henceforth, the Governors of states are required to lay before the State Legislature the recommendations made by the SFCs along with an explanatory memorandum containing action to be taken on it. Thus the suggestions and observations of SFCs shall have to be taken note of by the state governments. This is one of the most important aspects of the 74th CCA.

Though mandatory provision relating to constituting of SFCs is commendable, the poor fiscal health of the state governments themselves has constrained fiscal transfers according to the recommendations of the SFCs. The experience of transfers to the urban local self-governments gives enough evidence that the state governments have not accepted the recommendations of the SFC in totality. No state has as yet developed a convention of accepting the recommendations of the SFC in its entirety as has been the case with the central governments which has developed a healthy convention of accepting the recommendations of the FC in its totality.

The mechanism of SFC was looked upon as the only hope for refurbishing of municipal finance as the devolution of sources of revenue has been left to the state discretion. The recommendations of the SFCs was expected to fill this void as it has the mandate also to suggest taxes, duties, tolls, and fees to be devolved to the municipal authorities. However, hardly any SFC has suggested devolving new source of revenue to the urban local self-governments. A relevant issue relating to the mechanism of SFC pertains to the timing of its constitution by the state governments. If constituted well before the constitution of FC, it will go a long way in integration of non-plan municipal financial needs with state and federal finances through the mechanism of committed expenditure of the state governments. Amendment in the ToR of the Finance Commission was expected to help in devolving of functions by the state governments to the municipal authorities provided that the FC suggested fiscal transfers to the state governments only for such functions which are in the nature of state functions. The functions urban in nature and being performed by state agencies and parastatal organizations were expected to be transferred to the municipal authorities. But this again has turned out to be only a pious hope as this has not yet happened. It is worth stressing even at the cost of repetition, however, that the exercise of SFC is based on the functions performed by the municipal bodies. In case the functions are not devolved out of the Twelfth Schedule, the scheme of fiscal transfers to be suggested by the SFC continues to be short sighted, limited and partial.

Reports of the successive SFCs indicate that the various SFCs have adopted different approaches for transfers to the states. These can be grouped under three categories as mentioned below:

1. Transfers through Global Sharing
2. Transfers through sharing of specific taxes
3. Transfers in terms of an absolute amount

Fiscal transfer by the Finance Commissions in the past has been constrained by absence of SFC reports with the result that Finance Commissions could not discharge its constitutional obligation provided for in the amended Article 280 of the Constitution. This essentially requires that the reports of the SFCs should be available to the FC so that it could be in a better position to assess State's need on the basis of uniform principles. This has not been happening ever since the constitution of the Eleventh Finance Commission. It is worth mentioning that the Tenth Finance Commission gave an interesting observation that the 'measures' needed for augmenting the consolidated fund of the states does not involve fiscal transfers.[2] The Eleventh Finance Commission for the first time pointed to the constraints faced by it in addressing the amended ToR. It particularly referred to (i) non-synchronization of the period of the recommendations of the SFCs and the Central Finance Commission that is hindering availability of reports of the SFCs in time, (ii) delays on part of the state governments in taking action on the recommendations of the SFCs due to absence of defined time frame for this, and (iii) lack of clarity about assignment of powers, authority and responsibilities to the local self-governments that precludes estimating their fiscal needs.

For several reasons, the previous Finance Commissions could not base their recommendations entirely on the SFC reports. These included variations in the approaches adopted by the SFCs, difference in the periods covered by individual SFCs, non-synchronization of the SFC report periods with that of the Finance Commission report and the quality of SFC reports. Under the circumstances, the previous Finance Commissions recommended ad-hoc grants and suggested the steps that state governments could take to augment the consolidated fund of states to supplement the resources of local bodies.

The Twelfth Finance Commission (TFC) as well faced the same problem. It also referred to a number of constraints in proper addressing of the amended ToR. About the issue of synchronization of the two Finance Commissions, it suggested in precise terms that it would be desirable to constitute the SFCs at least two years before the required date of submission of their recommendations. It also suggested that the deadline for submission of SFC report should be decided such that it provides to the state governments at least three months for taking action on the recommendations and present the same in the state legislature. It clarified that 'Synchronization of the award periods of the SFC with the Central Finance Commission does not mean that they should be coterminous. What is necessary is that the SFC reports should be readily available to the Central Finance Commission, when the latter is constituted so that an assessment of the State's need could be made by the Central Finance Commission on the basis of uniform principles'. It, therefore, suggested legislative action on part of the state governments for facilitating the sequence of timing for constitution of SFCs and the action to be taken by the state governments. In its considered view, the Constitutional provisions for transfers to augment the consolidated fund of states do not merely imply additional transfers for supplementing the ULSG resources. Implication of such a constitutional provision has much wider ramification.

TFC observed two important intentions behind such a constitutional provision. First, special circumstances of the various states could be a reason for additional transfers to them. Second, implementation of some of the recommendations of the SFCs for augmenting the revenue of states may have centre-state and/or interstate ramifications. The FC could offer specific advice to the centre for resolving such intricate inter-state issues in financial administration. In view of these ramifications, TFC recommended that in order for the SFCs to effectively discharge their constitutional obligations, 'in future, the SFCs must clearly identify the areas, which require action on the part of the central government to augment the consolidated fund of the state and list them out in a separate chapter for the consideration of the Central Finance Commission'. Nevertheless, the TFC, with a view to augment the Consolidated Fund of states for supplementing the resources of the local bodies, suggested assignment of land tax, professions tax and also surcharge or cess on state taxes. It also suggested a number of measures for reforming Property Tax, Octroi/Entry Tax and user charges. In its considered view, the additional financial burden for implementation of SFC recommendations was already built into the system of transfers suggested by it. Therefore, there was no need for additional transfers. Nevertheless, it recommended an ad-hoc annual grant of Rs. 400 crore per annum for the ULSGs (Rs. 2,000 crore for five years).

TFC also pointed to a flaw in the methodology adopted by the SFCs. It, therefore, suggested that SFCs should follow the approach and the methodology adopted by the FC. This means that the SFC ought to estimate and analyse finances of both the state governments and the ULBs before and after the suggested transfers to get a scenario of their resource situations. Additionally, the SFCs would as well need to estimate the additional resource mobilization by the ULSGs as a result of implementation of policy measures suggested by the SFCs. Resource gap estimated in this manner will provide meaningful basis to the FC for their recommendation for augmenting the consolidated fund of states. TFC has also suggested that the SFCs should replace the existing practice of long term historical forecasts of revenue and expenditure by a forecast based on norms and standards for both revenue and expenditures. Revenue forecast should take into account the nature of local tax base, its buoyancy and the per capita norms. On the expenditure side, the norms would need to be based on per capita expenditure incurred by the best of local bodies in provision of local government services. Unfilled gap on the basis of such an approach adjusted to the resource transfers recommended by the SFC will provide to the FC an objective and meaningful basis for suggesting transfers to the states for enabling them to accept the recommendations of the SFCs. This is not happening at the moment.

13th CFC referred to the depleting fiscal health of ULSG by citing the memorandum submitted to the Commission by the Ministry of Urban Development. The expenditures incurred by all the ULSGs in the country declined from 1.74 per cent of the Gross Domestic Product (GDP) in 1998-9 to 1.56 per cent of GDP in 2002-3 and 1.54 per cent in 2007-8. Internal resources constitute less than half the total expenditure of urban local bodies.

The Thirteenth Finance Commission as well expressed views that things are not well with the way the SFCs are constituted. Non-synchronization of the period of recommendations of the SFCs and the FC, the methodology adopted by them for estimating the resource gap and the state action on the SFC reports were especially mentioned by it. Analysing the point of time when the various SFC were constituted by the state governments, the Commission observed that only three states appointed SFCs whose recommendations were coterminous with the period covered by the 13th FC (2010-15). Reports of the SFCs, therefore, did not help the FC in any way in quantifying transfers uniformly across all the states for supplementing the resources of the local self-governments both rural and urban. Moreover, the reports of the SFCs submitted to the 13th Finance Commission 'were widely divergent in the quality of their analyses and the scope and scale of their recommendations'. Referring to the constitutional provision for constituting SFCs every five years, the Commission observed that the basic rationale for this is that the recommendations given by the SFC must be used for a period of five years only; after this period, transfers to the ULSGs is supposed to be on the basis of a new SFC. But it found that this is not happening in actual practice. Late submission of the report was further aggravated by delayed action to be taken on the SFC report by the state governments. Naturally, in the interregnum period, transfer to the ULSGs continued only on the basis of the previous SFC.

By now about four generations of SFCs have already been constituted and the fifth generation should be now engaged in their exercise for suggesting transfers. The constitutional provisions require setting up of SFCs within one year from the commencement of the 74th CAA on a five yearly basis. Accordingly, the fourth round of SFC became due in 2009-10. The 14th Finance Commission has noted lags by the state governments in compliance to even such a mandatory provision of the Constitution. Only a couple of state governments constituted the fifth SFC, eleven of them constituted the fourth, another six states constituted the second SFC and one is yet to do so. This is yet another example of state governments to ignore mandatory Constitutional provisions of constituting State Finance Commissions 'at the expiry of every fifth year' as provided in Article 243I. The lackadaisical approach of the state governments in constituting the State Finance Commissions finds its full expression in the observations of the 14th Finance Commission quoted below:

> It emerged that States had constituted SFCs at different times and with varying regularity. As a result, the latest SFC constituted across States (barring one state) ranged from the second SFC to the fifth SFC. In certain States, the latest reports submitted by the SFC were still under consideration by State Governments. In other States, the SFCs were yet to submit their reports. (Report of 14th Finance Commission, www.finmin.nic.in)

This vividly depicts indifferent attitude of the state governments in strengthening urban governance. This is also corroborated by the observation of Chairpersons of the SFCs during interaction with the Finance Commission. They reported that the recommendations of the SFCs with respect to systemic changes are hardly acted upon by the state governments (14th Finance Commission Report). The 14th Finance Commission also noted reluctance of the state governments in accepting the recommendations of the SFC; the recommendations are rejected without giving any reason. It also observed that in some states, even when the recommendations were accepted, the timeframe for implementation was not specified in the Action Taken Report.

In view of non-availability of SFC Reports, the 14th Finance Commission suggested transfers to the local governments on basis of study of the SFC reports rather than on the basis of recommendations of the SFCs. Lack of proper sequencing in constituting the SFC (the 'synchronisation' issue) has continued unabated despite shrill and repeated observations of the FCs beginning from the 11th Finance Commission onwards. SARC as well has expressed strong views and has recommended amending Article 243Y of the Constitution for inserting the words 'or earlier' after the words 'every fifth year' (GoI 2007). The 13th Finance Commission endorsed this recommendation of SARC. The endemic issue of absence of synchronization of Finance Commission and the State Finance Commissions has continued despite the recommendations of the previous Finance Commissions which recommended amending the Constitution either to delete the requirement of the Finance Commissions to base its recommendations on State Finance Commission reports or to require it to recommend merely keeping in view the reports of the State Finance Commissions reports but not based on them. The 14th Finance Commission, going by the suggestion given by the Ministry of Panchayati Raj and some of the states (five in number), while suggesting transfers to the local government for the period 2015-20 had, therefore, opted to study the working of SFCs in detail and suggest transfers on the basis of such an in-depth study.

As for the methodology adopted by the SFCs for suggesting

transfers, the 13th Finance Commission lamented that despite a format suggested by the 12th Finance Commission for collection of data, the basis for determination of fiscal transfer to be given to the ULSGs is not uniform across SFCs. It also pointed out that the SFCs do not follow a uniform pattern in their analysis. This detracts the usability of the SFC reports. The 13th Finance Commission, therefore, developed a template for SFC reports and placed this template on the Commission's website. The 14th Finance Commission has though not given its views on this, it has given observations on the quality of data used by the State Finance Commissions. It came across data that were a decade old!

Another problem adversely affecting the quality of the SFC reports pertains to the composition of the SFCs in terms of specialities to be represented by its members. The 12th Finance Commission had suggested that the members of the SFC must be constituted with people of eminence and competence with qualification and experience in the relevant fields. Reiterating this recommendation, the 13th Finance Commission as well suggested the state governments to strengthen the composition of SFC. It emphasized that 'Important issues—legal, economic, financial and administrative, as well as those relating to decentralization—need to be examined and SFC members should be well equipped to meet these challenges. Article 243I (2) of the Constitution enables the state governments to legislate on the requisite qualifications of SFC members. It is desirable that all states legislate in this matter'. Another serious commentator on local government and local finance has expressed almost the same view by observing that the scant respect received by the SFCs is also because of membership composition of the SFCs that include even civil servants (Datta 2003). He also observes that the SFCs have not given much attention to improve fiscal administration of ULSGs that happens to be an important part of their ToR. He believes that addressing this ToR effectively is much more important than suggesting fiscal transfers. SARC as well echoes the same view. It suggests that SFCs should carry out a more thorough analysis of the finances of local bodies and make concrete recommendations for improvements in their working.

It needs to be mentioned that the submission of reports by the SFCs is not as important as the quality of the report in terms of approach and methodology adopted by them and the shape in which these are accepted by the state governments. Some of the important observations relating to deficiencies in the exercise of SFCs are mentioned below:

- SFCs generally take a long time in submitting their report.
- Most of the SFCs are not Commissions in the true sense of the term; in several instances, the Finance Secretary becomes a member of the Commission that makes it an extended arm of the state government.
- The SFCs are not headed by imminent experts in public finance or for that matter in local government finance.
- Most of the SFCs do not have experts in rural and urban local self-government.
- Most of the SFCs do not have legal experts.
- SFCs have not adopted a rational approach and methodology to get at revenue and fiscal gap at the local government level.
- Most of the SFCs have not addressed their ToR relating to assignment to and/or appropriation of taxes, toll, duties and fees by the local bodies.
- Most of the SFCs have faltered on suggesting concrete steps in improving financial management at the local level.

It is important to mention that the 13th Finance Commission expressed its pessimism on SFC in terms of their constitution, composition, the quality of report and also the not-so-prestigious clout enjoyed by them. It would be useful to quote from the Report of the 13th Finance Commission to flag its pessimism:

> The experience of SFCs has not been found to be successful for a number of reasons. SFCs themselves are hampered by lack of data. Limited capacity and poor ownership by State Governments compounds this problem. There is little incentive for them to produce a comprehensive report. Further, or because of these reasons, states are not overly keen either to accept their recommendations or to place the Action Taken Report before the state legislature in a timely manner. This situation provides a further disincentive for SFCs to produce good quality reports. There is, thus, a need for State Governments to ensure that the recommendations of SFCs are implemented without delay and that the Action Taken Report is placed promptly before the legislature.

Urban Planning

The 74th CAA envisages altogether a new paradigm of urban planning that is to be driven by the local political process and is to be informed by a participatory planning process. Article 243ZD has a mandatory provision that requires the state governments to constitute a District Planning Committee (DPC) at the district level in all the states (except in the Schedules Areas).[3] DPCs are required 'to consolidate the plans prepared by the Panchayats and the Municipalities in the district and to prepare a draft development plan for the district as a whole'. It enjoins the urban local self-governments to prepare local development plans. Preparation of participatory district plan through local political process is reflected in constitutional provisions relating to (i) the preparation of plans by the local self-governments (both rural and urban) and (ii) representation of local self-governments on the DPC. The nature of provision contained in Article 243ZD has implications also for a mandatory nature of plan preparation by the local governments even though urban planning as a function of urban local self-governments is contained in the 12th Schedule which is discretionary in nature. Preparation of plans by the local government is mandatory largely because the DPC has a mandate to 'consolidate' the plans prepared by the local governments. If plans are not prepared by the local governments, as is the case in most of the states, the DPC will be unable to discharge its mandate to consolidate the local plans for drafting a district plan. By implication, therefore, urban planning as a function of ULSGs is mandatory in nature.

Article 243ZD also requires the state legislatures to make provisions by enacting a law for the composition of DPC, the manner in which the seats in the DPC are to be filled up, the functions to be performed by the DPC and the manner in which the Chairpersons of the DPC are to be elected. As regards composition of DPC, the Constitution gives directive that not less than four-fifths of the total number of members of DPC are to be mandatorily elected by and from amongst, the elected members of the Panchayats and the Municipalities in the district in proportion to the ratio between the population of rural areas and urban areas in the district. Representation of the local governments, both rural and urban on DPC has thus built-in provision for planning to be driven by political process. The Constitution provides that a draft development plan has to be prepared by the DPC with respect to the matters of common interest between the Panchayats and Municipalities including spatial planning, sharing of water and other physical and natural resources, integrated development of infrastructure and environmental conservation. Plans so prepared are to be forwarded by the Chairperson of the District Planning Committee to the state government.

Constitutional provisions require nomination of one-fifth of the total members of the DPC by the state governments. Nomination happens to be an intelligent ploy not only to dilute representative character but also to scuttle popular will by the ruling party in a state for achieving its narrow political considerations (SARC 2007). Popular representation, on the other hand, happens to be the hallmark of democratic institutions. DPC does not stand out on this count. This is corroborated also by the fact that there was no room for participatory planning (DPC) in the Bills moved on the subject under two successive Prime Ministers after Rajiv Gandhi—V.P. Singh and Narsimha Rao. It is worth mentioning that the Bills on Panchayats and Municipalities were referred to a joint Parliamentary Committee. It was the wisdom of this Parliamentary Committee that led to the revival of DPC as a mechanism for promoting a planning process to be driven by the local communities. The original Bill drafted under Rajiv Gandhi's government contained provision for election of all the 29 members of the DPC from amongst the elected members of the Zila Parishad and the Municipalities in proportion to the ratio of rural and urban population (Sivaramakrishnan 2000). The provisions for constituting the DPC were also diluted by discretion given to the state governments about who is to chair the DPC. The 1989 Draft Bill envisaged locating DPC in the Zila Parishad provided that the Chairperson of the Zila Parishad was to chair the DPC as well. Provisions with respect to urban planning has attracted controversy also on the ground that even though planning is necessary to be conceived within the ambit of governance, the provisions especially for district planning makes the District Planning Committee a stand-alone entity. The issues involved in planning are discussed in greater detail in Chapter 5.

Article 243ZE has a mandatory provision for constituting Metropolitan Planning Committees (MPC) in metropolitan areas. MPC is also required to prepare a draft development plan for the metropolitan area. As in the case of DPC, the Municipalities are to be represented on the MPC as well. MPC is required to perform similar planning exercise for the metropolitan areas as is to be done by the District Planning Committee for a district. The intention of the Constitution of India is apparently clear—the planning process needs to be driven by the local political process so that the plans really reflect the felt needs of the local communities and its fulfilment. Article 243ZE also requires the legislatures of states to legislate on (i) the composition of the Metropolitan Planning Committees; (ii) the manner in which the seats in MPCs are to be filled up; (iii) functions relating to planning and coordination for the Metropolitan Area; and (iv) the manner in which the Chairpersons of MPC are to be elected. It also requires the state legislatures to provide for: (a) not less than two-thirds of the members of MPCs who must be elected by, and from amongst the elected members of the Municipalities and Chairpersons of the Panchayats in the Metropolitan area in proportion to the ratio between the population of the Municipalities and the Panchayats in a Metropolitan Area; and (b) representation of the Government of India and the state governments in MPCs and also of other organizations and institutions as may be deemed necessary for carrying out the functions of the MPC.

Executive System

The most conspicuous gap in the 74th CAA is its complete silence about the authority within the local government that should be vested with executive powers. Article 243W provides that

> Subject to the provisions of this Constitution, the Legislature of a State may, by law, endow: (a) the Municipalities with such powers and authority as

may be necessary to enable them to function as institutions of self-government and such law may contain provisions for the devolution of powers and responsibilities upon Municipalities, subject to such conditions as may be specified therein. . . .

It does not specify as to which organ of the local self-government should be exercising 'the devolution of powers and responsibilities'. The enabling laws in different states have specified the organs of the urban local self-governments that are vested with the authority to use powers contained in the different Municipal Acts. But the provisions vary a great deal across states. By and large, these include: (i) the Council, (ii) the Mayor/Chairperson, (iii) the Standing Committee, and (iv) the Commissioner. Which one of these organs should exercise the executive power? If the urban local governments have to be institutions of self-government, which they must be, the appropriate organ to be vested with executive power needs to be the Mayor/Chairperson who happens to be the elected head of the urban local self-government. The constitutional provisions with respect to the office of the Chief Minister in states and the Prime Minister at the centre designate them the chief executives. Being elected head of the ULSG institutions, the Mayors of municipal corporations and Chairpersons of the other types of urban local self-governments as well must be designated Chief Executive of the ULSGs. Even though the urban local governments have not yet been formally designated as the third tier of government in the Constitution, they have been given constitutional recognition and have a constitutional right to exist. It is, therefore, in the fitness of things that a political executive needs to be installed in the urban local self-government institutions. This is conspicuously absent in large number of states. Executive power[4], as a natural corollary of 'self-government' must vest with the elected Mayor/Chairperson. As against this, following the Bombay model of urban governance, in large number of states, executive power vests in the Commissioner/Chief Executive Officer who is appointed by the state government and, therefore, he is accountable to the state government. The concept of 'self-government' in such an executive system gets defeated. This has continued to be an anathema in so far as the concept of local self-government is concerned. The status of the political head—the Mayor/Chairperson—is reduced to becoming a mere nominal or ceremonial head. S/he has to be contended by presenting himself/herself as 'the first citizen' of the city/town whenever a dignitary visits the city/town. Such an insolent status of the political head is further exacerbated by giving him/her a brief tenure of office of one year in most of the municipal corporations that does not enable him/her to grapple with the nature of problems confronted by the city/town and forming a vision for effective governance and service delivery. The provision for reservation of offices of Chairpersons has further destroyed any semblance of motivation amongst them to perform.

Nature and Intent of Decentralization

Basic provisions in the Constitution and an evaluation of these provisions thus points to gaps in the constitutional provisions, some of which are quite conspicuous. Decentralization initiative through an amendment of the Indian Constitution in 1992 needs to be looked at and evaluated in the context of conceptual framework of decentralization discussed above. Viewed from this angle, the provisions incorporated in the Constitution through the 74th amendment seem to be wavering in its nature and intent. Political decentralization entails that there is clarity about devolving of functions to the decentralized level of government in terms of explicit list of functions over which it could take decisions in an autonomous manner. This has to be accompanied by assignment of sources of revenue that should match expenditure assignment which is reflected in the provisions with respect to municipal functional domain. Such a scheme of political and fiscal decentralization is not discernable in the constitutional provisions. Attributes of decentralization are conspicuously lacking in the 74th CAA. There is hardly any local list of functions and sources of revenue devolved to the urban local self-governments on which the urban local self-governments could take decisions in an autonomous manner. Wavering nature of the decentralization initiative is reflected also in the provision contained in Article 243W of the Constitution. It requires the states to endow to the Municipalities with such powers and authority as may be necessary for enabling them as institutions of self-government. The rigour of this seemingly laudable constitutional intent is lost by giving discretion to the states in doing so. This hardly leaves any constitutionality about the Twelfth Schedule. This also explains lack of will on part of the state governments in devolving such powers and authority to the urban local self-governments. Provisions for devolution of power and authority thus got constrained by the fact that local self-governments form part of the State List in the Seventh Schedule of the Constitution. Political decentralization has thus not actualized in true sense of this term (Jha 1993).

The wavering nature of 74th CAA is also reflected in silence of constitutional provisions about the executive system in the institutions of urban local self-government. If the local government has to be empowered, political decentralization must be accompanied by installation of political executive system and autonomy in its functioning especially in taking day-to-day decisions. This would also require relooking at the inter-government relations. This, in the existing scheme of decentralization, is characterized by a fragmented executive system. Even though Chairpersons of the three types of urban local self-government are supposed to have executive power, this, in a large number of states, is vested in the appointed Commissioner and Chief Executive Officers who enjoy both executive power and executive functions. Chairpersons continue to be mere figure heads of the urban local self-governments. Even though the statement of objects and reasons for enactment of the Consti-tution (74th Amendment) Act envisages to 'put on a firmer footing the relationship between the State Government and the Urban Local Bodies', the urban local self-governments and also the inter-government relations continue to be the same as they were before the enactment of this constitution amendment. Basic provisions in the Constitution and an evaluation of these provisions thus points to gaps in the constitutional provisions, some of which are quite conspicuous. Addressing these gaps require revisiting the 74th CAA.

In sum, though the 74th CAA has several infirmities, it is historic in many ways. First, it gives constitutional right to the municipal governments to exist. It provides for fresh elections within six months of dissolution of the Council. Second, it empowers the weaker sections and women by providing for reservation of seats. Third, it provides for creation of Wards/Ward Committees which will reduce the distance between the citizenry and the local government and will, hopefully, make it much responsive to the needs of the local communities and will ensure accountability. Fourth, the provision for constitution of State Finance Commissions and the amendment in the terms of Reference of the Central Finance Commission is expected to contribute to rationalization of transfer system that will strengthen fiscal capabilities of the municipal authorities.

Along with these brighter aspects of the Amendment there are, however, greyer areas as well. Provision relating to institution building got diluted in the amendment Act. It has missed a valuable opportunity to specify the functions and also the sources of local revenues. This would have prevented state encroachment into these spheres. By giving a lot of discretion to the state governments in these and other areas, the Amendment has left the issues unsettled. Experience in the past indicates that the state governments have not cared to make urban local self-governments vibrant units of self-government at the grass-route level. As the municipal authorities are the creatures of state government, the latter needs to fend for the former in the new reactivated environment of the 74th CAA. The experience in the past has not been rosy in this regard. The 65th Amendment Bill was qualitatively much different from the 74th CAA. It was not legislated by the Parliament chiefly on two grounds. First, the provisions were said to be an assault on the 'autonomy' of the state governments as it tried to thrust the provisions on the states that happen to be constitutionally autonomous entities. Second, the scope and the contents of the proposed Amendment Bill were said to be conceived in a great deal of hurry. As the ensued debate generated a great deal of political heat and high voltage political drama, the authors of the 74th Amendment perhaps became too conscious of the respect for 'state autonomy' and diluted the provisions substantially by giving discretion to the state government with respect to several important provisions of the Constitution Amendment Bill. As for a 'great deal of hurry' in pushing through the Amendments, the issues that were tried to be addressed by the 65th Amendment Bill have been debated since Independence and even before when the Local List of Revenues provided for in the Government of India Act, 1919 was removed in the Government of India Act, 1935.

NOTES

1. For a perceptive analysis of the thinking behind the decentralization initiative and documentation of processes that went into actualization of this initiative, see Sivaramakrishnan 2000.
2. The 74th CAA was introduced at a time when the Tenth Finance Commission was in the process of finalising its recommendations. It hardly had time to fulfill its constitutional obligation. Also, reports of the first round of SFCs could be available only around mid-1995. Recommendations of the TFC related to the time span of 1995-2000. Moreover, the Terms of Reference of the 10th Finance Commission did not include suggesting transfers for augmenting the Consolidated Fund of States.
3. Article 243ZC of the Constitution provides that Part IX A containing provisions of the 74th CAA is not to be extended to the Scheduled Areas referred to in Clause (1) and the tribal areas referred to in Clause (2) of Article 244 of the Indian Constitution unless the Parliament extends the provisions of this Part by enacting a law with such exceptions and modifications as may be specified in such law.
4. A distinction needs to be made between 'Executive Power' and 'Executive Function'. Executive power denotes powers to decide on policy, programmes, making decisions for effective governance and service delivery, authority to choose executive functionaries, appointing and removing them for lapse in their function, monitoring of implementation of policies, programmes and decisions made and ensuring effective, efficient, inclusive and responsive governance at the local level. Executive function, on the other hand, denotes performance of functions to ensure effective implementation of policies, programmes and decisions, keeping the chief executive (Mayor/Chairperson) informed about it as also the bottlenecks with regard to policy and governance in these regards, if any.

REFERENCES

AIR, 1973, *Kesvanand Bharti* vs. *State of Kerala*, SC, 1461.

Bennett, R., 1994, 'An Overview of Developments in Decentralization', in R. Bennett (ed.), *Local Government and Market Decentralisation: Experiences in Industrialized, Developing, and Former Easter Block Countries*, Tokyo: New York, Paris: United University Press, pp. 32-46.

Bird, Richard and Francois Vaillancourt, 1998, *Fiscal Decentralization in Developing Countries*. Cambridge: Cambridge University Press.

Bird, Richard, 1994, 'Financing Local Services: Patterns, Problems, and Possibilities', paper prepared for Global Report on Human Settlements.

Campbell, Tim, George Peterson and J. Brakarz, 1991, *Decentralization to Local Government in LAC*, Washington, DC: The World Bank.

Cheema, Shabbir G. and Dennis A. Rondinelli (eds.), 1983, *Decentralization and Development: Policy Implementation in Developing Countries*, Beverly Hills: Sage.

Datta, Abhijit, 2003, 'The National Finance Commission and Fiscal Devolution to the Local Bodies', paper prepared for the *National Seminar on Municipal Finance* sponsored by the 12th Finance Commission, at the Indian Institute of Public Administration (IIPA), New Delhi.

Horvath, Tamas M. (ed.), 2000, *Decentralization: Experiments*, Budapest: Public Service Reform Initiative, Open Society Institute.

Government of India, Committee on Plan Projects, 1957, *Report of the Team for the Study of Community Projects and National Extension Service*, vol. 1, (Chairman Balwantrai Mehta), New Delhi.

——, 1986, *Report of the Committee on Revitalization of Panchayati Raj Iinstitutions* (Chairman: L.M. Singhvi), Delhi.

——, 1988, *Commission on Centre-State Relations, Report*, Part I (Chair Justice R.S. Sarkaria, Nasik), Government of India Press.

——, 2007, *Sixth Report of the Second Administrative Reform Commission, Local Govenance: An Inspiring Journey into the Future*, New Delhi: Ministry of Personnel, Public Grievances and Pensions, Department of Administrative Reform and Public Grievances.

Jha, Gangadhar, 1993, 'Seventy-Fourth Constitution Amendment and the Empowerment of Municipal Government: A Critique', *Urban India*, XIII (2).

Martinez-Vazaquez, Jorge and Robert McNab (eds.), 1997, *Tax Reform in Transition Economies: Experience and Lessons*, International Studies Program Working Paper, Andrew Young School of Policy Studies, Georgia State University.

Owens, J. and G. Panella (eds.), 1991, *Local Government: An International Perspective*, Amsterdam, North Holland.

Prud'homme, Remy, 1991, 'The Dangers of Decentralization', *The World Bank Research Observer*, no. 10, pp. 201-20.

Peteri, Gabor (ed.), 2002, *Mastering Decentralization and Public Administration Reforms in Central and Eastern Europe*, Budapest: Local Government and Public Service Reform Initiative.

Report of the 14th Finance Commission, http://www.fincomindia.nic.in

Rondinelli, Denis A., 1981, 'Government Decentralization in Comparative Perspective: Theory and Practice in Developing Countries', *International Review of Administrative Science*, vol. 47.

Shah, Anwar, 2004, *Fiscal Decentralization in Developing and Transition Economies Progress, Problems, and the Promise*, World Bank Policy Research Working Paper 3282, Washington, DC: World Bank.

Sivaramakrishnan, K.C., 2000, *Power to the People? Politics Progress of Decentralisation*, New Delhi: Konark.

Wolman, Hal and Sharon McCormick, 1994, 'The Effect of Decentralization on Local Governments', in R.J. Bennett (ed.), *Local Government and Market Decentralized, Developing, and Former Eastern Block Countries*: Tokyo, New York, Paris: United University Press.

CHAPTER 4

State Municipal Laws in the Post-74th Constitution Amendment Regime

Article 243ZF of the 74th CAA required the state governments to bring changes in the laws relating to municipalities that existed immediately before the commencement of the 74th CAA so that the provisions in these laws are brought in conformity with the provisions contained in this Constitution Amendment Act. The new constitutional provisions became effective from 1 June 1993. Following this constitutional requirement, the state governments had to make amendments in these laws for bringing them in conformity with the new constitutional provisions before 1 June 1993. Though the state governments followed the constitutional provisions and incorporated the constitutional provisions in their existing municipal laws, the changes brought about in the conformity laws vary a great deal across the states. This is explained by discretionary nature of some of the constitutional provisions and the perception of the various state governments to customize some of the provisions in their respective states. It would be, therefore, in order to comprehend the manner in which the constitutional provisions have been incorporated in the municipal laws in the various states. These variations are analysed below on the basis of study of municipal laws in the major states.

NOMENCLATURE OF URBAN LOCAL SELF-GOVERNMENT

Though Article 243Q of the Indian Constitution provides for mandatory constitution of three types of urban local self-governments

(Municipal Corporation in larger urban areas, Municipal Council in smaller urban area and Nagar Panchayat in transitional areas), it gives discretion to the states about the nomenclature of especially the Nagar Panchayat. This explains variations in the nomenclature in different states. Information collected for some of the major states depicts these variations (Annex III). The states of Andhra Pradesh, Bihar, Gujarat, Madhya Pradesh, Uttar Pradesh, and Maharashtra have the names of the three types of ULSG that corresponds to the Constitutional provisions. On the other hand, in the states of Haryana, Karnataka, Odisha, Rajasthan, Tamil Nadu, and West Bengal, this is not so though 'larger urban areas' are constituted into a Municipal Corporation in all these states. Variation is found with respect of creation of Municipal Council and Nagar Panchayat. The state of Andhra Pradesh uses the nomenclature of 'Municipality' instead of 'Municipal Council' suggested in the 74th CAA. In the state of West Bengal, the situation is altogether different from the states referred to above. It uses the expression 'Municipal Area' for constitution of Municipal Council. For the purpose of application of the provisions of this Act, the West Bengal Municipal Act, 1993 classifies the 'Municipal Area' into five groups of A, B, C, D, and E (Annex III). It also provides for constitution of 'Notified Area Authority' to be created (i) in any urbanized area which does not fulfil the conditions for being immediately constituted into a municipal area or (ii) in any area which is comprised in a newly developing town, or (iii) in any area in which new industries have been or are being established. As for the nomenclature of Nagar Panchayats in some of the major states is concerned, it is called Municipal Committee in Haryana, a Town Panchayat in Kerala, Karnataka, and Tamil Nadu, a Notified Area Council in Odisha, and a Municipal Board in Rajasthan.

Great deal of variations found especially in the nomenclature of ULSG created in transitional areas raises a pertinent question about the justification for this. Of course, changing the name given in the 74th CAA, neither has financial nor policy implications. Nevertheless, using a single expression of Nagar Panchayat will be desirable for uniformity and avoiding confusion about it. These needs to be taken note of by the central government for further amendment of the Constitutional provisions in future.

DISCREPANCIES IN POPULATION THRESHOLD

The 74th CAA also gives discretion to the state governments in its perception of 'larger', 'smaller' and 'transitional' areas. As these have not been defined in terms of population, there exist quite varied practices in different states for constitution of ULSG in cities and towns of various size categories. Article 243Q of the Constitution gives discretion to the Governor of a state to specify the meaning of these three specific areas by public notification having regard to the following parameters:

1. Population of the area
2. Density of population in urban areas
3. Revenue generated for local administration
4. Percentage of employment in non-agricultural activities
5. Economic importance
6. Such other factors as the Governor of the state 'may deem fit'.

The discretion given to the Governor of states explains a great deal of variation in population and other parameters mentioned above in specifying larger, smaller urban areas and transitional areas. It is interesting to note that in the states of Kerala, Madhya Pradesh, Rajasthan and Uttar Pradesh, the municipal Acts do not define these three areas in terms of parameters suggested in the Constitution. The Municipal Acts in these states have simply reproduced the expression used in the 74th CAA. In the states of Andhra Pradesh, Gujarat, Haryana, Karnataka and Odisha for example, Municipal Corporations are created in a city with 3 lakh and more population. But Municipal Corporations in Bihar is created in cities with only 2 lakh population. In the states of Tamil Nadu and West Bengal, however, Municipal Corporation is created in a city with not less than 5 lakh population. Similarly, in the case of constitution of Municipal Council, one comes across great deal of variations in different states. This varies from a maximum population of 50,000 in Haryana to a minimum of 20,000 in Karnataka (Annex III). It is worth mentioning that in the state of Tamil Nadu, a transitional area with a population of 20,000 qualifies for creation of Town Panchayat (Nagar Panchayat). But for constituting a Nagar Panchayat, the State of Haryana has set a maximum population threshold of 50,000 for creation of Municipal Committee which is called counterpart of a Nagar Panchayat. In the states of Karnataka, Maharashtra, and Odisha this is only 10,000.

The range of population for constituting three types of urban local self-governments thus varies a great deal in different states. The different state governments have adopted different population thresholds for constituting the three different types of municipal governments. The discretion provided for in the 74th CAA has, in fact, led to too much of flexibility. The Constitutional provisions for creation of Municipalities do not specify the population threshold largely because of state specific conditions and realities. Nevertheless, great deal of variations in population threshold in different states suggests that there is need for a constitutional norm of population for creating the three types of Municipalities. As mentioned in Chapter 3, the original 65th Amendment Bill had provided specific population threshold irrespective of 'state specific' conditions. It had specified that a Nagar Panchayat was to be constituted in a transitional area with a population of 10,000 to 20,000, Municipal Councils in the town with a population of 20,000 to 3 lakh and Municipal Corporations in the cities of more than 3 lakh population. This was removed in the subsequent Bill. There does not seem to be anything wrong with the demographic norm that was contained in the 65th Constitution amendment Bill. These norms need to be provided for in the Constitution for creation of Municipalities of the three types.

DISCREPANCIES IN TERMS OF ECONOMIC CRITERIA

As mentioned earlier, the 74 CAA provides for certain economic parameters as well for the cities and the towns to qualify for creation of ULSG. These are: (i) revenue generated for local administration, (ii) percentage of employment in non-agricultural activities; and (iii) economic importance of cities and towns. These parameters are especially mentioned so that the economic base of the cities and towns will enable the ULSG in generating sufficient revenue for financing of municipal services and urban infrastructure. Here as well the practices in different states vary a great deal. First, in quite a number of states the enabling municipal Acts do not contain actual indicators for these parameters. These states have simply copied the provisions contained in this regard in Article 243Q (2). The enabling municipal Acts in these states require the Governor to notify creation of ULSG in larger urban areas, smaller urban area and transitional area if he deems it fit on the basis of the parameters contained in Article 243Q (2) of the Indian Constitution. The economic parameters have not been specified in terms of norms. Prevalence of these norms is left simply to the 'satisfaction' of the Governor. Some of the major states belonging to this category include, Gujarat, Haryana, Kerala, Madhya Pradesh, Odisha, Rajasthan, Uttar Pradesh and West Bengal especially in the case of creation of Notified Area Authority. In these states the parameters provided for in Article 243Q are not specified.

Barring the states mentioned above, in some of the other states, the municipal Acts contain actual indicators especially pertaining to revenue generation and proportion of employment in non-agricultural activities. The municipal Acts in the states of Karnataka, Tamil Nadu and West Bengal for Municipal Corporations and Municipal Councils provide for generation of minimum revenue for creation of these two types of Municipality and declaring an urban area as a municipal area. In Karnataka, creation of a Municipal Corporation is contingent on generation of revenue from Tax and non-Tax sources that should not be less than Rs. 6 crore in the year of the last preceding Census or a per capita income of Rs. 200 per year, whichever is higher. For creation of Municipal Council, the Karnataka Municipalities Act, 1994 provides that the annual revenue to be generated form Tax and non-Tax sources in the year of the last preceding Census should be Rs. 9 lakh or a sum calculated at the rate of Rs. 45 per capita per annum, whichever is higher. This, for constituting a Town Panchayat, needs to be Rs. 9 lakh per annum from Tax and non-Tax sources in the year of the last preceding Census or a sum calculated at the rate of Rs. 45

per capita per annum, whichever is higher. In the state of Tamil Nadu, the Tamil Nadu Local Bodies Act, 1998, for constituting a Municipal Corporation, simply provides that municipal income from taxation and other sources should be 'adequate for discharge of municipal functions'. However, for constituting the other two types of ULSG—Municipality and Town Panchayat, it provides for the revenue to be generated by them in precise terms. In the case of creation of Municipality, it provides that the annual income should not be less than Rs. 50 lakh in the last consecutive three years. This in case of Town Panchayat needs to be not less than Rs. 30 lakh per annum in the last consecutive three years when it was a Panchayat constituted under the Tamil Nadu Panchayat Act, 1994. The West Bengal Municipal Act, 1993 simply provides that municipal income from taxation and other sources must be 'adequate for discharge of municipal functions'. In the state of Andhra Pradesh, the Andhra Pradesh Municipal Corporations Act, 1994 does not provide for generation of revenue as a criterion for constituting Municipal Corporations. For creation of a Municipality in the state, the Andhra Pradesh Municipalities Act, 1965 provides different amount of annual revenue to be generated for different Groups in which the Municipalities are grouped (Annex III).

EMPLOYMENT IN NON-AGRICULTURAL ACTIVITIES

Though Article 243Q provides for 'the percentage of employment in non-agricultural activities' as one of the economic criteria for constituting Municipality, it has not specified actual proportion of such employment that urban settlements should have for qualifying to be constituted into the three varieties of ULSG as provided for in the Indian Constitution. The Municipal Acts in the states of Andhra Pradesh, Gujarat, Haryana, Kerala, Madhya Pradesh, Odisha, Rajasthan, and Uttar Pradesh do not have provision for this parameter. The states (Bihar, Karnataka, Maharashtra, Tamil Nadu, and West Bengal) that have provided for density of population as one of the criteria depict a great deal of variation amongst themselves in this regard. Also the expression used in the Municipal Acts in these states differs a great deal. In Bihar, the

Bihar Municipal Act, 2007 uses the expression 'non-agricultural population'. In Tamil Nadu, the Act uses the expression percentage of 'male population working in non-agricultural activities' and in the state of West Bengal, the Municipal Act provides for this only in the case of Municipal Corporation and the expression used is percentage of 'adult population' in pursuit of non-agricultural activities. Actual proportion of employment in non-agricultural activities in these states varies from a maximum of 75 per cent in Bihar to 25 per cent for Nagar Panchayat in Maharashtra (Annex III). It is curious to note that the Municipal Act in Maharashtra provides for constitution of Nagar Panchayat even in all Taluka headquarters. If a transitional area is located at a distance of more than 20 km from any Municipal Corporation or a class A Council, the percentage of such employment is required to be not less than 50 per cent. The degree of variation is thus awfully confusing and chaotic. The variation to such a large extent does not provide any justification for the relevance of economic criteria in constituting the three varieties of municipality.

In needs to be emphasized that urban local self-government is constituted only in settlements that are urban in nature. The Census of India defines an urban area in terms of the following criteria:[1]

1. All places with a Municipality, Corporation or Cantonment or Notified Town Area (for statutory towns); and
2. All other places which satisfied the following criteria (for identification of Census Towns):

   (i) A minimum population of 5,000;
   (ii) At least 75 per cent of the male working population was non-agricultural; and
   (iii) A density of population of at least 400 per sq km

Obviously, if the proportion of employment provided for in the Municipal Acts in the states mentioned above is taken into consideration, none of the towns having one or the other form of Municipality according to the provisions in their respective Municipal Acts, correspond to the definition of 'urban' adopted by the Census

of India. Even in Bihar where the proportion of employment in non-agricultural activities is provided in the Municipal Act to be more than 75 per cent, it does not comply with the Census definition. Whereas the expression used in the Bihar Act is 'non-agricultural population', the Census definition uses the expression 'at least 75 per cent of the male working population'. It thus indicates that the 'statutory' towns that are constituted into one of the three types of ULSG as provided for in the Indian Constitution, have employment in non-agricultural activities that is in variance with the second set of definition of urban adopted and practiced by the Census of India. This poses a question: should there be a uniform set of indicators for constituting the ULSG in the cities and the towns? The flexibility provided for in the Indian Constitution for larger, smaller urban areas and the transitional area seems to have become too flexible and has resulted in a great deal of variation in different states. In the states where this parameter is left to the 'satisfaction' of the Governor, there is lack of transparency with respect to this parameter. A possible consequence of such practice is an inevitable weak economic base of the ULSG after its creation. A weak economic base does not provide financial wherewithal to the municipal government; it strikes at its financial viability. Financial and economic criteria have important implications for generation of required revenue and the required economic base that would further strengthen the local resource base and could provide financial sustainability to the urban local self-governments. Great deal of variations found in different states indicates a casual attitude in constituting the three types of local government in urban areas. Such a casual attitude has adverse impact on financial viability of ULSGs and makes them dependent on subventions soon after they are created.

It is, therefore, absolutely necessary that population threshold should be accompanied by premeditated economic criteria for ensuring sufficient amount of revenue for the three types of Municipalities. This will provide to the Municipalities with the much needed fiscal wherewithal for discharging their devolved functions. The exiting Constitutional provisions as well allude to this in Article 243Q (2) wherein the Governor of a state is given the onus of specifying larger, smaller and transitional urban areas keeping in view 'the population of the area, the density of population therein, the revenue generated for local administration, the percentage of employment in non-agricultural activities, the economic importance or such factors as he deem fit, . . .' Strict adherence to these parameters in terms of norms would be absolutely desirable for a reasonable good fiscal health of the urban local self-government. Strong financial wherewithal, it needs to be emphasized, ensures addressing other parameters of capacity development of the urban local self-governments discussed in Chapter 8,

COMPOSITION OF URBAN LOCAL SELF-GOVERNMENTS

Municipal laws in the states, by and large, have incorporated constitutional provisions as enshrined in the 74th CAA. Representation of members of state legislatures and the Indian Parliament, as discussed already in the last chapter is not desirable. The Andhra Pradesh Municipal Corporations Act, 1994 has an unusual provision. It provides that even a member of the State Legislative Assembly and the two Houses of Parliament who in compliance of the provisions of the 74th CAA happen to be ex-officio members, if they are elected to the position of Mayor or Chairpersons, s/he shall cease to hold the office of Mayor unless, within 15 days from the date of election to such office, s/he ceases to be a member of the Legislative Assembly or as the case may be either house of the Parliament! Such a provision seems to be quite amusing by all means. The unpalatable provisions in the 74th CAA and the ones contained in the Andhra Pradesh Municipal Corporations Act notwithstanding, the experience of more than a couple of decades of working of the 74th CAA indicates not so active participation of members of State Legislature and the Parliament. This raises a question about the need to have such provisions at all in the Constitution and look afresh into the composition of municipal governments for addressing the existing provision that promotes political bureaucratization of urban local self-government.

EMPOWERMENT OF WEAKER SECTIONS

The 74th CAA provides reservation for weaker sections such as scheduled caste, scheduled tribes, women and backward castes. All the state municipal laws have religiously followed these provisions and have incorporated them in their municipal laws. Some of the state governments have enhanced the proportion of reservation for women. These states include Bihar, Karnataka, and Rajasthan. These states have already increased the reservation for women to an extent of 50 per cent of the total number of members to be filled through direct election. There is now a consensus at the national level as well to increase the reservation for women to 50 per cent by amending the Constitution of India. A Constitution (112th Amendment) Bill has been pending in the Parliament since 2009 for this amendment. After its presentation in the Lok Sabha, the Bill was sent to the Parliamentary Standing Committee on Urban Development.

An odd and ludicrous provision in the 74th CAA pertains to reservation of seats of Chairpersons for the scheduled castes, scheduled tribes and women. Article 243T (4) of the Constitution provides that offices of the Chairpersons in the urban local self-government institutions have to be reserved for Scheduled Castes and Scheduled Tribes and women. It has left to the State Legislatures to provide for the manners in which this provision is implemented. The Constitution also provides that reservation of seats for Scheduled Castes and Scheduled Tribes and the women belonging to these castes for the offices of the chairpersons is to continue till expiry of the period specified in Article 334 of the Indian Constitution.[2] The 74th CAA also gives discretion to the state governments to provide for reservation even for the backward castes. Operational implication of such a provision is that every municipality needs to have a roster for reservation of seats for candidates belonging to these castes and the women. Though this sounds quite progressive for uplifting the weaker sections, on a closer look, such a provision has been adversely affecting urban governance by killing the very motivation of Chairpersons occupying this office for being proactive in their outlook and endeavours. The system of caste based rotation of reservation for the office of Chairperson does not contribute to making the Chairperson pro-active and motivated in improving the quality and effectiveness of governance or service delivery as s/he very well knows that they cannot contest the election the second time. This decidedly odd system has led to (i) lack of incentives for the Mayors/Chairpersons and the Councilors to perform, and (ii) gives incentive to them to indulge in unfair and unethical practices as it makes very clear to them that they will not have opportunity for re-election. Strangely enough, though the concept of rotational reservation was conceived for promoting social justice, it has proved to be counterproductive by denying the performing Mayors/Chairpersons and the Councilors another term for demonstrating their abilities to perform and bring about change. The futility of such a practice of reservation is reflected in absence of such provisions in the Constitution for offices of the Prime Minister and the Chief Ministers. This also indicates the discriminatory attitude towards urban local self-governments.

It was because of these aberrations of rotational reservation that the Model Municipal Law drafted for the central government does not provide for such an incongruous provision. If such a system of reservation only for the office of the Chairpersons in the urban local self-governments is so virtuous, why not extend it to the offices of the Prime Minister at the centre or the Chief Minister? By all means, such a system of reservation only in the urban local self-governments demonstrates the attitude towards these institutions that are looked at as inferior institutions of local self-government. This is highly despicable. No wonder, therefore, that a petition has been filed in the Patna High Court challenging the constitutional provision for such discriminatory system of reservation especially for the position that is not more than one in number in a Municipality.

LOCAL GOVERNMENT STRUCTURE FOR INTRA-CITY DECENTRALIZATION

Constitutional provision with respect to intra-city decentralization, as discussed in the previous chapter, is discretionary. The states have discretion to create either a multiple Wards Committee or a Ward Committee in each ward especially in the cities and towns with more than 3 lakh population. As the actual structure for intra-city decentralization created in the cities is quite large in size, a need was felt subsequent to this amendment for further deepening of democracy at the sub-municipal level. The Ministry of Urban Development, therefore, got drafted a model Nagar Raj Bill (Community Participation Bill) that provides for creation of decentralized structures that could be much more amenable to (a) deepening of democracy, (b) bringing local government still nearer to the citizens and (c) provide space to the local communities for participation in governance that could promote local government accountability and transparency. Its prime objective is to institutionalize citizens' participation in discharge of municipal functions, e.g. setting priorities, budgeting process, planning for social and economic growth, etc., by constituting Area Sabha below the ward for one or more than one polling station. It also provides for creation of Ward Committee in each municipal ward. Creation of Area Sabha envisages to provide a platform to the adult population of about one thousand (the general number of voters register for a Polling Station) to participate in urban governance, decide the priority of schemes to be implemented in the Area Sabha, identify beneficiaries of a government programme, motivate taxpayers in prompt payment of tax, etc. The members of the Area Sabha become members of the Ward Committee that is to be composed of the Councilor elected from that ward who also chairs the Ward Committee. Besides them, it is also to have representation of not more than ten members of the civil society. Area Sabhas constituted within a ward are thus linked to the ward level Ward Committee through Area Sabha representatives, who act as community representatives. The ULSG will thus consist of a three tier decision-making structure in a municipality, namely, the Municipality, the Ward Committee, and the Area Sabhas. Ward Committee thus becomes a forum for broad-based participation of the local community and provides much needed participatory avenues for urban governance.

An important aspect of the Nagar Raj Bill having wider ramification for urban governance that is worth mentioning is that it intends to make a municipal ward the basic unit for planning, budgeting and service delivery. Plans are to be prepared for the wards by the members of the ward themselves and the plans thus prepared in each ward are to be consolidated into a development plan for the entire Municipality as a whole. Similarly, the budget would need to be prepared at the ward level and all the ward budgets are to be consolidated to form a budget for the Municipality. With a view to institutionalize this novel participatory structure, enactment of this Bill into law by the state governments was made part of the mandatory areas of state level reform for Jn-NURM and as one of the caveats for accessing Jn-NURM funds. However, as the state governments have created Wards Committees as well, the new urban local self-government structure will have a four tier structure such as (i) the Town Hall, (ii) Wards Committee for more than one ward, (iii) Ward Committee in every ward, and (iv) Area Sabha at the level of one or two Polling Stations. However, powers, functions, and responsibilities of the Ward Committee being much wider, existence of Wards Committee will become superfluous. It would be, therefore, advisable to abolish Wards Committee.

In addition, states may choose to create a structure at an intermediary level for administrative reasons by clustering multiple wards into a regional structure and locating it between the ward and the municipality exclusively for managing effective service delivery through de-concentration of municipal administration.

The states that have provided for creation of Area Sabha in their existing municipal laws are still quite less in number. Information contained in Annex IV for some of the major states reveals that hardly five states (Andhra Pradesh, Bihar, Karnataka, Kerala and Madhya Pradesh) have provided for this in their Municipal Acts. In Andhra Pradesh, there is provision in the enabling Acts and Rules for creation of both Area Sabha and Ward Sabha (in Municipal Councils with less than 1 lakh population). In Kerala, it is called Ward Sabha and is created only in the municipal areas that have less than 1 lakh population. In Madhya Pradesh, it is called Mohalla Samiti and is to be created in every municipal area. Constitution of Area Sabha is the only structure that provides a very wide space for the civil society to participate in urban governance. A counterpart of the Gram Sabha in the Village Panchayat under the Panchayati Raj system, it contributes to deepening of democracy right up to the polling station level. The provision for election of Area Sabha Representatives provides opportunities for the different segments of the population to participate in the process of governance.

Jn-NURM made it mandatory for states to either enact a separate Community Participation Law (CPL) or make appropriate amendments in their existing municipal laws. These enactments will need to ensure clarity about functions, duties and powers of each of these tiers, and provide for appropriate devolution of funds, functions and functionaries to these levels. Even though enactment of CPL was a mandatory state level reform under Jn-NURM, the number of states that have taken an initiative to provide for this in their municipal laws is still quite less in number.

It will be interesting to look into how the different states have adopted the provisions contained in the 74th CAA and in the model Nagar Raj Bill. Constitution of Wards Committee is a mandatory provision of the Indian Constitution. But even though it is mandatory provision of the Constitution, the states have discretion to create a multi-ward or a uni-ward committee. Creation and composition of decentralized structures of urban local governance are contained in Annex IV for some of the major states in India. A look at the information contained in Annex IV depicts a wide variation in the ways the different states have adopted this mandatory provision along with the creation of uni-ward committee and the Area Sabha.

The Municipal Acts in the states of Gujarat, Haryana, Odisha, Rajasthan, Tamil Nadu and Uttar Pradesh (only in Municipal Corporations) provide for creation of only Wards Committee that consists of more than one ward. Bihar is the only state that has provisions for creation of Wards Committee, Ward Committee and also Area Sabha. Municipal Laws only in two states provide for constitution of Ward Committee and Area Sabha. These states are Karnataka, Kerala (Ward Sabha in place of Area Sabha) and Madhya Pradesh. In Madhya Pradesh, the Act provides for creation of Wards

Committee and Mohalla Committee. In Karnataka, the Act provides for constituting the Ward Committees in each municipal ward and an Area Sabha in each 'Area'. The Karnataka Municipal Corporation Act provides for creation of an Area Sabha that, in any case, is not to consist of more than five polling stations. West Bengal, the Municipal Corporation Act, 2006 provides for constituting a Borough Committee in every Municipal Corporation (to be created in a municipal area that has a population of 5 lakh and more). Borough Committee is required to be created by grouping the wards of the municipality in such a manner that each Borough consists of not less than six contiguous wards. Borough Committee is then constituted for each Borough. The West Bengal Municipal Act, 1993 as well contains provisions for creation of Borough Committees in municipal areas that have a population of 3 lakh and more. It is created by grouping the wards of the Municipality into five Boroughs so that each Borough consists of not less than six contiguous wards. A Borough Committee is created in each Borough thus created in a municipal area. Below the level of Boroughs, both the West Bengal Municipal Corporation Act, 2006 and the West Bengal Municipal Act, 1993 provide for constitution of a Ward Committee in each Municipal Ward. The Municipal Act for Municipal Councils in the state of Uttar Pradesh provides for creation of only a Ward Committee.

Madhya Pradesh has entirely a different structure of intra-city decentralization. It has Wards Committees that are created by pooling together more than one ward especially in the cities that have more than 3 lakh population. The Madhya Pradesh Municipal Corporation Act, 1956 also provides for creation of Wards Committee in cities with less than 3 lakh population. It has an interesting practice of determining the number of Wards Committees to be created. The number of Wards Committees to be created in a municipality is arrived at by dividing the total population of the municipal area by 100. In addition to Wards Committees, the Madhya Pradesh Municipal Corporation Act, 1956 and the Madhya Pradesh Municipality Act, 1964 provide for creation of Mohalla Samitis (Committee). The Municipality Act also provides for constitution of Wards Committee in Municipal Councils and Nagar Panchayats if the Municipal Council and Nagar Panchayat so decide. Bihar Municipal Act, 2007, a unified municipal law, provides for creation of Wards Committee in every Municipal Corporation area that has a population of 3 lakh and more. In order to constitute Wards Committee, the different wards of the Municipal Corporation are first grouped in such a manner that each group of wards consists of not less than three wards. Wards Committee is then created for each group. The Bihar Act also provides for constitution of Ward Committee in each municipal ward. Down below the ward there is one more structure—the Area Sabha. Area Sabha is constituted in each 'Area' that happens to be the body of all persons registered in electoral rolls pertaining to every polling booth in an Area especially in cities with more than 1.5 lakh population. Ward Committee and Area Sabha are, however, not yet created.

A synoptic view of legal provisions for creation of decentralized structures in some of the major states thus indicates great deal of variation in the conformity laws across states. The conformity legislations do not seem to be 'conforming' to the constitutional provisions largely due to ambiguity about the constitutional provisions itself. The parameters for constituting municipalities are not specified in terms of specific norms. The confusion with respect to Wards/Ward Committee is the result of an option provided for in Article 243S that provides for its constitution in 'one or more wards'. This has led to a variation in legal provisions and hence in creation of these decentralised structures. Inserting the alphabet 's' to the word 'ward' has further compounded the confusion. The expression 'wards' has perhaps led quite a large number of states to believe that this Committee needs to be a multi-ward committee. In some other states, notably Kerala and Karnataka, the Acts provide for constitution of only the Ward Committee in each ward and not the Wards Committee consisting of multiple wards. The analysis of legal provisions with respect to decentralized structures also reveals that some of the states have gone for creation of structure down below the ward for widening the space for participation by complying with the caveat for accessing the Jn-NURM funds and have simply replicated provisions of the model Community Participation Bill in their newly amended laws. The states of Bihar, Karnataka, Kerala, and Madhya Pradesh belong to this category of states. It needs to be mentioned that creation of a three-tier decentralized structure such as (i) Wards Committee by pooling more than one ward together, (ii) Ward Committee in each ward and (iii) Area Sabha/Mohalla Committee (Madhya Pradesh)/Ward Sabha (Kerala) needs to be avoided. A two-tier structure consisting of only the Ward Committee and the Areas Sabha/Ward Sabha/ Mohalla Committee makes the multiple Wards Committee not only superfluous but it is also prone to bureaucratization of local governance. A three-tier decentralized structure is likely to be infested with inter-committee conflicts, coordination problems and above all, conflicts primarily arising out of search for more authority that contributes to added conflict.

The analysis of decentralized structures also depicts that only a few states have provided for creation of Wards Committee and the sub-ward structures (Area Sabha, Wards Sabha and Mohalla Committee) largely because of, curiously enough, resistance from the Ward Councilors! The Councilors believe that creation of structure down below the ward may curtail their own authority over the ward. This, in a way, also depicts replication at the ward level of the usual apprehension observed at the state level for not empowering the institutions of urban local-self government as this may jeopardize their political prospects! Therefore, the mindset obtaining in large number of states makes them reluctant to strengthen the grass-root institutions of governance; there is a feeling that they should not be allowed to take roots. The states of Kerala, Karnataka, West Bengal, and to some extent, even the state of Rajasthan, however, happen to be notable exceptions largely due to enactment of relatively much more progressive municipal legislations.

COMPOSITION OF DECENTRALIZED STRUCTURES

Wards Committee

Multi-Wards Committees are required to be constituted in cities with a population of 3 lakh and more. The Councilors elected from the wards that happen to be the constituents of the Wards

Committee constitute the Wards Committee and they elect one of the members from amongst themselves as the Chairperson. The 74th CAA has a discretionary provision for nominating additional members on the Wards Committee. Municipal laws in the states of Bihar, Haryana, and West Bengal (Borough Committees) do not provide for nomination of members. Wards Committees in these states are composed of only the elected Councilors from the constituent wards. However, in states such as Gujarat, Madhya Pradesh, Odisha, Rajasthan, and Uttar Pradesh, the Acts also provide for representation of persons other than the locally elected Councilors (Annex IV). In the state of Gujarat the law provides for representation of three recognized Non-government Organizations (NGO) and the Community-based Organizations (CBO) that are engaged in social work within the wards that form part of a Wards Committee. In addition, an officer of the Municipality designated as Officer-in-charge of the territorial area of the Wards Committee is also required to be made a member of the Wards Committee. In Madhya Pradesh, Wards Committee is required to be composed of elected Councilors and two persons residing within the territorial area of this Committee who has knowledge and experience of municipal administration. The municipal law in the state requires the Mayor to nominate the members to the Wards Committee. But s/he is required to do this on the recommendation of the Chairperson of the Wards Committee. In Rajasthan and Uttar Pradesh, besides the elected Ward Councilors, five persons are required to be nominated as members. The law also provides that the persons to be nominated should have knowledge and experience of municipal administration. Whereas in Rajasthan the nomination is required to be made by the Municipality, in Uttar Pradesh, nomination is required to be made at the highest level—by the state government. This seems quite unusual and cumbersome a practice. Such a practice is also contrary to the import and ethos of self-government.

In West Bengal, the counterpart of the Wards Committee is called the Borough Committee and the municipal laws provide for its constitution 'in municipal areas' that have a population of 3 lakh and more. The law also provides that Borough Committees may be created even in territorial areas of Municipal Council if its population exceeds 3 lakh.

The municipal laws in the states mentioned above, provide for constituting Wards/Borough Committees. As discussed subsequently in this chapter, these committees serve a very large number of population that defeats the very objective of the constitutional provisions for creation of decentralized structure. The Second Administrative Reforms Commission cites example of Mumbai where it serves about 7 to 11 lakh people. In Delhi, it is created for a population of more than 1.5 million persons.

Ward Committee

The Composition of Wards Committee discussed above indicates limited representation of non-officials on these Committees. Compared to the Wards Committee created for a number of wards, the states that have provided for constituting Ward Committee for each ward in their municipal laws also provide for better representation of non-officials and civil society on this committee. Mention must be made of five states where the municipal laws provide for composition of Ward Committee that is quite broad based. These states are (i) Andhra Pradesh, (ii) Kerala, (iii) Karnataka, and (iv) Uttar Pradesh and (v) West Bengal (Annex IV). In Kerala, the Councilor elected from the Ward becomes the Chairman of the Ward Committee. In addition to the Councilor, Section 43 of the Kerala Municipality Act, 1994 provides for representation of residents' associations, neighbourhood groups, educational institutions, cultural organizations, voluntary organizations, industrial and commercial establishments, professionals and trade unions. Thus a very wide segment of the different shades of persons and groups are required to be represented on the Ward Committee. In terms of numbers, the law provides that 15 persons are to be elected from among the members of the residents' association of that ward provided these associations are registered in the Municipality. Another 20 members are required to be elected from among the members of the registered neighbourhood groups of that ward; one person each is to be nominated by every political party having representation in the Municipality. It also provides that heads of all recognized educational institutions functioning in that ward become the member. Besides these members, the Chairperson of the Ward Committee nominates 20 persons of whom (i) 10 are from persons representing cultural organizations, voluntary organizations, educational institutions, and industrial-commercial establishments which are functioning in that ward but not necessarily residing in the ward; (ii) 5 happen to be from persons representing those working in that ward as professionals such as experts in agriculture, industry, health, education, engineering, etc., not necessarily residing in the ward; and (iii) five persons from the registered trade unions. Obviously, attempt has been made to give representation on the Ward Committee of a cross-section of persons and groups of the society. However, the number of members represented on the Ward Committee is too large. In such a situation where the number of members is quite large especially on a structure created for smaller areas, there is likelihood of lack of focus on specific issues to be discussed in the Committee. Representation of too many diverse groups has also the likelihood of conflicting interest of different groups that are represented on the Committee.

Ward Committees in Kerala have been entrusted with a number functions that are relevant for development of the ward such as service delivery and maintenance, development works, and expenditure proposals with assigned priority. The Ward Committee Rules in Kerala (Annex V) require the Ward Committee to hold its meeting every three months. The rules also enjoin upon the Ward Committees that in a meeting to be held three months before the end of every financial year, it should prepare development schemes for the next financial year along with an expected estimate of the expenditure for each item in the order of priority and submit the same to the Council through the Chairperson.

In Andhra Pradesh the enabling municipal laws do not provide for creation of Wards Committee (meant for multiple wards). There is provision for constituting Ward Committee in every ward of the Municipal Corporation and Municipal Councils. The Committee is chaired by the Councilor elected from the ward. Besides the

Chairperson, the law provides that the committee shall consist of not less than four and not more than 10 electors from the ward on the basis of population. Members to be nominated must represent the civil society. Nomination is required to be made by the Council of the Corporation. The Andhra Pradesh Municipalities (Constitution, Conduct of Meetings, Powers and Functions of Ward Committees, Area Sabhas and Ward Sabhas) Rules, 2010, also contains definition of civil society that includes President/Secretary representing registered Residents Welfare Associations in the ward, member of registered Tax Payers Association/Rate Payers Association, President/Secretary of slum level federation of a slum. In case a ward does not have slums, the representative of self-help group, member of registered Association/Institution/NGO/Mahila Mandal/ Trade Union/Chamber of Commerce/Medical Council, and any other prominent citizen in the ward needs to be ensured. Functions required to be performed by Ward Committees, by and large, conform to the list of functions provided for in the Nagar Raj Bill.

In Karnataka as well, the enabling laws and rules provide for composition of Ward Committee having broad-based representation. Besides the elected Councilors, 10 other members are made members through nomination by the Corporation. Of the 10 nominated members, two must belong to Scheduled Caste and Scheduled Tribes, three must be women, and two is required to be nominated from Residents' Associations. Besides these members, an Officer of the Corporation is also designated by the Commissioner to be the Secretary of the Ward Committee. In the State of West Bengal, as well Ward Committees are required to be constituted both in Municipal Corporation and Municipal Councils. The enabling laws provide for a broad-based representation of civil society. In Municipal Corporations, it is to consist of 17 members to be nominated by the Councilor and the Municipal Corporation from among the residents of the ward. Of the 17 members, at least three members are required to be nominated from the representatives of Community Development Society (CDS), and in case CDS does not exist, then such number of members are nominated from among the women members of the families belonging to below poverty line (BPL) but residing within the area. The members to be nominated must be engineers, doctors, cultural activists, social workers, educationists, etc., residing in the territorial areas of the Ward Committee.

The West Bengal Municipal Act, 1993, though provides for broad-based representation of civil society on the Ward Committee, the nature of provision in this regard is somewhat different from the ones contained in the West Bengal Municipal Corporation Act, 2006. The Municipal Act provides that besides the Councilor elected from the ward who chairs this Committee, the Ward Committee also has minimum of 9 and a maximum of 17 other members to be nominated by the Councilor and the Municipality from among the residents of the ward. For a population up to 2,500 the number of other members is capped at 9, and thereafter for every 500 additional population or part thereof, the Act provides for one additional member subject to a maximum of 17. If the number of other members varies from seven to nine then two, and if the number exceeds nine then at least three among them are required to be nominated from the representatives of CDS. The type of members to be nominated on the Ward Committee is almost the same as in the case of Municipal Corporation. Ward Committee, in its 1st meeting, is required to select a Member Secretary from amongst the members. He is authorized to convene meetings of Ward Committee in consultation with the Chairman and gives secretarial assistance to the Committee. Ward Committee Rules in this State (Annex VI) requires that the Committee must meet at least once every month.

The West Bengal Ward Committee Rules has further elaborated the role and the functions of the Ward Committee as the prime mover of the ULSG in the state. One of the important functions of the Ward Committee is to prepare Draft Development Plan for the ward. Ward Committees identify the programmes on the basis of priority for the ward and prepare Draft Development Plan through a participatory approach. The Draft Development Plans, after preparation, are submitted to the Municipal Council for approval. The plan, after approval, is sent to the District Planning Committee. Apart from this the Ward Committee is also empowered to supervise and monitor civic services provided in the area, and assist the Municipality in various works related to the ward concerned. It is required to convene an annual general meeting of the citizens of the ward up to 30 June of every year (i) to apprise them of the actions taken by the Municipality in the previous year and also (ii) to interact with them on municipal administration of the area. Similar half yearly meeting is also required to be organized by the Ward Committee in October-November each year for public interaction. An interesting aspect of Ward Committee rules in this state is that the responsibility of the Municipality is as well defined for giving proactive support to the Ward Committees. These include providing to the Ward Committees decisions of the Standing Committee, decisions and resolution of the Board of Councilors, ward wise budgetary allocation made by the municipality, ward wise details of municipal properties, annual financial statements, annual administration reports, and the ward map.[3]

In the state of Uttar Pradesh as well, the Ward Committee (created only in the Municipal Council and Nagar Panchayat areas), the Uttar Pradesh Municipalities Act, 1916 provides for representation of 10 nominated members by the Municipal Council from within the ward who should be office bearers of citizens' welfare societies and representatives of non-government organizations having special knowledge or experience of municipal administration. In Bihar, however, the Bihar Urban Local Body (Community participation) Rules, 2013 does not provide for representation of non-officials. The Ward Committee (not yet constituted) is to be composed of only the Ward Councilor and the Area Sabha Representatives.

Composition of Ward Committee thus depicts that the provisions in some of the conformity laws depict a broad-based representation of civil society groups. This is quite enabling a composition that besides providing opportunities for participation, also promotes transparency and accountability in urban governance. But as discussed above, only a few states have such provisions in their respective Municipal Acts.

Area Sabha

Constituting Area Sabha does not form part of the 74th CAA. It was part of the state level mandatory reforms under the Jn-NURM. Study of Municipal laws in states indicates that only four states have provided for constitution of Area Sabha. The Bihar Urban Local Body (Community Participation) Rules, 2013 does not provide for nomination of members on it; it is to consist of only the Area Sabha Representatives. Area Sabha is not yet implemented in Bihar. Mohalla Committee provided for in the Municipal Acts in Madhya Pradesh as well is yet to be implemented. Only in the states of Karnataka and Kerala, the municipal Acts provide for a different composition (Annex IV). The Karnataka Municipal Corporation Act, 1976 provides that the Area Sabha is to consist of all persons registered as voters in the electoral rolls of the polling stations that are included to form the Area Sabha. It has thus replicated the Gram Sabha of a Village Panchayat that is created under the Panchayati Raj laws in the Panchayati Raj institutions. The Karnataka Act provides that the Area Sabha representatives are to be nominated by the Councilor of the ward. The Kerala Municipal Act (a unified law) does not provide for representatives to be elected or nominated to the Ward Sabha. It has the provision that Councilor of the ward of which the Ward Sabha is a constituent, shall become its Convener and all persons enrolled as elector in the ward become its members. Obviously, the territorial area of the Ward Sabha in Kerala is much larger than that of an Area Sabha.

In Andhra Pradesh, the enabling law provides that Area Sabha is required to be constituted in Municipal Corporations, Municipal Councils and Nagar Panchayats. The rules provide for a threshold population for the Area Sabha. It provides for constituting one Area Sabha for every 2,000 population in the Municipal Corporation that has a total population of up to 5 lakh. The population threshold for creation of Area Sabha in Municipal Corporation with more than 5 lakh population is provided as 3,000. In the Municipal Corporation with a population of more than 10 lakh, the Act provides for creation of Area Sabha for a population of 3,000 and one Area Sabha for every additional population of 5,000 (with 10 per cent variation). In the case of Municipalities and Nagar Panchayats, provisions with respect to constitution of Area Sabha are almost similar to those for the Municipal Corporations. The rules mentioned above, provides for constituting of Ward Sabhas in a municipality with less than 1 lakh population, Ward Sabhas are to be constituted in different Wards after the constitution of Ward Committees. But the rules also provide that Area Sabha will not be constituted in the Municipal Councils and Nagar Panchayats that already have a Ward Sabha. All electors of the ward become members of the Ward Sabha and the elected ward member is its convener.

Functions to be performed by the Ward Committee, Area Sabha and Ward Sabha are provided in detail.[4]

Enactment of Community Participation Law only by four states, out of 28 states (Telangana, the 29th state of the Indian Union had not taken its birth then) indicates an aberration in ensuring implementation of state level mandatory reforms envisaged under Jn-NURM. Accessing funds under this mega urban sector project was contingent upon implementation of a series of state and municipal level mandatory reforms.

Composition of decentralized structures for devolved democracy and for participatory urban governance has depicted varied practices in different states. The states of Andhra Pradesh, Karnataka, Kerala and West Bengal stand out in providing for representation of quite a cross section of focus groups (Annex IV). As the remaining states have different type of composition discussed in detail in the preceding paragraphs, the objective of participatory urban governance is largely defeated. Lesser the degree of participation in plans and programmes of the ULSGs, less transparent and accountable the local government is supposed to be. The analysis of structures for intra-city decentralization has also revealed that a three-tier local government structure consisting of (i) Town Hall (the Municipality), (ii) Ward Committee in each municipal ward, and (iii) Area Sabha is the ideal structure. In such a scheme of intra-city decentralization, continued existence of Wards Committee constituted presently by pooling more than one ward, becomes superfluous.

Executive System

Cities across the globe have two variants of executive system in local government. First is the Strong Mayor system. The Mayor/ Chairperson, under this system, is vested with executive power that enables him/her to be in perfect command of governance of the city, develop a vision for development and urban governance, ensure its effective implementation and monitoring and review of implementation of policies and programmes. The appointed Commissioner under such a system performs only executive functions. This also makes him/her accountable to the local government for the decisions taken for implementation of policies and programmes adopted by the executive—the Mayor/Chairperson. Cities in Europe, the USA, and South-East Asia, and even in some of the countries in Africa (South Africa, for example) have a Strong Mayor system. As against this, the second variation of executive system is a Weak Mayor system. Under this system the Mayor/Chairperson happens to be merely a titular head of the local government; the executive power vests in an appointed functionary. Weak Mayor System is epitomized by the Bombay model of urban local governance contained in the Mumbai Municipal Corporation Act, 1888—an Act enacted during the colonial rule, about more than 125 years ago and just a few years after the local government Resolution of Lord Ripon that heralded an organized system of local government in India. Though India has emerged as the largest vibrant and democratic nation of the world, the Mumbai Municipal Corporation Act—an antique piece of municipal legislation enacted during the colonial rule, has not only survived but has travelled to many states and implanted a Weak Mayor system in India's burgeoning cities. Even the big bang decentralization initiative conceived in the 74th CAA could not make a dent on abandoning such a bureaucratic system of local government.

Annex VII depicts the executive system provided for in as many as 20 Municipal Acts that are operating in some of the major states. The information culled from these laws and tabulated in this Annex is quite revealing. Of the 20 municipal laws studied for this purpose, as many as nine laws provide for a Weak Mayor system. The states where these laws are operating are Andhra Pradesh, Gujarat (both for municipal corporation and municipal council), Haryana, Madhya Pradesh (both for Municipal Corporations and Municipal Councils), Maharashtra (in case of municipal councils and municipal corporations especially Mumbai), Tamil Nadu and

Uttar Pradesh (especially in municipal corporations). It is interesting and at the same time perplexing as well to mention that the much hyped Mayor-in-Council form of government implanted in Madhya Pradesh having semblance of a cabinet form of local government that is next only to the similar system established first in West Bengal, the Mayor does not enjoy executive powers! Sub-section (3) of Section 69 of the Madhya Pradesh Municipal Corporation Act, 1956 provides that 'Subject to the approval or sanction of the Corporation or of the Standing Committee, wherever it is in this Act expressly so directed and subject also to all other restrictions, limitations and conditions imposed by this Act, the entire executive power for the purpose of carrying out the provisions of this Act vests in Commissioner. . . .' Sub-section (2) of Section 50 of the Madhya Pradesh Municipality Act, 1961 and the Chhattisgarh Municipality Act, 1961 as well have similar provisions. Incongruity of such a glaring legal provision especially in a cabinet form of local government is further heightened by the provision in this Act for direct election of the Mayor. It is all the more a glaring legal provision. If the Mayor does not enjoy any executive power, direct election—yet another hype being passionately professed in the country—can neither make him the real executive head of the local government nor bring executive power to the Mayor. Direct election cannot be a proxy for executive power. If the Municipal Act does not designate him/her as the chief executive by bestowing the required executive powers, direct election is unlikely to bring it through a back door! If s/he is a weak Mayor in law, s/he has to be so irrespective of the mode of election.

The situation in the State of Uttar Pradesh and hence in Uttarakhand as well (the Uttar Pradesh Act is adopted by Uttarakhand with minor modifications), the situation is quite indeterminate and confusing. Sub-section (2) of Section 117 of the Uttar Pradesh Municipal Corporations Act, 1959 provides that 'Except as otherwise expressly provided in this Act, the Executive Committee shall be vested with, on behalf of the Corporation, with the superintendence of the municipal administration of the City'. The Mayor according to the provision in Section (51)(1)(a), happens to be the Chairman of the Executive Committee and, therefore, by implication, the Mayor should be the chief executive. But then sub-section (5) of Section 117 of this Act provides that 'Subject to the general control and direction of the Mayor . . . the executive power for the purposes of carrying out the provisions of this Act shall be vested in the Municipal Commissioner. . . .' Inherent contradiction in such a provision between the expression 'Subject to general control and direction of the Mayor' and vesting executive power to the Municipal Commission is awesome. One keeps on guessing as to how the Municipal Commissioner who is enjoying executive powers under the law can also at the same time be subject to general control and direction of the Mayor! Nevertheless, as the Commissioner is vested with executive power in unambiguous terms, one can only say that the Municipal Corporations in Uttar Pradesh are working with a Weak Mayor system.

Municipal laws (for constituting Municipal Councils) prevailing in the states of Bihar, Kerala, Karnataka, West Bengal, Odisha, Uttar Pradesh, and West Bengal provide for a Strong Mayor system meaning thereby that the elected head in the municipal councils in these states happens to be the real executive and that s/he is formally vested with executive powers. The Commissioner/Chief Officer performs only executive functions. The picture seems to be quite hazy with regard to the Municipal Corporation in the state of Uttar Pradesh where the provision with respect to executive power and function is quite ambivalent.

In recent years, a trend towards directly elected Mayor/Chairperson is discernable in some of the states in India. Such practice has existed for quite some time in Europe, USA and even in some of the African countries and in South-East Asia. Citing examples from abroad for directly elected Mayor, SARC has quite forcefully argued for adopting a practice of an elected Mayor/Chairperson. Reasons given for its replication in India are basically two. First is the stability it provides to the system as an elected Mayor need not depend on political support of the majority political party as is presently the case with an indirectly elected Mayor/Chairperson. Second, it is argued that an elected Mayor/Chairperson has altogether a different image due to his/her election directly from the city-wide constituency by the citizens of the city at large.

So far as the stability argument is concerned, every municipal law has provision for a vote of no-confidence. The election of the Mayor directly or indirectly becomes immaterial with such provision in the municipal law. Even the Indian Constitution has provisions for no-confidence motion against the Prime Minister and the Chief Ministers. As regards the prestige and 'concentrated attention' received by an elected Mayor, these do not carry any meaning if s/he is not vested with executive power under the law. Direct election of Mayor from a city-wide constituency is surely not going to arm the Mayor with executive powers if the enabling Municipal Act does not give such powers to the Mayor. There are at least a couple of cases in point that can be cited in this regard. In the state of Tamil Nadu, the Mayor is elected directly. But the Tamil Nadu Local Bodies Act, 1998 does not vest any executive power to the Mayor. It is the Municipal Commissioner who wields executive powers for carrying out provisions of this Act. The Mayor-in-Council in the state of Madhya Pradesh is yet another example. The Mayor is elected directly in the state. Despite this, s/he does not have any executive power. It lies with the appointed Commissioner. As discussed above, direct election of Mayor/Chairperson is apparently irrelevant; what is relevant is the executive powers vested to him/her in law. Offices of the Prime Minister and the Chief Ministers are powerful by all means even though the incumbents to these offices are not elected directly; the Constitution has armed them with powers and authority. What is, therefore, important is empowerment of the offices of Mayor in Municipal Corporations and Chairpersons in the Municipal Councils and Nagar Panchayats in law, not through the process through which they are elected. Direct election without any executive powers is a misnomer. This also points to absence of empowerment in true sense of the term.

Term of Office

Lack of executive powers of the Mayors/Chairpersons is exacerbated by a very short term of office provided in some of the Municipal Laws. Not all the Municipal Acts in all states provide for a five year term for the elected Council of Municipal Corporations and other varieties of urban local self-government. The term of office of the Mayor in Municipal Corporations and Chairperson/President of Municipal Councils and Nagar Panchayats needs to be co-terminous with that of the Council. This provides the elected head sufficient time horizon to develop his/her own vision for development of the city, governance and service delivery. It also enables the elected head to become conversant with municipal affairs, needs of the cities/towns and also the dynamics of municipal politics that comes handy for developing the vision for the city/town. Looking at the provisions in municipal laws in some of the major states, the largest number of Municipal Acts (out of 20 Acts) provide for five-year term for the elected head. The states having such provisions are Bihar, Kerala, Madhya Pradesh, Odisha, Rajasthan, Tamil Nadu, Uttar Pradesh and West Bengal. All the three types of urban local self-governments in these states have a term of five years for the Mayor/Chairperson. In the remaining states (Annex VIII), the Municipal Acts provide for less than five years. In the states of Andhra Pradesh, Karnataka (in Municipal Corporation), and in Mumbai Municipal Corporation, the Acts provide for a term of office of only one year for the elected head. In the national capital of Delhi (not included in this Annex) as well the Mayors have a term of office of only one year. In the states of Gujarat, Maharashtra and Karnataka (in Municipal Council), the term of office provided for is two and half-a-year. This is yet another indicator of scant importance given to the office of Mayor/Chairperson in the institutions of self-government. This is in glaring contrast to the executive system and the term of office of the elected head in the Panchayati Raj Institutions.

Analysis of important provisions contained in the municipal laws that were amended for incorporating the provisions of the 74th CAA or enacted subsequent to this constitutional amendment reveals a great deal of variation in the legal provisions in these laws in different states. The enactment of the Constitution (74th Amendment) Act has not made much of dent on municipal laws. The analysis of some of the important aspects of this decentralization initiative in major states reveals that in the matters of constituting of municipalities of the three types, consideration of the parameters for their constitution, creation of decentralized structures, composition of the decentralized structures, powers and functions of the municipalities and the decentralized structures vary a great deal not only from the constitutional provisions but also in different states. Such a wide variation is further accentuated by absence of executive powers to the Mayors/Chairpersons and very short-term of office provided in some of municipal laws. Even though quite a big and bold step was taken in 1992 by the Indian Parliament for strengthening decentralization and empowerment of the institutions of urban local self-government, it is characterized by (i) gaps in the Constitution Amendment Act itself and (ii) gap between the provisions in the 74th CAA and the conformity legislations. These gaps indicate that empowerment of urban local self-governments is even now largely a myth.

NOTES

1. Whereas the first set of criteria is used in identification of statutory towns, the second set of criteria is used to identify the Census towns.
2. Article 334 provides that reservation of seats for the scheduled castes and the schedules castes in the Lok Sabha and in the Legislative Assemblies of the States is required to continue for seventy years from the commencement of the Constitution, i.e. 26 January 1950. But as this has become highly politicized, it is doubtful if provisions in Article 334 could be abolished even after seventy years (in 2020).
3. For details and a study of working of Ward Committees in West Bengal, see Prabhat Datta and Dipankar Sinha, 2007; *Participatory Governance: Ward Committees in Action,* Dasgupta and Co., Kolkata.
4. Andhra Pradesh Municipalities (Constitution, Conduct of Meetings, Powers and Functions of Ward Committees, Area Sabhas and Ward Sabhas) Rules, 2010.

CHAPTER 5

Views of Constitution Review Commission and Second Administrative Reforms Commission

The central government took two important steps to review the working of the Constitution and public administration system prevailing in the country. These steps were taken to get insights into constitutional provisions and whether these have worked for helping the polity in enhancing the quality of life of the citizens. Another related purpose was to identify bottlenecks, if any, in working of the Constitution and the public administration system that has been operating for fulfilling aspirations of the people. It, therefore, constituted two Commissions such as (i) National Commission to Review the Working of the Constitution, and (ii) the Second Administrative Reforms Commission. These Commissions also looked into the legal framework for local self-government in both rural and urban areas and the obstacles in smooth and effective functioning of local government. The views of the two Commissions pertaining to urban local self-government are discussed below.

CONSTITUTION REVIEW COMMISSION

The Constitution was adopted on 26 January 1950. After it came in force, gradual socio-economic changes required introducing changes in the Constitution for facilitating national economic and social development. By February 2002 when the Report of the Commission was submitted, after about 52 years of the working of the Constitution, as many as 85 amendments had already been made in the Constitution. These changes notwithstanding, the need for a comprehensive, objective and transparent exercise was felt for getting insights into the working of the Constitution and evaluating its achievements as well as failures. Need for a comprehensive exercise was also felt to have knowledge about fulfilment of the objectives of the Constitution as also to comprehend additional changes that would be required in years to come for effective governance of the polity and the required socio-economic development. In 2000 the Atal Behari Vajpayee government then in power, therefore, decided to constitute a National Commission to review the working of the Constitution. Consequently, the Government of India, Ministry of Law, Justice and Company Affairs (Department of Legal Affairs), vide its Resolution, dated 22 February 2000 resolved to constitute 'the National Commission to Review the Working of the Constitution' to make suitable recommendations. The Commission was chaired by M.N. Venkatachaliah, a former Chief Justice of the Supreme Court of India. The Terms of Reference given to the Commission required it to

> . . . examine, in the light of the experience of the past 50 years, as to how best the Constitution can respond to the changing needs of efficient, smooth and effective system of governance and socio-economic development of modern India within the framework of parliamentary democracy and to recommend changes, if any, that are required in the provisions of the Constitution without interfering with its basic structure or features.

Before constitution of this Commission, the Constitution (74th Amendment) Act, 1992 had already been enacted by the Parliament. It inserted a new part—Part IXA in the Constitution. The National Constitution Review Commission (hereinafter to be referred to as the Constitution Review Commission), therefore, also reviewed the provisions relating to decentralization of urban governance contained in the newly introduced Part IXA of the Constitution. While reviewing the constitutional provisions with respect to institutions of self-government—both Panchayati Raj institutions and the municipal governments—the Commission found several gaps in the framework of decentralization and the process of implementation of 73rd and the 74th Constitution Amendment Acts.

It observed that 'The Union Government and the State Governments continue to exercise powers in planning and the Panchayats and Municipalities do not enjoy autonomy—financial or administrative—as institutions of local self-government' (GoI 2002). The Commission, therefore, suggested several steps for addressing the gaps as also aberration in the functioning of local self-government institutions. Important suggestions that have bearing on imparting elements of 'autonomy' to the institutions of urban local self-government are very briefly discussed below.

To begin with, the Constitution Review Commission also observed 'considerable gaps' in the implementation of both the 73rd and the 74th CAAs. In precise terms, the Commission observed two types of gaps. First, the state governments still exercise powers in the sphere of planning. This observation of the Commission is perhaps impelled by absence of institutionalization of altogether a new paradigm of planning contained in the 74th CAA that is primarily to be driven by local political process resulting in a bottom-up process of planning. This has been also discussed in detail in Chapter 6 with similar conclusion. Second, the Commission found that the institutions of local self-government—both rural and urban—do not enjoy either financial or administrative autonomy. The Commission, therefore, evaluated the provisions in the Constitution with respect to decentralization of urban governance as well. In doing so, the Commission has given valuable suggestions for bridging the gaps in constitutional provisions.

Local Government Election

Conducting elections in fair and objective manner happens to be the essence of transparency in local government elections. The Constitution Review Commission, however, noticed political considerations in conducting of local government elections largely because the state governments retain powers relating to conduct of elections under the State Acts and Rules. Moreover, the State Election Commissions have to depend on the state governments for getting financial, staff and logistics support for conducting local government elections. State governments also have powers with respect to issuing notifications for conduct of local government election, delimitation of local government constituencies, and earmarking of reserved seats in local government electoral wards. The Commission also felt that interference of state governments in these matters are borne by experience in the past. According to the Commission, experience has shown that some of the state governments have assumed responsibility especially in matters of delimitation of territorial constituencies, reservation of seats and its rotation. The state governments thus intervene in the composite and integrated process of conducting of elections. The Commission, therefore, recommended that functions and responsibilities relating to delimitation, reservation and rotation of seats and the matters connected with these should be vested in a delimitation commission to be constituted by law made by the appropriate Legislature and not in the State Election Commission. It did not favour delimitation of local government constituencies before local government elections. It suggested that this should be adjusted after every Census, and that such a provision should be put in the Constitution itself. It, however, felt the need for Guidelines that could be provided under the state laws for delimitation work. In this regard, the Commission observed that 'The State laws should provide guidelines for the delimitation work such as parity, as far as possible, in the ratio between the population of a territorial constituency and the number of seats within the same class of Panchayats or Municipalities. The extent of permissible variations should also be mentioned.' The Commission also pointed out a discrepancy in constitutional provisions with respect to parity for the two sets of local governments; the requirement of parity is provided for in the proviso to Article 243C of the Constitution for the Panchayati Raj institutions, but not for Municipalities.

In view of state government interference in matters relating to local government election and lack of teeth in the State Election Commission, the Constitution Review Commission felt the need for strengthening the State Election Commissions so that accountability of States for timely and fair local government elections are ensured and the State Election Commissions are enabled to 'function independent from the State Governments'. The Commission also suggested that the Election Commission of India should as well have some role in ensuring fair local government election. It, therefore, suggested that the Constitution itself should have provisions that would enable the State Election Commissions function independent from the state governments and draw expertise and guidance from the Election Commission of India. The Constitution Review Commission, therefore, recommended amending Article 243ZA of the Constitution for defining the role of the Election Commission in terms of giving it powers to issue any direction or instructions to the State Election Commission for the discharge of its functions. Accordingly, the Commission recommended substituting Clause (1) of Article 243ZA by the following new constitutional provisions: 'The Election Commission shall have the power to issue any directions or instructions to the State Election Commission for the discharge of its functions under clause (1)'.[1]

The Constitution Review Commission also referred to yet another important issue that is quite germane for conducting of fair local elections. Articles 243K and 243ZA provide for preparation of electoral rolls by the State Election Commission. Though generally the electoral rolls prepared for holding Lok Sabha and State Assembly elections are used for conducting local government elections. At times, especially in the event of discrepancy between the electoral rolls for conducting elections for the higher levels of government and the local government, the State Election Commission prepares fresh electoral rolls all over again. The Constitution Commission has pointed to this practice and has suggested that there should be common electoral rolls for conducting elections for all levels of government be it the Panchayats, the Municipalities, the State Assemblies and the Lok Sabha. What is, therefore, suggested by the Constitution Review Commission is that there should be a common electoral roll for holding all elections and that this should be prepared by the Election Commission under Article 327 of the Constitution read with the Representation of the People Act 1950. In the Commission's view, this could be updated by the State Election Commission. To quote from the Report of the Commission, 'The processes for preparing the roll as also its periodical revision should be uniform throughout the country'.

Reservation of Seats

The 74th CAA provides for reservation of seats in the municipal governments of the three types especially for empowerment of the weaker sections of the society. It, therefore, provides for reservation of seats for Scheduled Castes, Scheduled Tribes and women. In addition, it also provides for reservation in the offices of Chairpersons in the Municipalities. The Constitution Review Commission has raised a couple of very pertinent questions with respect to rotation of reservation in different local government electoral wards and in the system of reservation in the office of Chairpersons. First, it observed 'some ambiguities about the rotation of such reserved seats'. The 'ambiguity' pertains to the use of expression 'may' in clause (1) of Article 243T of the Constitution. It provides that for the election of Councilors, seats shall be reserved for Scheduled Castes and Scheduled Tribes and such reserved seats 'may be allotted by rotation to different constituencies in a Municipality'. Thus rotation of reserved seats for these castes seems to be discretionary (due to the use of expression 'may'). But it is not so in case of reservation of offices of the Chairpersons'. Clause (4) of Article 243T provides that 'The Offices of Chairpersons in the Municipalities shall be reserved for the Scheduled Castes, the Scheduled Tribes and women in such manner as the Legislature of a State may, by law, provide'.

The Constitution Review Commission points out to yet another ambiguity with respect to frequency of rotation that is not clear from the constitutional provisions. Should it be in every election or should it be at the time of delimitation of local electoral wards?

In addition to these 'ambiguities', the Commission has raised a fundamental issue with respect to rotation of reservation. The Commission rightly observed that in case rotation of reserved seats is effected during every election, it does not allow the person elected on the reserved seat to get re-elected; in fact s/he cannot even contest the election. This kills the very motivation of the occupier of such seat not to perform and nurture his/her constituency. In addition to such a very pertinent view of the Commission, such a system of rotation also does not enable the person holding such a reserved seat in getting the much needed training in managing public affairs—an objective that came to the fore so conspicuously and extensively during the British rule. The Constitution Review Commission, therefore, has recommended removing this ambiguity and flaw in rotation of reserved seats by amending Article 243T to provide for rotation of seats only at the time of delimitation of local electoral wards and not in between. It also suggested that State laws should provide the guidelines for the process of reservation which should ensure transparency and adequate opportunities for eliciting voter response.

Constitutional provisions for reservation of seats include providing reservation of seats that are filled up through direct election and reservation for the offices of Chairpersons in the both types of local self-government—rural and urban—also for the backward castes. It, however, does not provide for a ceiling for the total number of seats and offices to be reserved. Provision for reservation of not less than one-third of the total number of seats for women is specified in the Constitution, additional reservation for the backward castes, according the Constitution Review Commission may put a claim on large proportion of the total number of seats and offices in the Municipalities. Therefore, the Commission has suggested that the precise position with regard to reservation needs to be clarified by specifying the total number of reserved seats and offices in Panchayats and Municipalities.

Dissolution of Municipalities

In pre-74th CAA days, urban local self-governments were dissolved by the state governments every now and then generally by ascribing to their purported failure in discharge of functions devolved to them. As mentioned in Chapter 2 as of 1989, as many as 39 out of 71 Municipal Corporations were dissolved in the country. After dissolution, elections were not held for years together. In order to ward off such a situation, the 74th CAA provides a safeguard. A Proviso to Article 243U(1), therefore, provides that 'a Municipality shall be given a reasonable opportunity of being heard before its dissolution'. Sub-clause (b) of Clause 3 of this Article also gives a mandate to the state governments for holding fresh elections for constituting of the Municipality 'before the expiration of a period of six months from the date of its dissolution'. The Constitution Review Commission, however, alludes to treating dissolution of urban local self-governments by the state governments rather casually. In the opinion of the Constitution Review Commission, it is the political expediency that is generally the motivation for dissolution. It has, therefore, recommended that 'whenever a Municipality is superseded, a report stating the grounds for such dissolution should be placed before the State Legislature'. In the opinion of the Commission this will 'be a deterrent to treating supersession casually and resorting to it because of political expediency'.

Functional Domain

Views of the Constitution Review Commission on the status of the 12th Schedule are not very different from what has already been discussed in Chapter 3. The Commission as well has looked at this Schedule as a mere illustrative list of functions that a municipality is expected to perform. In the opinion of the Commission, it 'does not guarantee assignments of a set of exclusive functions'. It has also pointed to the shrinking municipal functional domain discussed in quite some detail in Chapter 2. The Commission felt that enactment of the Constitution (74th) Amendment Act was an opportunity to reverse this trend 'and once again entrust the responsibilities for the upkeep and development of towns and cities to Municipal governments. Pointing to provisions in Article 243W, it observes that the intention of the Constitution is endowing such powers and authority to the Municipalities under the state laws that could enable them to function as 'institutions of self-government'. However, the newly appended 12th Schedule merely lists altogether 18 functions and that the Schedule itself is merely illustrative. In the opinion of the Commission, this Schedule is neither exhaustive nor does it signify a variety of functions. A Consultation Paper on Decentralization prepared by the Constitution Review Commission observes that the 12th Schedule 'leaves much to be desired' (GoI 2001). It refers to the original 65th Amendment Bill introduced in the Lok Sabha in 1989 and observes that the 12th Schedule as conceived in this Bill was much larger and that it had listed municipal functions that were both obligatory and discretionary. The functions listed in this Schedule incorporated the functions that were already assigned to the urban local self-governments in different states under the State laws. In addition several new functions were added to the municipal functional domain such as welfare of the weaker sections, women and child development, family welfare, urban electrification, non-conventional energy, urban poverty alleviation, public distribution, etc. This Consultation paper also refers to a dichotomous approach in treating the two Schedule of functions—the 11th Schedule of the Constitution (73rd Amendment) Bill for the Panchayati Raj Institutions prepared then as part of the 64th Constitution Amendment Bill and the 12th Schedule. Whereas the 11th Schedule was retained in its original form, the 12th Schedule was prepared all over again. In the process of recasting of the 12th Schedule, some of the local government functions such as non-conventional energy, adult education, family welfare or women and child development which were considered legitimate activities for Panchayats and, therefore, were included in the 11th Schedule, were, however, excluded in the case of Municipalities in the 12th Schedule.

The Consultation Paper quite forcefully pleads for having a common Schedule of functions for both the types of local self-government—rural and urban—that could be applicable to both of these types of local government.

The Commission, however, did not finally suggest a common Schedule. Nevertheless, it observed that being not autonomous institutions of self-government, the role to be played by the municipalities in urban governance is inevitably contingent on the regime controlling the state government. The Commission, therefore, recommended that the Panchayati Raj institutions and the Municipalities need to be categorically declared as 'institutions of self-government'. This, in view of the Commission, requires assigning exclusive functions to them. It has, therefore, recommended amending Article 243W of the Constitution in a manner that transforms the existing provision from discretionary to mandatory. For this it has suggested two changes to be made in the existing provisions. First, the expression 'may' wherever appearing in this Article that denotes discretionary power of the state governments is suggested to be converted into 'shall' so that it becomes a mandatory provision. Second, it has suggested to substitute the word 'endow' (appearing after the words 'the Legislature of a State May, by law') by 'vest'.[2]

Fiscal Domain

In the fiscal domain, the 74th CAA could not make any change with respect to the sources of own revenue of the urban local self-governments. The Consultation Paper of the Constitution Review Commission referred to the issue of creating a separate tax domain for the urban local self-government institutions. It noted that as in the pre-74th CAA regime, financial domain of the Municipalities is determined by the will of the State Governments. Tax authority of urban local self-government institutions is derived from municipal laws enacted by the legislatures in the different states. Through these laws the state governments have delegated tax authority to the Municipalities from the State List contained in the 7th Schedule of the Constitution. Many such laws provide that the urban local self-governments need approval of the respective state governments even for determination of tax rates. Such a legal provision has continued even after 74th CAA. Article 243X for municipalities and Article 243H in the case of Panchayats lay down that the Legislature of a state may, by law, authorize a municipality 'to levy, collect and appropriate such taxes, duties, tolls and fees in accordance with such procedures and subject to such limits' as may be specified in the law'. The other provisions in this Article regarding assignment of taxes, grants-in-aid from the Consolidated Funds of the state to the Municipalities are also not new. These constitutional provisions are not different from the provisions in the existing state laws.

Obviously, in its existing form, the constitutional provisions are discretionary in nature. It gives discretion to the State Legislatures for authorizing the municipalities in respect of levy, collection and appropriation of taxes, duties, fees and tolls as well as for the creation of a fund within the Municipal institutions to regularize and control inflow and outflow of financial resources. The Constitution Review Commission recognized the futility of such a discretionary constitutional provision that is unlikely to strengthen municipal finance. With a view to making the provisions in these two Articles (243X and 243H) meaningful, these need to be made mandatory. In fact, the Commission treaded altogether a new ground by observing that these Articles do not serve their purpose 'since some State Governments appear to be reluctant to share their fiscal powers with the local self-government institutions'. It even accepted the need for a separate tax domain for the local government—both urban and rural. The Commission, therefore, felt that 'the only way out is to introduce the concept of a separate tax domain for the local bodies. Having expressed such bold and enabling thoughts for local self-government institutions, the Constitution Review Commission made a strange turnaround by observing that 'it would be too early to consider such a proposal'. One keeps on wondering as to how long will it take to provide for a local list of local revenue?

The suggestion given by the Constitution Review Commission with regard to devolving of local fiscal tools is quite ambivalent and appears to be too vague to be made anything out of it. To quote from the Commission's Report, 'the Twelfth Schedule should be restructured in a manner that creates a separate fiscal domain for . . . Municipalities'. It is not clear as to how a restructuring of the 12th Schedule that contains only the list of illustrative functions will be able to carve out a separate fiscal domain for the local government! The Consultation Paper on Decentralization, somehow demystifies this ambivalence by forthrightly suggesting that the 12th Schedule could be restructured such that it would contain both functions as well as the sources of revenue for the Municipalities. However, such a restructuring will be contrary to the Commission's considered view that such a fiscal arrangement will be 'too early to consider'! Nevertheless, the Commission finally recommended as mentioned below:

The Commission recommends that the concept of a distinct and separate tax domain for municipalities should be recognized. This concept should be reflected in a list of taxes in the relevant schedule. Carving out items from the existing State lists such as item 49 (taxes on land and buildings) and item 52 (taxes on entry of goods into a local area for consumption) should not be difficult.

The Commission then goes on to suggest amending Article 243X in a manner that makes it mandatory for the State Legislature to enact laws that will devolve powers to the municipalities.

In the sphere of fiscal transfers, the Constitution Review Commission also refers to the issue of non-synchronisation of the period of Finance Commission and State Finance Commissions. Sub-clause (bb) of Clause (3) of Article 280 that deals with the terms of Reference of the Finance Commission requires it to recommend 'measures needed to augment the Consolidated Fund of a State to supplement the resources of the Municipalities in the State on the basis of the recommendations made by the Finance Commission of the State'. As discussed in Chapter 3, the 11th Finance Commission for the first time raised this issue that as the timing of constituting the Finance Commission and the State Finance Commissions are not synchronized, the Finance Commission is not in a position to recommend the measures on the basis of the recommendations made by the State Finance Commissions. The Constitution Review Commission considered this issue and recommended that sub-clause (bb) and (c) should be suitably amended by replacing the words 'on the basis of the recommendation' by the words 'after taking into consideration the recommendations' of the State Finance Commissions.

SECOND ADMINISTRATIVE REFORMS COMMISSION

The Second Administrative Reforms Commission (SARC) was constituted by the President of India in August 2005 with a quite wide Terms of Reference for suggesting 'measures to achieve a proactive, responsive, accountable, sustainable and efficient administration for the country at all levels of the government' with specific mention of key areas of public administration such as organizational structure of the Government of India, ethics in governance, refurbishing of personnel administration, strengthening of financial management systems, steps to ensure effective administration at the state level, steps to ensure effective district administration and other aspects of public administration. Local self-government and Panchayati Raj institutions as well formed part of the specific areas to be looked into by the Commission. With respect to local self-government, the specific Terms of Reference of the Commission required it to suggest measure for:

(i) Improving delivery mechanism of public utilities and civic services like water, power, health and sanitation, education, etc., with greater citizens' and stakeholders' involvement in such processes;
(ii) Empowerment of local self-government institutions for encouraging participative governance and networking; and
(iii) To encourage capacity building and training interventions for better performance of local bodies.

The Commission, having enquired into and studied the existing structure of local government—both urban and rural—submitted its observations, views and suggestions in its Sixth Report in October 2007 with an interesting caption—'Local Governance: An Inspiring Journey into the Future'. This chapter gives a flavour of the thoughts of the Commission specifically on the urban local self-government. The Commission examined the local government structure, its functioning, empowerment and the constraints in these in a quite wider context of Gandhi's dream of integrating institutional reforms in local government with economic reform as his vision for 'Poorna Swaraj'. It also took into account the onset of economic reforms that began in 1991, and political consensus in the country for empowerment of local self-government in the country. But at the very outset, the Commission observed that 'in practice, real empowerment as envisaged has not taken place'.

Referring to the Constitution (74th CAA) 1992 as altogether a new chapter in the process of democratic decentralization, the Commission mentions a basic weakness in the constitutional scheme.

Local government being part of the State List under VII Schedule of the Constitution, implementation of the provisions with respect to empowerment of the urban local self-government is dependent on the intention and the strength of the state enactments. In order to be implementable, the enabling state legislation for empowerment would need to be in complete harmony with the constitutional provisions. Although the state governments complied with the mandate of the Constitution to bring their existing laws in conformity with the constitutional provisions within one year of the enactment of the 74th CAA, the Commission has observed a slow and hesitant devolution of functions and finances to the urban local self-governments. The Commission also notes creation of specific purpose state-wide authorities such as housing boards, urban development authorities, slum development agencies and water and sanitation boards which has led to fragmented approach to urban development and service delivery. Such an approach has also contributed to decline of urban local self-government. Weakening of the urban local self-government has resulted in their inabilities in managing urbanization and inadequate and inequitable delivery of basic urban service. It would be worth to quote here from the Commission's Report:

> The State Governments have created a large number of functional bodies in the form of development authorities, housing boards, slum development agencies and water and sanitation boards. The growth of these specialised agencies has weakened the authority of municipal bodies and contributed to their atrophy. This has also led to a fragmented approach, with a large number of bodies working in isolation. Consequently, ULBs remain ill-equipped in terms of technical manpower and organisational ability and are unable to deal with the spread of urbanisation to the rural areas. In addition, our mega cities are characterised by specific problems of mounting infrastructural constraints, large scale in-migration and governance structures that remain unprofessional, unresponsive and lacking in transparency.

Such a weak institutional capacity of urban local self-governments impelled the Commission to reiterate the need for autonomy without which no amount of reform will be meaningful. According to the Second Administrative Reform Commission (SARC), local government institutions constitute 'an integral part of the country's governance system' and, therefore, an autonomous space needs to be created for them so that they could replace the existing administrative structure with regard to functions devolved to them. It has even gone to the extent of observing that the local self-government must have autonomy with respect to the functions devolved to them and must be free from the bureaucratic control of the state governments. According to SARC, evolution of the Constitution has tended to greater empowerment of states without weakening of the Union. There is need now to empower the local government without weakening the states. Relations between states and local government need to be lifted from its present infancy towards maturity. To this end in view, SARC has enunciated a set of core principles mentioned below:

1. Application of the principle of subsidiarity in the context of decentralization;
2. Clear delineation of functions of local governments vis-à-vis state governments and among different tiers of local governments;
3. Effective devolution of these functions and resources accompanied by capacity-building and accountability;
4. Integrated view of local services and development through convergence of programmes and agencies; and
5. 'Citizen-centricity'.

Principle of Subsidiarity

This principle brings citizens at the centre stage of governance. The sovereign citizen who also happens to be the users of local services needs to exercise as much authority as possible. This principle, therefore, requires that the sovereign citizen-consumer of services—should delegate only such powers upwards that need the benefit of economies of scale, technological and managerial capacity. In the context of local governments, therefore, the higher levels of government should perform only such functions that cannot be performed effectively at the local level. In the words of SARC, the Principle of Subsidiarity entails that 'functions shall be carried out closest to citizens at the smallest unit of governance possible and delegated upwards only when the local unit cannot perform the task'. SARC notes especially three benefits of this principle. First, local decision-making improves efficiency, promotes self-reliance at the local level, encourages competition and nurtures innovation. Second, It enables the democratic system to derive its full legitimacy as it puts the citizens at the centre stage by making them sovereign in making decisions that are in their best interest. Third, once decision-making and its consequences are integrally linked at the local level, people can better appreciate that the hard choice needed for effective performance have to be made. Such awareness promotes greater responsibility, enlightened citizenship and maturing of democracy. In view of these advantages of the Principle of Subsidiarity, SARC suggests that local government reform package must be essentially informed by this principle.

Clear Delineation of Functions of Local Governments vis-à-vis State Governments

Though the Principle of Subsidiarity is cardinal in any scheme of local government, it can be effectuated only through effective decentralisation. The 74th CAA tried to do it by creating enabling structures, the authority to devolve functions continued to vest with the state governments. Delineation of functions, therefore, needs to be such that it conforms to the principle of subsidiarity. Such a system of delineation will also establish, in a much more effective manner, the local government efficiency in discharge of the devolved function.

Effective Devolution of Functions and Resources Accompanied by Capacity-building and Accountability

A federal structure of governance consists of more than one level of government. It is, therefore, all the more essential that the roles and responsibilities of each level of government must be defined in clear terms. There is hardly any ambiguity about it with respect to functions of the Union and the States. But since the local governments are devolved with delegated functions of states, the roles of state governments and the urban local self-government need to have clarity both with regard to functional and fiscal devolution. According to SARC, the Principle of Subsidiarity and democratic decentralization, in order to be meaningful, has to be accompanied by devolving authority to the urban local self-governments which 'should be effectively empowered to frame regulations, take decisions and enforce their will within their legitimate sphere of action. Such empowerment should be clearly and unambiguously defined by the Constitution and State legislatures'. This needs to be also accompanied by devolving to the ULSG control over their staff. Fiscal empowerment entails that the ULSGs have autonomy in using the sources of revenue devolved to them and generate resources for meeting their obligation for good governance and effective, inclusive and responsive service delivery.

Convergence of Programmes and Agencies

This principle is germane especially in a multiple agencies operating at the local level such as parastatals, state government departments, and the field administration of the state governments. The services provided by them and also their operations need to converge at the local level in a coordinated manner.

Citizen Centricity

Citizens have to be at the centre stage of every level of government. This principle is especially important for local government as the proximity between the citizens and the government is the closest. Yet, the citizens get alienated from the local government. SARC, therefore, suggests involving the citizens in local governance especially at the community level that is quite amenable for participation like the Gram Sabha in case of the Panchayati Raj Institutions.

Devolution for Implanting Local 'Self-Government'

The observation of SARC on the contemporary state of urban local government is quite candid. It observes several lags in evolution of democratic decentralization as conceived in the 74th CAA. These lags are manifested in slow and late constituting of local self-government, reluctance of state governments, state legislatures and civil servants for effective empowerment of ULSGs, ignoring implementation of even mandatory provisions for constituting District Planning and Metropolitan Planning Committees, and some of the legislators acting like 'executive' by intervening in transfers, postings, sanctioning of local government contract and tenders, etc. SARC refers to Objects and Reasons of the Constitution (74th Amendment) Act and also to Article 243P(e) that gives clear intention of the Constitution about local 'self-government' and observes that whereas the former laments that the 'urban local bodies are not able to perform effectively as vibrant democratic units of self-government', the latter (Article 243P(e)) defines local government as 'institutions of self-government'. Yet, in view of SARC, Article 243W that has provisions relating to power, authority and responsibilities of Municipalities is 'less categorical' especially because when it comes to take action for making local governments institutions of 'self-government', the balance of convenience lies in favour of minimum local empowerment.

Having observed that Article 243W is less categorical about empowerment of ULSGs as institutions of self-government, SARC points out to a dilemma as well as a difficulty in this regard. The dilemma is about the autonomy of states granted by the Constitution that needs to be respected in bringing about major constitutional changes for additional devolution to the local government. The 'difficulty' is about suggesting a solution (one shoe fits all) that should be applicable in diverse situations obtaining in different states. It also doubts if the local government institutions will be in a position to discharge responsibilities because, according to SARC, the ULSGs have not fully handled the functions listed in the 12th Schedule of the Constitution 'even in the best of circumstances'. This is a complex dilemma that the policy makers have not been able to resolve.

SARC refers also to the observations of the National Commission to Review the Working of the Constitution (discussed earlier in this chapter) and its recommendation to replace 'may' by 'shall by law vest' in Article 243W. After examining these and not so exhaustive nature of the 12th Schedule, SARC recommended an amendment in Article 243W on the basis of two cardinal principles—(i) the Principle of Subsidiarity, and (ii) as the functions listed in the Twelfth Schedule are not to be wholly transferred to the ULSGs, their empowerment needs to be limited to specific functions. The Principle of Subsidiarity demands that the local self-government should be vested with adequate powers and authority to enable them to function as institutions of self-government in respect of functions that can be performed at the local level. The second principle entails that they should be empowered with respect to specific functions that can be performed at the local level. Accordingly, the Commission recommended amending this Article by recasting it. It recommended to amend Article 243W as: 'Subject to the provisions of this Constitution, the Legislature of a State shall, by law, vest the Municipalities with such powers and authority as are necessary to enable them to function as institutions of self government in respect of all functions which can be performed at the local level including the functions in respect of the matters listed in the Twelfth Schedule'.

The amendment suggested by SARC is more comprehensive as compared to the suggestion given by the Constitution Review Commission. Recommendation of SARC is not restricted to specific functions, rather it is quite wide and provides for vesting to the ULSGs with 'all functions which can be performed at the local level including the functions listed in the Twelfth Schedule'. This also means that the existing provision of Article 243W (a)(i) and (ii) and (b)[3] will no longer form part of this Article.

FRAMEWORK LAW FOR EMPOWERMENT OF LOCAL GOVERNMENT

Article 243W that provides for enabling the Municipalities to perform as institutions of 'self-government' has continued to be the bone of contention and quite eluding with regard to empowerment of local government both rural and urban. It has continued to be on the statute book without any initiative to give it an operational form. The states have been dithering on this for more than two decades of enactment of the 74th CAA. SARC, therefore, has raised an issue about the manner in which the Union could intervene to ensure that the local government is duly empowered by the states. The Commission rightly points to the emerging role of ULSGs that has a great deal of impact on the national economy—making the cities livable, enhancing the quality of urban life, efficient, effective, equitable and responsive provision of urban infrastructure and services that become instrumental in attracting investments. Moreover, central schemes for local governments are abounding with impressive financial assistance to the local government institutions. This additionally justifies the interest of the central government in empowerment and strengthening of urban local self-government. The Commission has, therefore, examined three options with regard to empowerment of local government through statutory means. These are:

1. Transferring Item 5 of List II (local governments) of the Constitution to List III (Concurrent List) along with functions that even though are with the Union or the States but they are relevant for all the three tiers of government (Union, State, and Local). Such a transfer will transform 'functions' into 'subject' and will, according to SARC, enable the Parliament to legislate appropriate, hierarchical and framework legislation on the subject 'Local Government'. The Union could thus 'mandate the devolution of powers, functions and responsibilities to the local governments'.
2. Second option examined by SARC for empowerment of local governments and for activating the 74th CAA is a bit more unusual. Under this option, certain legislative powers could be devolved to the third tier of government (Local Governments) along with functions. In order to give it a constitutional basis, List IV within the 7th Schedule could be created in the Constitution of India for giving limited legislative authority to the ULBs. In case this new list consists of two sets of functions—one for rural and the other for urban local self-governments, the new list could contain two parts—one each on rural and urban local self-government.

3. Impelled by the framework laws in South African model of municipal governance, SARC has examined a yet third option which, according to it, seems to be 'more integrated one'. Under this option, SARC favours 'introducing a single, legally binding legislative framework under which the States and the local bodies would function, somewhat on the lines of the South African model for municipal systems'. Such framework laws exist in some other countries as well. The European Union Directives, for example, is in the nature of framework legislation.

SARC has laid a great deal of emphasis on the South African model of framework legislation. In order to get a proper perspective of the framework law in South Africa that SARC wishes to replicate in India, it is desirable to look into constitutional provisions in South Africa that have made urban local self-government institutions a constitutional entity which is markedly different from the constitutional provisions inserted in the Indian Constitution through the 74th CAA. There are quite a few unusual provisions in the South African Constitution that distinguishes it from the provisions relating to local government in the Indian Constitution. These are mentioned below:

1. Article 40 of the Constitution of South Africa provides that the government of the Republic is constituted of (a) national, (b) provincial, and (c) local spheres of government.
2. All the three spheres of government are 'distinctive, interdependent and interrelated'.
3. All spheres of government are mandated by the South African Constitution to 'observe and adhere to the principles' enunciated in the Constitution and must conduct their activities within the parameters provided for in the Constitution.
4. This Principle is contained in Article 41 of the Constitution which lays down the 'Principle of cooperative government and inter-governmental relations'.

The Principle of cooperative government requires that all spheres of government (national, provincial, and local) and all organs of state within each sphere must:

a. respect the constitutional status, institutions, powers and functions of government in the other spheres;
b. not assume any power or function except those conferred on them in terms of the Constitution;
c. exercise their powers and perform their functions in a manner that does not encroach on the geographical, functional or institutional integrity of government in another sphere; and
d. cooperate with one another in mutual trust and good faith by
    (i) fostering friendly relations;
    (ii) assisting and supporting one another;
    (iii) informing one another of, and consulting one another on, matters of common interest;
    (iv) coordinating their actions and legislation with one another;
    (v) adhering to agreed procedures; and
    (vi) avoiding legal proceedings against one another.

The Constitution of South Africa further re-enforces the concept of 'Cooperative Government' by giving further mandates to all the three spheres of government as mentioned below:

1. Municipalities must exercise their executive and legislative authority within the constitutional system of cooperative government envisaged in Article 41 of the Constitution.
2. The national and provincial spheres of government must, within the constitutional system of cooperative government envisaged in Article 41 of the Constitution, exercise their executive and legislative authority in a manner that does not compromise or impede a municipality's ability or right to exercise its executive and legislative authority.
3. For the purpose of effective co-operative government, organized local government must seek to:
    (a) develop common approaches for local government as a distinct sphere of government;
    (b) enhance cooperation, mutual assistance and sharing of resources among municipalities;
    (c) find solutions for problems relating to local government generally: and

(d) facilitate compliance with the principles of cooperative government and inter-governmental relations.

The Indian Constitution, on the other hand, makes local government as creatures of state governments. The above provisions for making local government a part of a cooperative federalism, also mandates the South African Parliament to:

(a) establish or provide for structures and institutions to promote and facilitate inter-governmental relations; and
(b) provide for appropriate mechanisms and procedures to facilitate settlement of inter-governmental disputes.

The South African Constitution with the above mentioned quite valuable and interesting constitutional provisions, enabled the South African Parliament to enact a framework legislation called the Municipal Systems Act of South Africa, 2000. This Act, besides containing several interesting provisions for empowerment of local government, specifically provides 'to establish a framework for support, monitoring and standard setting by other spheres of government in order to progressively build local government into an efficient, frontline development agency capable of integrating the activities of all spheres of government for the overall social and economic upliftment of communities in harmony with their local natural environment; to provide for legal matters pertaining to local government; and to provide for matters incidental thereto'. This Act especially provides that the Council of Municipality (i) has the right to govern on its own initiative, the local government affairs of the local community, and (ii) exercise municipality's executive and legislative authority without improper interference.

Even though the Report of SARC contains extensive reference to the South African constitutional provisions, it has not favoured making local government part of the Concurrent List of the Constitution for enabling the Union Government to enact a framework law for local government. Nevertheless, it favours enactment of a framework law by the Parliament under Article 252. This Article empowers the Parliament to legislate for two or more states by consent and the piece of legislation enacted in this manner should be adopted by other states. Such a law, besides providing for rights and duties of the citizens in relation to local government and its responsibilities towards the citizens, will also provide for principles for detailing of activities to be performed by the local government. It should also, the SARC Report observes, lay down guidelines for devolution of responsibilities, powers and functions by the states. The Commission suggests that the proposed framework law should be based on the principle of subsidiarity, democratic decentralization, delineation of functions, and devolution in real terms, convergence and citizen centricity. The ideas given in the SARC Report seem to be quite interesting and also desirable in the existing situation when the state governments have vacillated in empowering the local government despite addition of Part IXA to the Constitution through the 74th CAA. This leads one to doubt if the states would agree to enactment of a framework law by the Parliament.

STRENGTHENING THE VOICE OF THE LOCAL GOVERNMENT

Recognizing local government—both rural and urban—as the third tier of government, SARC suggests that this level of government needs to be given a much needed voice so that it could be audible to higher levels of government. It feels that the third tier of government should have a stake in legislative enactments in a state. With this end in view, SARC has given a suggestion having far wider implications for strengthening voice of the local government. Article 171(2) of the Constitution contains provisions for composition of the Council of States or Legislative Council and one-third of the total number of members of this body is suggested to be elected by the local governments which is not enough. Noting that not every state has a Council of States or Legislative Council, it has recommended that this Council should be recast as a Council for Local Govern-ment. Article 171 also provides an opportunity for recasting of the Council of States. While recasting the Council of States, it should be solely composed of members elected by the elected representative of local governments. SARC observes that this recasting will not need any amendment of the Constitution; only an enactment by the Parliament to this effect will be sufficient.

URBAN GOVERNANCE STRUCTURE

The Second Administrative Reforms Commission has thoroughly reviewed the urban local governance structure contained in the 74th CAA and has suggested changes in it. In doing so, it acknowledges the diversity in geographical locations across the country that precludes designing a single structural model which could be replicated in all types of urban settlements. Nevertheless, it has tried to develop an overall structure keeping in mind certain common basic structural features that could be further fine-tuned according to obtaining situations. Accordingly, it has suggested a new local government structure that is based on a set of core principles discussed earlier in this chapter (such as (i) the principle of subsidiarity; (ii) clear delineation of functions of local governments vis-à-vis state governments and among different tiers of local governments; (iii) effective devolution of these functions and resources accompanied by capacity-building and accountability; (iv) integrated view of local services and development through convergence of programmes and agencies and above all, (v) 'citizen-centricity').

Evaluating the local government structure provided for in the 74th CAA, it rightly observes that it does not lay down the parameters for categorizing urban settlements into (i) Municipal Corporation, (ii) Municipal Council, and (iii) Nagar Panchayat. States have discretion to decide on this. This, according to SARC, precludes a uniform pattern of categorization across the states (as discussed also in Chapter 3 while evaluating constitutional provisions in this regard and also in Chapter 4 while analysing the nature of Conformity legislations in major states). The Commission, therefore, has suggested a scheme of categorization for two reasons. First, 'it would reduce the lack of clarity that exists in understanding the nature of the urban bodies across the states. Second, it would help in adoption of a structured approach leading to a more systematic national planning process and in the devolution of funds through National and State Finance Commissions'. Guided by these considerations, the Second Administrative Reforms Commission has suggested the following categorization of urban local governments institutions.

TABLE 5.1: CATEGORIZATION OF URBAN LOCAL GOVERNMENTS RECOMMENDED BY THE SECOND ADMINISTRATIVE REFORMS COMMISSION

S. No.	Size	Nomenclature
1.	ULSGs with a population up to 20,000	Town Panchayats
2.	ULSGs with a population between 20,000 and 1,00,000	Municipal Councils
3.	ULSGs with a population 1,00,000 and 10,00,000	City Municipal Council
4.	ULSGs with a population between 10,00,000 and 50,00,000	Municipal Corporations
5.	ULGs with a population above 50,00,000	Metropolitan Corporations

Source: Second Administrative Reforms Commission, Part II, p. 206.

PARTICIPATION IN LOCAL GOVERNMENT

WARD COMMITTEE

SARC has stressed on the need for a structure of urban local self-governments that could be amenable to participation. It observes that the existing structure of urban local governance is not amenable to participation of average citizens and providing opportunity for playing their role. Second, it does not have checks and balances to make the elected local councilor accountable. Referring to the provision for creation of Wards Committee, it observes that even though the intent of Constitutional provision was to ensure citizens' participation in local decision making process, these Committees have been created for a population exceeding three to five lakh population. Thus, Wards Committees have been created 'merely to fulfil the constitutional obligation of creating Wards Committees'. According to it 'Such a perfunctory creation of decentralized structures clearly violates the letter and spirit of the Constitution'. (GoI 2007). This has defeated the very concept of participatory governance. Such a structure with large jurisdiction and huge population is not amenable to participation and associating the local population in the local decision making process. This also reduces transparency and accountability. SARC, therefore, has recommended creation of Ward Committee in each ward. It has rightly suggested scrapping the existing practice of constituting Wards Committee consisting of more than one ward and creating instead Ward Committee in every ward even in small towns with a population of less than 3 lakh. The Councilor elected from the ward besides being the member of the Municipal Council, will also be the Chairperson of the Ward Committee. In such a scheme of things, the Ward Councilor will be able to perform a dual role; as the Chairperson of the Wards Committee: to perform executive role in the ward, and as the Ward Councilor, represent the ward in the Municipal Council.

As for composition of Ward Committee, besides consisting of Area Sabha Representatives, the Ward Committee is suggested to have representation of non-residential stakeholders as well who do business in the ward but reside outside it. The Ward Committee will meet regularly with the citizens they represent through Area Sabha to review programmes and their planning and implementation. In order to enable effective functioning of Ward Committees, the Commission suggests that these Committees must have 'legitimate functions and financial devolution'. It has suggested an elaborate list of functions to be performed by the Ward Committees. The suggested functions include all activities which can be handled at the ward level such as street lighting, sanitation, water supply, drainage, road maintenance, maintenance of school buildings, maintenance of local hospitals/dispensaries, local markets, parks, playgrounds, etc. With a view to enable the Ward Committees perform its functions, the municipal staff in respect to all the functions delegated by the Municipal Council shall be accountable to the Ward Committee. A radical suggestion given by the Commission envisages that salaries of such employees shall be authorized/paid by the Ward Committee on the basis of their performance. Also the funds allocated to the functions that are entrusted to the Ward Committees shall be transferred en-block to the Ward Committees and the overall municipal budget of the Municipality concerned will take into account the budgets prepared by the Ward Committee. It also suggests that the Ward Committee will be given a share in Property Tax collected from the ward depending on the economic profile of the locality. These suggestions are extremely useful and need to be put in the legal framework for urban local self-governments.

Area Sabha as a Space for Participation

SARC has suggested creating a space for participation at the micro level by creating Area Sabha that would provide opportunity for participation of every citizen in local governance—a semblance of direct democracy. The Commission suggests that Area Sabha needs to be a functional equivalence of Gram Sabha in a Village Panchayat. In suggesting this, the Commission is guided by low representation ratio between the citizens and their elected representatives. This is almost ten times larger (3,400: 1) than in rural areas (380: 1). Urban local self-government intuitions, according to the Commission, do not provide space for participation of every citizen in the affairs of local government. The Gram Sabha, in a village Panchayat, on the other hand, provides this space in the form of Gram Sabha which is a body consisting of all the voters registered in the electoral rolls for a village forming part of the Village Panchayat. Such a forum is conspicuously absent in the present structure suggested by the 74th CAA. The Commission, therefore, suggests constituting Area Sabhas at the level of Polling Stations in every municipal ward. A polling Station generally has about 1,000 to 1,200 registered voters that is an ideal for managing participation of citizens in the local government activities. The Commission, however, suggests that an Area Sabha should cover preferably not more than 2,500 voters. Each Area Sabha is suggested to elect a small Committee of Representatives once in every five years who will elect from amongst themselves a person to chair the meetings of the Area Sabha. The Chairperson thus elected will represent the Area

Sabha in the Ward Committee. This will offer a fair and legitimate opportunity to all the citizens to participate. SARC suggests that 'The Area Sabha should be a legitimate, formal space, which would need to be explicitly defined in terms of constitution, composition, functions, duties and responsibilities.' Referring to the model Nagar Raj Bill circulated by the Ministry of Urban Development in 2006 (discussed in detail in Chapter 3 of this book), SARC suggests that the Area Sabhas should perform functions as delineated in this model Bill.

Guided by the considerations discussed above, SARC has proposed a three-tier structure of urban local self-government consisting of (i) Municipal Corporation/Council, (ii) Ward Committee, and (iii) Area Committee or Area Sabha, as depicted in Figure 5.1. Town Panchayat/Nagar Panchayat being small in size, was not thought to have the three tier structure suggested above.

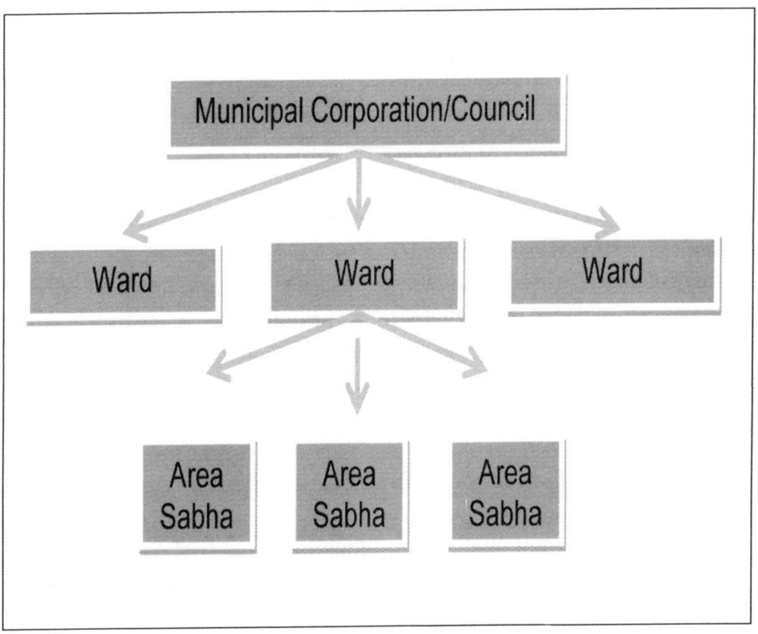

Figure 5.1: Structure of Urban Local self-Government Suggested by the Second Administrative Reforms Commission

SARC suggests that delineation of functions amongst the different tiers of urban local government as suggested above would need to be very much on the lines of delineation of functions in case of rural local government. But the guiding principle in allocation of functions will have to be according to the principle of subsidiarity. For this it has also suggested that a process of activity mapping shall have to be done by the ULSG institutions as is done by the Panchayati Raj Institutions.

De-concentration of Municipal Administration: Municipal administration especially in very large cities becomes quite complex in terms of space, population and span of control. These factors have contributed to a trend towards centralization of municipal administration in the Town Halls of very large cities. This has also contributed to erosion in efficiency and effectiveness in service delivery. Municipal administration in such cities is also not amenable to redress of citizens' grievances on a day-to-day basis. SARC, therefore, suggests creation of administrative zones in large cities and de-concentration of functions to the zones. Very large cities such as Delhi, Kolkata and Mumbai have adopted de-concentration of municipal administration down below the Town Hall. In Delhi, municipal administration and service delivery is shifted to the zones that have zonal offices. Whereas Kolkata is divided into Boroughs as an additional tier of governance, in Mumbai there is a Ward Officer who has delegated authority to take decisions, provide services and execute public works in the area. SARC, therefore, suggests creation of Zonal Offices preferably for a population of 5 lakh or less. It has laid emphasis on delegation of powers to the Zonal Offices by the city governments.

LOCAL GOVERNMENT ELECTION

Like the Commission to Review the Functioning of Constitution, SARC as well has looked into the issues in local government elections. It has given suggestions for further empowerment of State Election Commission by entrusting it also with the responsibility of delimitations of local government constituencies. With a view to enable development of leadership over a period of time, it has recommended for rotation of reservation after two terms of five years each. The Commission is of the view that the imposing presence of Members of Parliament and the State Legislature in local government would subdue the emergence of local leadership which is a *sine qua non* for development of vibrant local self-governments. Therefore, the Commission is of the view that Members of Parliament and State Legislatures should not become members of local bodies. This would enable the elected councils of urban local self-governments to have free and frank discussion on various local issues will also endow them with decision-making capabilities.

LOCAL GOVERNMENT FUNCTION

SARC rightly observes that the functions listed in the 12th Schedule are only illustrative in nature. It is also not exhaustive. According to it, this Schedule covers a vast range of functions and there are also certain incongruities in the 12th Schedule functions. It refers to 'economic and social development' and feels that it is restricted to only planning for it. It, therefore, felt the need for further delineation of functions between state and local government for most of the matters listed in the Twelfth Schedule. The Commission, however, did not favour reviewing the list of functions and emphasized that this Schedule needs to be recognized as only illustrative.

Even though considerable period of time has elapsed since the enactment of the 74th CAA, SARC laments once again that 'the progress of devolution of powers and responsibilities to local governments at various levels is poor and uneven'. It points out multiplicity of public agencies—Union, State, and Local—engaged in performing a function even within a single sector. Branding it as an 'organisational jungle' the Commission observes that it has created confusion, unnecessary duplication, inefficiency, wastage of funds, and poor outputs and outcomes. Local government which should be at the centre stage for performance of local functions, is at best 'a small part of the implementation, occasionally consulted but, in most cases, bye-passed and ignored'. It refers to the Standing Committee on Urban and Rural Development, 2004 (13th Lok

Sabha) which noted that the union and the state governments have failed in implementing the provisions of the Constitution.

In such a confusing functional domain that is fragmented amongst multiple levels as mentioned above, SARC has taken a view about devolution of functions to the ULSGs by questioning the very root of such a fragmented provision of services. Referring to Article 243ZF of the Constitution, it says that all the laws containing provisions that are not consistent with the constitutional provision relating to Municipalities was required to be amended or repealed within a year. As the 74th CAA came in to force in June 1992, all such laws were required to be amended or repealed by June 1993. But despite an elapse of long period of time since the enactment of the 74th CAA, the states have not even identified the laws that are inconsistent with the constitutional provisions except the state of Kerala that identified and amended about dozen of such laws. Such laws, therefore, even now need to be suitably amended and alternative statutory arrangements made to transfer powers to the Municipalities. For devolving functions to the Municipalities, the Commission (SARC) has suggested:

> . . . a fresh, more comprehensive, set of functions should be laid down for urban bodies, to include all the activities that need to be performed at the local level. In addition to the functions already listed in the Twelfth Schedule, functions like school education; public health including community health centres/Area hospitals; traffic management and civic policing activities; land management, including registration, etc., may also be included.

DEVOLUTION OF FUNDS

The views of the Second Administrative Reforms Commission on the state of municipal finance are not very different from the views expressed recently by the official Committees and Working Groups. As discussed in Chapter 3, fragile resource base of the ULSGs is documented by almost all the official Committees and Commission constituted on urban sector in recent years.

Views of SARC on the state of municipal finances in the country are not different from the observations of various Official Committees discussed earlier in Chapter 3. It has observed that even though urban population is rising at a rate that is higher than the national average, the urban local self-governments have become increasingly dependent on the Union and the states for financial resources. Revenue from their own sources is declining. Yet another characteristic of municipal finance is a mismatch between functions and sources of revenue devolved to them because of delegation of inadequate tax authority and absence of buoyancy in the sources of local revenue. In order to mitigate such a situation, SARC suggests reforming Property Tax by switching over from the existing annual rental value system to either the unit value or the capital value systems, widening of the tax net through periodical verification of properties and preparation of computerized data base using the GIS mapping, minimizing the number of properties that are exempted from property tax, and improving collection efficiency.

EXECUTIVE SYSTEM

Article 243 R(2)(b) of the Constitution uses the term 'Chairpersons' that is a generic name for offices of elected heads of the ULSG institutions and as such it includes the office of the Mayor as well. SARC, while dealing with the office of political heads in municipal governments, has not discussed powers of these offices. But it has discussed in greater detail the position of Mayor, his/her powers and the mode of election. It as well observes the mere ceremonial status of Mayor with exception to West Bengal, and Madhya Pradesh even though in the latter state the Mayor does not have executive power under the law. It also observes that the Commissioner is appointed by the state government and s/he enjoys executive power in most cases. Referring to the appointment of Netaji Subhas Chandra Bose as the Chief Executive Officer of the Calcutta Municipal Corporation by the elected Council and the Mayor, Deshbandhu Chittaranjan Das, during the colonial era in 1924, the report of the SARC laments the existing practice of appointment of the Chief Executive Officer/Municipal Commissioner by the state governments in an independent India. Municipal laws in different states generally, do not have provision for the Chairperson/Mayor to be the real executive authority. The laws also do not provide for appointment of Chief Executive Officer by the ULSGs. SARC, therefore, observes that 'This dilution of the role of the Mayor/Chairperson is clearly violative of the spirit of self-governance and local empowerment'. In general, the Chairperson/Mayor chairs the council meetings and has only a peripheral role in urban governance.

SARC also refers to the manner of election and term of office of the Mayor/Chairperson that varies from state to state. In most major states, the Chairperson is indirectly elected by the elected Councilors. It also notes different terms of office of the Mayor in different states as discussed in Chapter 4 of this volume. It discusses in greater detail the manner of election of Mayor in different countries where the Mayor is directly elected as chief executive in most cities. SARC, as well has favoured a directly elected Mayor by considering a few key factors that, according to SARC, should guide election of the Mayor/Chairperson. These include (i) Stability, (ii) Accountability, (iii) Cohesion, and (iv) Representation.

The office of an indirectly elected Mayor, according to SARC, is vulnerable to instability largely due to his/her dependence on the majority support in the Council. This also promotes what SARC calls 'horse trading' that further weakens the office of Mayor. A directly elected Mayor is not susceptible to these pulls and pressures primarily because of a fixed tenure of office that largely prevents his/her ousting from the office. SARC, therefore, suggests that in view of rapid urbanization and complex challenges confronted by the cities, the Mayor needs to have a long-term vision of the city's development and service delivery. The office of the Mayor, therefore, needs to have a fixed tenure of five years that will promote stability in urban governance. Nevertheless, the SARC Report is also conscious of the much needed system of accountability on part of the Mayor/Chairperson, for, a popularly elected Mayor may have tendency to become unaccountable. It, therefore, suggests certain checks and balances. First, the Council is the most important mechanism of accountability as the budget is approved by it and it could as well frame regulations and major policies besides exercising oversight on the functioning of Mayor. Second, according to SARC, institutional checks, strong public opinion and free press go a long way in guaranteeing checks and balances in the working of Mayor. It also refers to its recommendation about appointment of an Ombudsman for local government that will act as an additional safeguard against abuse of authority, if any, by the Mayor. Separation of power could have a built-in mechanism for defining the role of the Mayor and the Council. In the words of SARC, each of them 'acts as a check against the other, but cannot stop legitimate exercise of power'. Yet another factor it refers to seems to be highly optimistic by indulging in a wishful thinking. It believes that in a situation when the Council is led by an opposition political party, there is an opportunity for the Mayor to strengthen city governance by taking along the Council with him/her!

SARC's predilection for a directly elected Mayor is also based on the quality of leadership. Under a system of indirectly election of Mayor, it believes that a Councilor elected as a Mayor may not have the skills and leadership quality to develop the required vision and implementation processes for translating the vision into action. In a system of a directly elected Mayor, the political party will place the best candidate for the office of Mayor. This, according to SARC, becomes all the more important in a system that has a practice of reservation for empowerment. As the Constitution provides for reservation for the office of Mayor/Chairperson for Scheduled Castes, Scheduled Tribes, women and even for backward castes, the Councilor elected from these constituencies may not be having the required quality of leadership. In a directly elected system of Mayor, the political party will decide to present the Mayoral candidate that has these qualities.

In view of the above, SARC recommends a directly elected Mayor and such a Mayor should have a fixed tenure of five years. For putting a mechanism of checks and balances, the Council should have powers of budget approval, oversight and framing regulations and major policies. SARC quite emphatically and rightly suggests making the Mayor/Chairpersons as the Chief Executive in the urban local self-governments. The views expressed by SARC are cited below for appreciating the case for it.

The Commission is of the firm view that executive power must be exercised by the elected Mayor/Chairperson because basic democratic legitimacy demands that power is exercised by the elected executive. The whole logic of local government empowerment is to facilitate people's participation and democratic governance as close to the people as possible. Only when the elected executive exercises real authority can people understand the link between their vote and the consequences of such a vote in terms of provision of public goods and services. Such a clear link also ensures fusion of authority and accountability. If the elected local government has no real authority and if executive powers are vested in an unelected official appointed by the state government, then local governance is reduced to mere symbolism. The Commission is, therefore, of the view that the Mayor/Chairperson should be the Chief Executive of a city or urban government, and the city government should have the power to appoint all officials including the Commissioner and to hold them to account (GoI 2007). It also suggests that the city governments should have powers to appoint all officers including the Commissioner and hold them to account.

Though the persuasive arguments for appointment of all officials including the Commissioner/Chief Executive Officer is a welcome suggestion especially under a scheme of 'self-government', the case for a directly elected Mayor is quite contentious. It is true that if elected directly from the city-wide constituency, it imparts enhanced visibility to the office of Mayor. The Mayor, under such a system gets concentrated attention. But if the office of Mayor is only ceremonial and executive power is vested in the appointed Commissioner/Chief Executive Officer as is the case in several states, direct election of Mayor becomes altogether irrelevant. Office of an elected Mayor makes sense only if s/he is the real executive and executive powers are devolved to this office in the enabling municipal Acts. It is a well known fact that direct election of Mayor belongs to the presidential form of government; it does not go with the parliamentary system of governance that has been in vogue in India since Independence. The states of West Bengal, Madhya Pradesh and Chhattisgarh have a cabinet form of local government in urban settlements. Called Mayor-in-Council in Municipal Corporations and President-in-Council in Municipal Councils and

Nagar Panchayats, the Mayor/Chairperson forms a mini cabinet by inducting the members from amongst the Councilors who get elected as members of the municipal council. The Mayor/Chairperson also allocates portfolios to the members of the Mayor-in-Council/President-in-Council thus constituted. But the mode of election of Mayor, in the two states differs a great deal. Whereas, in West Bengal, following the parliamentary system of governance, the Councilors belonging to the political party that wins the largest number of seats elects the Mayor, in Madhya Pradesh and Chhattisgarh, the Mayor is elected directly. There have been several instances when the Mayor and the majority political party in the Council in the states of Madhya Pradesh and Chhattisgarh do not belong to the same side. In such situations, the party in majority in the Council keeps on creating innumerable problems that do not permit smooth functioning of the Council and the Mayor/Chairperson. This has even culminated in situations when the Mayor/Chairperson was not allowed to constitute the Mayor-in-Council/President-in-Council. Observation of SARC that such situations provide the Mayor to show his leadership qualities do not work especially due to aggressive local politics that at times acquire even a militant attitude on part of the members of the majority political party. It was because of these maladies that the state of Rajasthan abandoned the system of direct election of Mayor. In West Bengal where the Mayor is elected indirectly, the system of Mayor-in-Council/Chairman-in-Council has been working smoothly. It needs to be appreciated that if the Mayor has a fixed term that is coterminous with the life of the Council and if the enabling municipal Act vests the Mayor with executive powers, the mode of election becomes immaterial. What is critically important is vesting the offices of Mayor and Chairpersons with executive powers in law, not the mode of election.

As for the argument of SARC that the practice of an elected Mayor will contribute to putting the best candidate for the office of Mayor, a fixed term of five years for the office of Mayor/Chairperson will itself contribute to such a practice as is the case for the offices of Prime Minister and the Chief Ministers. Elections to these offices are not held directly though there have been occasional debate about switching over to a presidential form of government. But the existing parliamentary system of governance need not, and should not be mixed up with the presidential form of governance. Mixing these two systems together will create utter confusion and sustained conflict as is testified by the Madhya Pradesh and Rajasthan examples. Direct election of Mayor has created a fine mess especially in the case of a cabinet form of governance. SARC has recommended having a cabinet form of governance especially in very large cities so that the Mayor could be assisted in his/her day-to-day work for effective urban governance. SARC also cites example from UK where in London where the Mayor is directly elected even though UK has a very long tradition of working with parliamentary system that travelled across the globe as the Westminster model of governance to several countries. It also cites example of cities across the globe that have an elected Mayor. But the examples cited by SARC do not have a cabinet form of local governance. Also politics in these countries is not as aggressive as in this part of the world. Incongruities of an elected Mayor in a cabinet form of urban local self-government are obvious. If direct election of Mayor is that virtuous, offices of the Prime Minister and the Chief Ministers could as well be filled up through such a mode of election. The argument of SARC that an elected Mayor is immune from logjam in the Council on the issue of vote of no-confidence against the office of Mayor also does not hold ground. Every municipal Act contains provisions for vote of no-confidence irrespective of the fact whether the Mayor is elected directly or otherwise.

DECENTRALIZED PLANNING

SARC is not enamoured by the framework of planning provided for in the 74th CAA though it is in agreement with the concept of participatory and bottom up planning process. It goes on to comment that of all the provisions of the 73rd and the 74th CAA, the institution of District Planning Committee (DPC), in particular, has failed to emerge as effective institution of planning in all the states. To quote from the Report of the SARC:

> . . . of all the institutions created by the 73rd/74th Constitutional Amendments, the District Planning Committee (DPC) is one, which in most States, has so far failed to emerge as an effective institution. Some States have not formed the DPC. Besides, there are some inherent problems with this institution. In a developmental State, planning is an essential function of government at any level. Creating a separate authority independent of the structures of governance for undertaking the exercise of development planning has no logic.

SARC has pointed out some inherent organizational problems in the scheme of planning envisaged by the 74th CAA. In its considered view, planning essentially needs to be part of the functional domain of the government at any level. Therefore, it does not find any logic in creating DPC as a planning institution located outside the government structure. The Commission has strong feelings with respect to the practice of nomination of one-fifth of its members. The system of nomination, the Commission rightly felt, is guided by the partisan and narrow attitude of the ruling party in states to nominate preferred persons. It mentions the practice of making even a minister to chair the DPC (as in Madhya Pradesh) that converts the DPC into a centre of power that, by all means, is stronger than the elected local self-government itself. The practice of a mix of elected and nominated members makes it unaccountable to the people and the Panchayats and the municipal governments. It points out to yet another flaw with respect to rural urban continuum and absence of organic link between the two types of settlements. DPC has become a stand-alone institution that is not in a position to deal with issues of common interest of rural and urban local self-governments. These weaknesses have not enabled it to contribute to the process of decentralization. Kerala is the only exception where the DPC plays commendable role in providing planning guidelines to the local governments, performing technical examination of local plans, preventing duplication and overlapping of schemes in preparation of district plan.

Referring to the district as the traditionally indispensable unit of administration, the Commission pleads for creating a representative body at the district level that will facilitate democratic decentralization. According to its considered opinion, Zila Parishad created at the district level provides the much needed organic link amongst the different tiers of Panchayati Raj institutions. The urban local self-governments, on the other hand, is completely detached not only from each other but also from the rural local government. In the planning framework provided for in the 74th CAA, DPC has to contain two different components of district plan, one for the rural and the other for urban areas. The Commission rightly felt that the nature and character of a plan acquires newer dimensions in terms of perspective and priorities as one moves from the village having a micro plan to the higher meso-and-macro levels. Article 243ZD recognizes this fact and, therefore, suggests that a district plan should have regard to the 'matters of common interest between the Panchayats and the Municipalities'. Planning, therefore, needs to recognize inter-dependence and complementarity between rural and urban areas, the latter needs to grow in relation to its hinterland and the former has to thrive by benefitting from specialized services rendered by urban areas. In its present form, DPC is not in a position to address the issues emanating from a rural-urban divide.

URBAN-RURAL DIVIDE AND THE CONCEPT OF DISTRICT COUNCIL

SARC looks at planning in the context of rural-urban divide that needs to be addressed. Urban-rural relationship and a divide between these two types of settlements has been an endemic issue in governance.[4] SARC observes that a divide between the two is only artificial as these two types of settlements have common needs and aspirations. The boundary between the two keeps on shifting in the wake of urbanization. Even within urban settlements, a large number of people reside in peri-urban areas that have rudimentary urban services or even complete absence of these services. Needs of the people residing in these areas as well have to be met in an integrated manner. It has also felt that there is a need for coordinating the working of rural and urban local governments within a district. A unified single, undivided local government, which is needed to address the existing artificial divide, is non-existent at present. The need for this in the past had led to creation of different institutions. Karnataka, for example, made an experiment by creating a District Government in 1980 and Kerala constituted District Councils in 1991. Similar suggestions were given by the Institute of Social Sciences and the National Advisory Council in its Memorandum to SARC. It has been suggested to create an elected representative District Council by abolishing the DPC. The 74th CAA has provided for District Planning Committees (DPC). But the Zila Parishad which is the apex institution in a district under the Panchayati Raj framework and the Municipalities within the district, function without any coordination for addressing common needs of both rural and urban population. This has brought the Collector to be the real authority in the district. In the opinion of SARC, DPCs are 'too weak and non-starters in many States'.

Evaluating the progress made in these regards, SARC observes that complete re-orientation of the district level planning mechanism is required for bringing the local governments at the centre-stage for their involvement in the participative planning process from the village and urban settlements levels upwards. SARC has, therefore, looked into altogether another institutional option for district planning on the ground that planning at the district level is more than a mere integration of Panchayat and Municipal plans. There could be several dimensions that are unlikely to be resolved at the micro-level (Panchayats and Municipalities) but could be solved only at the macro-level. It also involves planning and coordination of trans-Municipal and trans-Panchayat functions that need to be planned at a higher level. This requires expanding the jurisdiction of the Zila Parishad to the entire district including the urban areas so that it could not only prepare District Plan but could also be better positioned to coordinate planning and plan implementation in the district with the Panchayats and the Municipalities. SARC, therefore, suggests that Article 243ZD should be repealed for creating altogether a new institutional structure at the district level as the apex district level composite local government for both the rural local and urban areas within the district. In order to coordinate planning exercise of various local bodies, technical guidelines would need to be provided to them. Also it will need to examine local plans for ensuring technical and financial viability, prepare district plans and prevent overlapping and duplication of schemes. SARC, therefore, suggested creating a Planning Committee within the District Council to address these issues. District Council will be responsible for the discharge of all local functions including the functions listed in the 11th and the 12th Schedules including planning for social and economic development in the entire district. In such a scheme of things, SARC has not favoured dismemberment of the office of Collector. The institution of Collector, SARC suggests, should be utilized for strengthening the District Council by making him its Chief Officer. Appointment of Collector will then have to be made in consultation with the District Council and the Collector will have to play a dual role of being Collector of the district and also the Chief Officer of the District Council. As a Collector, he will be responsible to the state government and as the Chief Officer of District Council, he will be accountable to the District Council.

The organizational framework for planning suggested by SARC is conceived within the context of elected and representative self-governance and not as a detached and stand-alone institution like the DPC provided for in the 74th CAA. It also has several merits for unified planning and development of rural and urban areas. The provision of DPC, therefore, needs to be revisited for putting in place a representative district government to be entrusted with performance of planning functions in the entire district constituting of both rural and urban areas. SARC has, therefore, suggested creation of an elected representative District Council by abolishing the DPC. District Council is suggested to function as the district level local government representing both rural and urban population.

NOTES

1. Article 243ZA presently reads as: (1) The superintendence, direction and control of the preparation of electoral rolls for, and the conduct of, all elections to the Municipalities shall be vested in the State Election Commission referred to in article 243K.

(2) Subject to the provisions of this Constitution, the Legislature of a State may, by law, make provision with respect to all matters relating to, or in connection with, elections to the Municipalities.

The suggested Constitutional provision for substitution of Clause (1) of Article 243ZA reads as:

(1) Subject to the provisions of clause (1A), the superintendence, direction and control of the preparation of electoral rolls for, and the conduct of, all elections to the Municipalities shall be vested in the State Election Commission referred to in article 243K.

(1A) The Election Commission shall have the power to issue any directions or instructions to the State Election Commission for the discharge of its functions under clause (1).

2. The changes suggested in Article 243W are shown by words written in bold italics. The Article 243W will then read as 'Subject to the provisions of this Constitution, the Legislature of a State *shall*, by law, *vest:*

   (a) the Municipalities with such powers and authority as *are* necessary to enable them to function as institutions of self-government and such law *shall* contain provisions for the devolution of powers and responsibilities upon Municipalities subject to such conditions as shall be specified therein, with respect to:

   (i) the preparation of plans for economic development and social justice;

   (ii) the performance of functions and the implementation of Schemes as may be entrusted to them including those in relation to the matters listed in the Twelfth Schedule.

3. Article 243W presently reads as: 'Subject to provisions of this Constitution, the Legislature of a State may, by law, endow:

   (a) the Municipalities with such powers and authority as may be necessary to enable them to function as institutions of self-government and such law may contain provisions for the devolution of powers and responsibilities upon Municipalities, subject to such conditions as may be specified therein, with respect to—(i) the preparation of plans for economic development and social justice; (ii) the performance of functions and the implementation of schemes as may be entrusted to them including those in relation to the matters listed in the Twelfth Schedule;

   (b) the Committees with such powers and authority as may be necessary to enable them to carry out the responsibility conferred upon them including those in relation to the matters listed in the Twelfth Schedule.

4. For detailed discussion on this see, Government of India (Ministry of Health and Family Welfare), *Report of the Rural-Urban Relationship Committee,* Government of India Press, 1966.

REFERENCES

Government of India, Ministry of Health and Family Welfare, 1966, *Report of the Rural-Urban Relationship Committee*, New Delhi: Government of India Press.

——, National Commission to Review the Working of Constitution, 2001, *A Consultation Paper on Decentralization and Municipalities.* New Delhi: Government of India Press.

——, 2002, *Review of the Working of the Constitution, Report of the National Commission to Review the Working of the Constitution*, vol. 1, New Delhi: Government of India Press.

——, 2007, *Sixth Report of the Second Administrative Reform Commission, Local Govenance: An Inspiring Journey into the Future,* New Delhi: Ministry of Personnel, Public Grievances and Pensions, Department of Administrative Refom and Public Grievances.

CHAPTER 6

Implementation of 74th Constitution Amendment

A policy initiative is said to be as good as it is implemented. It would be, therefore, worthwhile to see how the decentralization initiative introduced through an amendment of the Constitution in 1992 has been implemented in different states. Implementation of the 74th Constitutional Amendment Act (CAA), it needs to be emphasized, is the constitutional responsibility of the state governments. This onus of the state governments for implementation, one would expect, should have ensured that the constitutional provisions are implemented by the state governments in letter and spirit of the Constitution on their own. Nevertheless, the state governments were given incentive as well to implement it. In order to provide incentive to the state governments for implementation of the constitutional provisions, the Ministry of Urban Development (MoUD) now renamed as Ministry of Housing and Urban Affairs, Government of India also decided to leverage urban reforms through financial assistance to the state governments. Implementation of the 74th CAA was, therefore, included as one of the mandatory state level reforms under the ambitious urban sector programme—the Jawaharlal Nehru National Urban Renewal Mission (Jn-NURM). The guidelines for Jn-NURM clearly provided that implementation of the reforms conceived at the state and urban local self-government levels were part of an essential caveat for accessing the Jn-NURM funds by the state governments. In order to monitor implementation of the reform agenda and the projects under this Mission, MoUD devised mechanisms such as holding periodical review meetings with the state governments and involving National Institute of Urban Affairs, National Institute of Public

Finance and Policy and Administrative Staff College of India in project monitoring that included monitoring of the reform agenda. MoUD also periodically submitted Delivery Monitoring Unit Reports to the Prime Minister's Office on the progress achieved in project implementation. Despite such an elaborate arrangement for monitoring of implementation of the reform agenda and the Jn-NURM projects, curiously, the outcome of these mechanisms of monitoring and review does not throw light on effective implementation of the 74th CAA in various states. Monitoring of implementation was done in a mechanical manner without throwing any light on implementation of the reform agenda vis à vis the objectives of the constitutional provisions.

An objective evaluation of implementation of 74th CAA is constrained by paucity of required information on this. The information contained in the official monitoring and evaluation reports is firstly characterized by inconsistencies in information collected and presented. The data on implementation also suffer from limitations some of which are quite confusing and even daunting. Moreover, the data are, by and large, quite inconsistent. Inconsistencies vary according to the sources from which these are collected; the information collected from one source is quite different from the information collected on the same from another source. Second, the available information is mostly quantitative rather than qualitative in nature. It only suggests that so many states have transferred so many functions to the urban local self-government, DPC is constituted in so many states, local elections have been conducted in so many states and so on. There is hardly any qualitative information on implementation that could throw light, for example, not only on actual status of devolution to the urban local self-governments but also on actual performance of the 'devolved' functions by them. Third, the available information gives an account of only creation of the institutions that are required to be created by the state governments in compliance with the provisions of the Constitution. It does not indicate if the created institutions are structured and composed according to constitutional provisions and are actually working as well. Information such as mere enactment of conformity legislation or Acts and Rules for creation of DPC, MPC and Ward(s) Committee, 'transfer' of a function to the urban local self-governments do not even remotely indicate if the institutions of DPC, MPC, Ward(s) Committees are actually functioning according to constitutional provisions or if a particular function is transferred to the urban local self-governments, it is actually being performed by the local self-governments in the different states. Fourth, even if the available information indicates that these institutions have become operational, such information does not indicate the extent to which the functions performed by the above mentioned institutions are actually in consonance with the constitutional provisions. For example, if DPC is created and is also functioning in a state, it does not help in knowing if the District Plans are prepared actually by consolidating the plans prepared by the local self-governments.

Due to unavailability of qualitative data on implementation of constitutional provisions, the analysis of implementation of the 74th CAA is, therefore, based on the available quantitative information only. This is supplemented by limited qualitative information from a few micro evaluation studies conducted on certain aspects of the 74th CAA wherever such information is available from various sources.

DEVOLVING OF FUNCTIONS

Despite inconsistencies in the available information mentioned above, it depicts that implementation of the 74th Constitution Amendment is quite inadequate and unsatisfactory. Before elucidating inadequacies in implementation of the 74th CAA, inconsistencies in the available data and the confusion emanating from the inconsistent data need to be mentioned. A much hyped official evaluation report of the MoUD on Jn-NURM (Grant Thorton 2011) indicates that as many as eight states implemented transfer of the 12th Schedule functions to the urban local self-governments even before December 2005 when Jn-NURM was launched (Table 1 in Annex IX). It further shows that transfer of functions was in 'progress' in 14 other states and it had made 'significant progress' in another six states at the time of conducting of evaluation study of the Jn-NURM (the study was conducted in 2011). The states that transferred the 12th Schedule functions to the urban local self-governments are said to be Madhya Pradesh, Chhattisgarh, Gujarat, Kerala, Maharashtra, Bihar, Tripura and West Bengal. On the contrary, the fact remains that in all these states even now urban planning and town planning which is a function listed in the 12th Schedule, is performed either by the State Town Planning Department or by the urban development authorities. This is buttressed also by the fact that barring the local governments in the mega cities, none of the urban local self-governments in other cities and towns have urban planners or a town planning department in these states which could perform this function. Also there is hardly any information available to suggest that the state town planning departments in these states have been preparing plans on behalf of the ULSGs.

Yet another example is the state of Bihar which after enactment of the 74th Constitution Amendment Act, was the first to abolish the then existing Patna Regional Development Authority (PRDA)—the only such organization in the state, and merged it with the Patna Municipal Corporation in the name of compliance with the 74th CAA. Merging of PRDA, however, never became effective in performing regional or urban development functions in Patna or in its region. Over the years, PRDA has gradually declined because of attrition of its officials and staff and their non-replenishment through fresh recruitments. PRDA has become completely defunct by now. Performance of urban planning function at the state level also became ineffective as the State Town and Country Planning Department as well became non-operational over the years because the state government could not fill up the positions vacated by the retiring planners and the support staff. Yet the Jn-NURM evaluation report mentioned above indicates that urban planning function is devolved to the urban local governments in Bihar even before the state level reforms were introduced by leveraging the funds under Jn-NURM and in some other states after the launching of Jn-NURM. No urban local self-government in the state of Bihar is presently preparing any local development plan largely because of absence of urban planners and urban planning departments/sections in them. Similar is the situation with performance of water supply function. In Bihar, barring the cities of Patna, Muzaffarpur and Bhagalpur, and also in many other states water supply function even now vests with the state level Public Health Engineering Department. It is worth mentioning that despite data gaps and inaccuracies in the available information, Table 6.1 clearly shows that implementation of the 74th CAA with respect to devolving of the Twelfth Schedule functions is not yet implemented satisfactorily.

This is also supported by information provided by the Minister of Urban Development while answering a question in the Rajya Sabha on 31 July 2014. Accordingly, the 12th Schedule functions have been transferred to the urban local self-governments only in 11 states; in the remaining 18 states, functions are not yet transferred. Based on the information contained in the Minister's reply to a Rajya Sabha question, a synoptic view of status of functional shifts in the 29 states in the country is contained in Table 6.1.

TABLE 6.1: STATUS OF TRANSFER OF TWELFTH SCHEDULE FUNCTIONS TO THE URBAN LOCAL SELF-GOVERNMENTS IN VARIOUS STATES

States that are said to have transferred the Functions	States that are not said to have transferred the Functions
Chhattisgarh	Andhra Pradesh
Gujarat	Arunachal Pradesh
Himachal Pradesh	Assam
Jammu & Kashmir	Bihar
Jharkhand	Goa
Kerala	Haryana
Madhya Pradesh	Karnataka
Maharashtra	Manipur
Meghalaya	Mizoram
Odisha	Nagaland
Punjab	Rajasthan
	Sikkim
	Tamil Nadu
	Telangana
	Tripura
	Uttar Pradesh
	Uttarakhand
	West Bengal

Source: Culled from the information given by the Union Minister of Urban Development and Housing and Urban Poverty Alleviation in the Rajya Sabha on 31 July 2014.

The information given in Table 6.1, being basically quantitative in nature, it does not indicate that these functions are actually performed by the urban local self-governments. The information contained in the table is based on the information collected from the states which, under the Jn-NURM caveats for accessing the financial assistance provided by the centre were required to implement the 74th CAA. In most cases the states mechanically intimated the MoUD that they have transferred the 12th Schedule functions to the urban local governments just to have an acess to the funds. No attempt was made by the MoUD to verify if functional shifts have actually taken place and, most importantly, if the transferred functions are actually being performed by the urban local self-governments. This is corroborated by the information available from yet another source.

Relatively more reliable data on devolving of functions by the states to the urban local self-governments, even though quantitative in nature, is contained in a World Bank supported Capacity Building for Urban Development (CBUD) Project in the MoUD.[1] An initiative was taken under this project to collect baseline information from the project cities for evaluation of impact of the initiatives taken under the CBUD project in terms of urban governance, service delivery and institutional capacity of the urban local self-governments. As part of a Rapid Baseline Assessment (RBA) studies, information was also collected on implementation of the 74th CAA also. However a limitation of this information is that it pertains to only devolving of functions to the urban local self-governments. Information with respect to other provisions of the 74th CAA was not collected under this study. It also needs to be mentioned that the information collected under this study pertains to the project cities that were spread into 19 states and a Union Territory (Table 3, Annex IX)). Even though the information was collected at the city level, since implementation of 74th CCA is not city-specific, generalization about implementation of the constitutional provisions at the state level can be safely made.

Table 4 (Annex IX) containing information for 19 states (out of 29 states) and a Union Territory depicts that not all the functions listed in the 12th Schedule are transferred yet to the urban local self-governments. Much on the contrary to the data contained in the Grant Thornton evaluation report of Jn-NURM (Tables 1 and 2, Annex IX), urban planning along with some of the other functions are not yet transferred to the urban local self-governments in all the 19 states for which information is available from the RBA study. Much to the contrary of information contained in Table 2 (Annex IX), these states include the Union Territory of Chandigarh and the states of Gujarat, Himachal Pradesh, Jammu & Kashmir, Jharkhand, Kerala, Madhya Pradesh, Maharashtra and Odisha which, according to information contained in Table 2 (Annex IX), are said to have already transferred the 12th Schedule functions to the urban local self-governments. In addition to urban planning, other functions not yet devolved to the urban local self-governments in the 19 states and the Union Territory of Chandigarh include regulation of land use, water supply, urban forestry, protection of environment and ecology, planning for economic and social development, slum improvement and up-gradation, roads and bridges and fire services. It also corroborates that in these states, urban planning and regulation of land uses are performed either by the state level Town Planning Department or by the Urban Development Authorities. Water supply as well is not yet part of the functional domain of the urban local self-governments in nine states (Assam, Chhattisgarh, Goa, Haryana, Himachal Pradesh, Jammu & Kashmir, Karnataka, Kerala, and Sikkim). Table 4 in this Annex also depicts the existing organizational arrangement at the state level for performance of functions that are not yet devolved to the urban local self-governments.

Inherent gap in devolving of functions to the ULSGs as revealed by quantitative data analysed above, is corroborated also by empirical micro studies of a few aspects of the 74th CAA. Such studies as well are quite limited in number. A Progress Review Report prepared after a review meeting of MoUD, indicates that the functions listed in the Twelfth Schedule have been transferred to the urban local self-government (GoI 2010) and that water supply is transferred in as many as 17 states. Evidence from Tamil Nadu, which happens to be one of the 17 states, indicates that out of six water supply projects, five projects were still being implemented by the State Water Supply and Sewerage Board. In West Bengal as well 18 water supply projects were implemented by non-municipal agencies (Sivaramakrishnan 2011). Even though town planning and regulation of land use and buildings are said to have been devolved to the urban local self-governments in the state of Uttar Pradesh, an empirical study sponsored by the Centre of Policy Research reveals that the Municipal Corporations in the cities of Agra and Meerut do not have any role to play in sanctioning of building plans which is under the purview of the Development Authorities (ibid.). Functional shifts to the urban local self-governments from the domain of the state governments and from the state level entities created by them have thus not actualized. Such pitfall in the claim about transfer of the 12th Schedule functions are the result of basic flaw in the methodology adopted for monitoring and review of implementation of the 74th CAA. The monitoring agencies should have verified if the functions purported to have been transferred, have actually been transferred and that the transferred functions are being actually performed by the urban local self-government. As the state governments were interested only in accessing the Jn-NURM funds, they simply indicated in a facile manner that the 12th Schedule functions have been transferred to the urban local self-governments. No attempt was made by the central government or its agencies to get the veracity of such assertions verified. Such a flawed monitoring of 74th CAA implementation might be guided by the sheer concern of the MoUD to depict enhanced disbursement of Jn-NURM funds and demonstrate an impressive account of implementation of Jn-NURM!

In view of the above, one needs to ponder over the fact as to why, despite more than a couple of decades of enactment of the 74th CAA, the 12th Schedule functions have not yet been devolved to the urban local self-governments. There are important reasons which explain the gaps in transfer of functions to the urban local self-governments. First, there exists a gamut of urban local self-governments (ULSGs) that belong to different demographic size categories. The ULSGs functioning especially in India's small and medium towns do not have the required organizational capacity to perform several functions that are listed in the 12th Schedule much less for projectizing, financing, implementing and maintaining a water supply and sewerage plant. The number of such ULSGs is presently the largest. A Municipal Council created in a city of less than 3 lakhs, or, for that matter, a Nagar Panchayat constituted in a town of 25,000 population, for example, does not have the required resources—both financial and human, and the skills to set up a water supply system, or a sewerage system and also maintain it in operational fitness. There are other examples of such functions that are beyond the existing capacity of a very large number of ULSGs. Entrusting such functions to them requires existence of the required institutional capacity to perform. 'One size fits all' suffers from inherent limitations. This perhaps explains the discretionary nature of provisions of Article 243W and the 12th Schedule. In view of weak organizational capacity of a very large number of ULSGs, performance of functions that are resource-intensive and require the necessary skills need to be provided through specific organizational arrangement by the state governments. Transferring such functions to the ULSGs in small and medium towns would make sense only when the local governments in these size categories of towns acquire the required organizational wherewithal. Functional shifts, therefore, need to be tailored according to prevalence of organizational capacity in terms of resources that could enable them to perform such functions. This points to the need for focused capacity development interventions for the ULSGs for strengthening their financial resource generation and financial management capability, staffing, work management system, reporting system, organizational development; the contemporary strategy for this even at the centre and in the states is limited only to training. Training and capacity building seem to have become synonymous in public policy which they are not.

Capacity development, on the other hand, is much broader a strategy than mere training. Chapter 8, therefore, discusses conceptual groundings of capacity development and how to go about it. Therefore, till the ULSGs acquire the needed organizational capacity, a mechanism would need to be devised at the state or regional level for provision of services for which the urban local self-governments do not have the required organizational capacity. Nevertheless, a mechanism for ensuring accountability of service providers to the urban local self-government would as well need to be put in place as, under the law, only the urban local self-governments are legally accountable to the citizens for provision of services. Such a mechanism must include representation of the elected head of the local self-government on the Board of Directors/Managing Committee of the service providing agencies and designating him even as the Chairperson of the Board/Committee. It would also require to make the service producer accountable to the ULSGs.

The second related reason is the nature of the 12th Schedule itself. It, at most, contains the list of functions that are in the nature of subjects. It does not give an account of specific activities that need to be performed under each function (subject) that the state governments are expected to transfer to the ULSGs. These subjects that are listed as functions need to be unbundled through a process of activity mapping. This will help in elaboration and identification of various activities required to be performed under each function. Activity mapping also helps in analysing the nature of each activity and relating the same with the existing organizational capacity of the ULSGs. This will provide a better basis for deciding if the ULSGs are in a position to discharge each activity under each function. Water supply, for example, involves activities such as development of water source, project development for water treatment, distribution system, operations and maintenance of the systems, and billing and collection. In such a mix of activities, it would be a daunting task for the local governments constituted especially in small and medium towns to perform all these activities. They could, at the most, be entrusted with the task of performing activities relating to distribution, billing and collection. Transfer of the 12th Schedule functions, therefore, essentially requires activity mapping so that a judgment on entrusting a particular activity to the ULSGs is made on the basis of the nature of the activity and the capability of the ULSGs to perform it. This will also require going through a process of consultation with the local self-government concerned before actual transfer of functions takes place.

Third, most of the state governments have been dithering on

functional shifts also because of an attitude of indifference towards strengthening of urban local self-government. Though traditionally ULSGs have been responsible for delivery of essential public service such as health care, water supply, sanitation, primary education, provision and upkeep of public works and regulation of private activities such as trade, profession, building plans, markets, place of entertainment, there has been a trend towards creating specific purpose authorities for performing quite many of these traditional municipal functions. Specific purpose authorities have in fact proliferated over the years. These have been created for water supply and sewerage, slum clearance and improvement, and urban planning and development even in large cities where the ULSG has the capacity to perform such functions on its own. Continued presence of such parastatals and state level specific purpose authorities is also explained by a sense of predilection of the state governments towards these authorities as these specific purpose authorities happen to be apolitical organizations and suits the convenience of the state governments. Moreover, diminution of power and authority is not a pleasant thing; entrusting these functions to representative local governments and its bureaucracy, therefore, does not suit the preference of the state governments. The trend towards creation of state level parastatals began in the 1960s when, on the plea of 'weak capacity' of urban local self-governments, the state governments started constituting a spate of state level parastatals and urban development authorities (Jha and Vaidya 2011). This substantially contributed to weakening of institutions of self-government (Shah and Shah 2006; Datta 1999; Datta and Chakravarty 1981; Bhattacharya 1978; Sivaramakrishnan and Green 1986). Proliferation of specific purpose authorities, besides weakening the ULSGs, has also adversely affected accountability in service provisions and has undermined the perception of local self-government amongst the users of services provided by the specific purpose authorities. No care was taken to strengthen institutional capabilities of the ULSGs by diverting the resources that went into creation of specific purpose authorities for performance of urban sector functions. The same resources could have been used for strengthening of ULSGs.

The State Government of Kerala, on the other hand, has effectuated functional transfer to the ULSGs in a much more elaborate manner. Under Section 30 of the Kerala Municipality Act, 1994, 165 functions have been grouped into 21 heads under the 1st Schedule of this Act and these have been transferred to the ULSGs. The Act provides that the Municipality 'shall have powers and responsibility to prepare and implement schemes for economic development and social justice in relation to the matters enumerated in the First Schedule' of the Kerala Municipality Act, 1994. Complying with provisions in sub-section (3) of this section (Section 30), the State Government also transferred institutions, schemes, buildings, other properties, assets and liabilities connected with the matters mentioned in the 1st Schedule of the Kerala Municipal Act. The Government also allocated a proportion of Central and State Plan allocations and annual budget allocation in respect of the subjects transferred to the Municipalities. This, however, has not motivated other state governments yet for replicating similar exercise in their own states.

STRUCTURES FOR INTRA-CITY DECENTRALIZATION

As discussed in detail in Chapter 3, the Constitution provides for structures to be created below the Town Hall especially for deepening of democracy and bringing local governance nearer the citizeans. Multiple Wards Committees or a Ward Committee in each municipal ward is envisaged to provide a space that could be amenable to participation of citizens in urban governance. Provision for nomination to the decentralized structures was especially conceived as a mechanism for giving opportunities to the focus groups of citizens and the civil society to participate in inclusive urban governance so that the element of 'self-government' could be reinforced further and transparency and accountability in urban governance could be enhanced. An objective evaluation of realization of these objectives through creation of participatory structures provided for in the Constitution is as well constrained by paucity of qualitative data. A study conducted for MoUD by The Energy

Research Institute (TERI) on participation through the institutions of Ward Committee provides only a grim picture. According to this study, only 19 states including the Union Territory of Chandigarh enacted the enabling legislation for constituting Ward Committee. While evaluating constitution and functioning of Ward Committee, this study observes thus:

- Not all the states have enabling legislation for constitution of Ward Committee;
- Not all the cities in states having the enabling legislations, have Ward Committees; and
- Wherever Ward Committees are functioning, they are not delegated proper functions and finances (TERI 2010).

The last bullet point above corroborates that even when created and also functioning, the decentralized structures are not functioning according to stipulations of the Constitution—quite a plausible hypothesis of this volume.

The observation cited above is not very different from that of the Second Administrative Reforms Commission. The Commission also observed that even if Wards (or Ward Committees) are constituted in the states, 'they are hampered by the combination of various factors like the nomination process, limited citizen representative and an ambiguous mandate' (GoI 2007). It has also castigated the state governments by observing that Ward Committees have been created only to fulfil constitutional obligation. Analysis of the population served by each Ward Committee in some of the cities indicates that it is too large to achieve the constitutional objective of participatory governance and deepening of democracy. This is evident from the data on the number of Wards Committee created in some of the cities and the average population for each of them as contained in Table 5 in Annex IX. In the Municipal Corporation of Greater Mumbai, for example, the average population in a Wards Committee is about 5.20 lakh. Such a large population amounts to the creation of a Municipal Corporation itself. In the erstwhile Municipal Corporation of Delhi (MCD), the average population for Wards Committee was about 9.17 lakh. Even after partition of MCD into three municipal corporations, the situation remains the same as the Wards Committees coincide with the administrative zones of the erstwhile MCD. Table 5 also depicts that average population per Wards Committee is quite large in all the cities for which data could be available. This once again indicates the casual manner in which the decentralized structures have been created. In most of the very large cities, Wards Committees have been created to coincide with the administrative zones that are diametrically opposed to the concept and objectives of creating the Wards Committees discussed in Chapter 3. The Constitution provides for creation of Wards Committee (or Ward Committees) in the cities with more than 3 lakh population. Table 5 (Annex IX) shows that due to large number of average population per Ward Committee, the objective of bringing local self-governments nearer the citizens have not yet been addressed properly. In some of the cities, the Ward Committee itself has about 3 lakh population or more (Delhi, Mumbai, Borough Committee in Kolkata, Chennai and Bangaluru).

In some of the states, Ward Committee has been created in each ward (Kerala, Karnataka, West Bengal, Andhra Pradesh, and Gujarat). But wards, as well, mostly have quite large population that is not amenable for meaningful participation and proximity of citizens and the local government. Also, Ward Committees have been devolved with limited functions; in most states Ward Committees are only an advisory body without having any power. They also have limited financial powers (TERI 2010). Discretionary provision of the Constitution with respect to nomination of members on the Ward Committees has led to nomination of favourites as members by the political parties thereby defeating the very purpose of participation of civil society members. Only in the states of Kerala and West Bengal, composition and functioning of Ward Committee is qualitatively different. These have been discussed in detail in Chapter 4. Lately, in West Bengal, however, functioning of Ward Committee (created in each Ward) has become dormant following changes in priorities and focus of the state government by the ruling political party on governance.

As discussed in Chapter 4 in detail, Gram Sabha created in every Village Panchayat, on the other hand, imparts meaningful participatory space to the local citizens because of small population threshold. The concept of Area Sabha was, therefore, developed to form a third tier in urban local government structure by replicating the concept of Gram Sabha that is prevalent in the Panchayati Raj Institutions. MoUD also included creation of Area Sabha among the mandatory reforms required at the state level for accessing the In-NURM funds. However, the experience of creation and functioning of Area Sabhas is also not encouraging. There are gaps in creation and functioning of Area Sabhas at two levels. At the first level, enactment of the Nagar Raj Act (Community Participation Law) is not in conformity with the Jn-NURM guidelines of the MoUD and the Nagar Raj Bill of the Ministry (ibid.). According to the information available in MoUD, only 12 states enacted Community Participation Law and created Ward Committees under these laws. Some of the states, instead of enacting this law, merely inserted the provision for creation of Ward Committee by amending the existing Municipal Acts and subsequently framed the Community Participation Rules. In the states of Andhra Pradesh, Tamil Nadu, Delhi, and Haryana, Ward Committee is composed of only the elected councilor (ibid.). The state of Bihar is also an example of this. The rules framed by the state government of Bihar does not provide for representation of civil society on the Ward Committees. Composition of Ward Committees in such a manner is obviously against the spirit of the Community Participation Law that essentially provides to the civil society a space for participation in urban governance and thereby contribute substantially to enhancing local government accountability and transparency.

INSTITUTIONS FOR URBAN PLANNING

District Planning Committee

Situation with respect to constitution and functioning of District Planning Committees (DPC) is as well not very different from the fate of other provisions of the 74th CAA discussed above. Information on constitution of DPC as contained in an answer to a question in the Rajya Sabha by the Urban Development Minister is presented in Table 2 in Annex IX. Information contained in the appraisal report of Jn-NURM by the much hyped Grant Thornton Report depicts that, as of 2011, as many as 11 states had created DPC even before 2005 when Jn-NURM was launched by the Government of India (Table 1, Annex IX), another three states did so after December 2005 and that creation of DPC was 'in progress' in as many as 12 states. There are reasons to believe, however, that the information contained in the Grant Thornton Report cannot be relied upon for the simple reason that some of the states mentioned in both pre and post-Jn-NURM phase have not yet actually created the DPC; the states of Bihar and Gujarat which are purported to have created DPC, have not yet created the DPC though the laws for creation of DPC have been enacted. Yet another example of facile information contained in the Grant Thornton Report and also in Table 2 (Tables 1 and 2 in Annex IX) pertains to the state of Madhya Pradesh that is depicted to have created DPC even before the launching of Jn-NURM. Much to the contrary, DPC in this state became quite controversial immediately after its creation as they were converted into semblance of a district government headed by the Minister-in-Charge of the district, thus obfuscating the real objective for which these were conceived in the Constitution. Thus, paucity of information and inconsistencies in the available information constrain, in a big way, an objective analysis of creation and actual functioning of the DPC. Nevertheless, the information contained in some of the studies conducted on DPC provides evidence that the institution of DPC as a vehicle for participatory urban planning has not got off the ground in most of the states. The information culled from these micro studies is contained in Table 6 in Annex IX. A look at this table indicates that DPC is not constituted yet in a large number of states. The status of creation of DPC in 29 states and union territories for which information on DPC could be available, is presented in Table 6.2. The information contained in this table is classified into three broad categories on the basis of (i) creation of DPC, (ii) non-creation of DPC and (iii) actual functioning of DPCs. Table 6.2 contains a summary of information presented in Table 6 in Annex IX).

TABLE 6.2: STATUS OF CREATION OF DPC IN THE STATES AND THE UNION TERRITORIES

DPC not Created	DPC Created but not Functioning	DPC Created and Functioning
States and Union Territories	States and Union Territories	States
Andhra Pradesh	Andman & Nicobar	Karnataka
Arunachal Pradesh	Bihar	Kerala
Assam	Chhattisgarh	Rajashtan
Chandigarh	Dadra & Nagar	–
Gujarat	Daman & Diu	–
Jharkhand	Goa	–
Punjab	Haryana	–
Puducherry	Himachal Pradesh	–
Tripura	Laksh Dweep	–
Uttar Pradesh	Madhya Pradesh	–
Uttarakhand	Maharashtra	–
	Odisha	–
	Sikkim	–
	Tamil Nadu	–
	West Bengal	–

Source: Summary of Table 6 in Annex IX.

It is obvious from Table 6.2 that DPC has not yet been created in as many as 11 states and union territories of India. It has been constituted in 15 states and union territories but these are not functioning and, most important, it is functioning in only three states such as Karnataka, Kerala, and Rajasthan. Getting insights into the 'actual functioning' of DPC is, however, further constrained as the available information contained in Table 6.2 does not throw light on the functioning of DPCs according to constitutional provisions. It does not indicate if the plans are prepared by the local governments, if prepared, they are consolidated in preparation of District Plan, and that the District Plans are implemented fully either on its own by the DPC or through their inclusion in the State Plans. A study conducted by PRIA on the status of DPC in a dozen of state is revealing with respect to implementation of DPC and achieving its objectives as provided for in the Constitution

form to the process of district planning. Yet, the objectives of preparation of District Plan could not be achieved. Serious thinking that went into developing systems, procedures and modalities for district planning could not lead to a sustained process for district planning.

It is not denying the fact that the 74th CAA has conceived all together a different bottom up urban planning process. This is, however, contingent upon effective implementation of such a revolutionary bottom up process of urban planning. There are indications that neither the basic issues involved in such a planning process are sorted out yet nor the state governments have taken the required steps for operationilization of such a bottom-up planning process. Evaluating the progress made in these regards, SARC observes that it requires complete re-orientation of the district level planning mechanism for bringing the local governments at the centre-stage for their involvement in the participative planning process from the village and urban settlements levels upwards. In order to facilitate such a participatory planning process, the erstwhile Planning Commission as well requested the states in October 2005 to establish DPC in accordance with provisions contained in Article 243ZD of the Constitution so that the Eleventh Five Year Plan (2007-12) and the Annual Plans of the states could be founded on District Plans as provided for in the Constitution. This could not be actualized. SARC also refers to yet other unsettled issues such as the very nature of District Plans that, according to the constitution, involves 'consolidation' of Panchayat and Municipal Plans. It rightly raises another important related issue that in preparation of a District Plan; there could be several dimensions that are unlikely to be resolved at the micro-level (Panchayats and Municipalities); these could be resolved only at the macro-level. SARC has raised yet another important basic issue with respect to planning: devolution of functions to the Municipalities in a half-hearted manner. According to it, if the functions presently performed by the state governments are not devolved to the municipalities, the planning exercise will not be meaningful. Moreover, there is presence of urban development authorities that are as well engaged in urban planning. Urban planning initiative in such a functionally fragmented situation will contribute to duplication and also inter-organizational conflicts. In view of these unsettled issues, SARC has very rightly suggested to bring clarity on the issues discussed above.

The initiatives discussed above for translating the concept of decentralized and participatory planning process as also the views of the SARC for redesigning altogether a new organizational framework for decentralized participative planning are quite elaborate, varied and focused. Yet, it has not actualized. Reasons are quite many. The first and the foremost reason is the lack of will at the state level to be receptive to the concept of decentralized planning. There could be conceptual and institutional issues in institutional design provided for in the constitution as the DPC. In its present form and structure, DPC happens to be a standalone institution without having any link with the district level local government—the Zila Parishad (GoI 2002; Sivaramakrishnan 2011; GoI 2007). But provided the will, these could be addressed by devising appropriate strategies for addressing these issues. The Ministry of Panchayati Raj, for example, invited the views of the State Chief Secretaries for amending the provision of DPC in the constitution (Article 243ZD) by creating institutional mechanism that is very much similar to the suggestions offered by SARC. The Ministry of Panchayati Raj proposed constituting elected District Councils within the district that is to be vested with the responsibility of performing all functions listed in the 11th and the 12th Schedules. It also suggested that the District Councils shall have jurisdiction over both rural and urban areas within the district with the District Collector as its Chief Executive Officer. DPC was suggested to be a technical and professional arm of the District Council. All these efforts notwithstanding, the states have been found wanting in giving operational form to such an endeavour. Second, there is also the problem of funding for both preparation and implementation of decentralized plans. Third, local governments happen to be critically important players in such a scheme of things. But neither the rural nor the urban local self-governments have the required capacity for preparation of local plans that could be used by the DPC in formulation of district plans. The functionaries of the DPC as well lack the required capacity for preparation of district plans. These constraints could be effectively addressed provided there is a will as one comes across largely in the states of Kerala, Karnataka and to some extent in Rajasthan as well. In the mean time, the Planning Commission itself has been abolished. It is not yet clear if the planning process at the sub-national levels as well will survive and get strengthened. It is unfortunate that despite a series of creative ideas going into giving operational form to the concept of participatory district planning, the concept itself should become a non-issue after the abolition of the Planning Commission and absence of any synergy between the ministries of Panchayati Raj and Housing and Urban Affairs in working together by picking up the lost thread and move forward. Under the dispensation of new government elected to power in 2014, the official thinking of the new government and also the state governments on participatory urban and rural planning is not yet clear. This puts a big question on translating a wealth of ideas on participatory district planning.

It is more than a couple of decades of enactment of the 74th CAA that the various steps taken in the past to put in place a process of meaningful decentralized participatory and inclusive planning could not be implemented. This also indicates disregard for even mandatory provisions of the Constitution. One will have to wait and watch if the NITI Ayog that has succeeded the Planning Commission will pick up the lost thread and steer a policy process for taking decentralized and participative planning forward at the local and district levels in different states. But there seems to be little hope for this to happen. The new government elected to power in 2014 does not seem to be favourably disposed towards the concept of planning as a strategy for development. This may lead to abandoning of planning at the sub-national and local levels as well. In the existing policy environment, there is a great deal of uncertainty about further refurbishment of Constitutional provisions for district planning and its effective implementation.

METROPOLITAN PLANNING COMMITTEES

The 2011 Census reported a total number of 53 metropolitan cities. Another eight cities marginally missed to acquire the status of a metropolitan city (Table 7 in Annex IX). They were Bareily

(979,933), Mysore (983,893), Tirupur (962,982), Solapur (951,118), Hubli-Dharwad (943,857), Salem (919,150) Aligarh (909,559) and Gurgaon (901,968). Thus, it is safe to assume that there are at present about 61 metropolitan cities in the country that are spread into 17 states and two union territories.[2] The 74th CAA provides for constituting Metropolitan Planning Committees for an orderly growth of metropolitan areas with adequate provision of civic services. Uttar Pradesh has the largest number of nine metropolitan cities. This is followed by Tamil Nadu and Kerala with seven metropolitan cities each and Maharashtra with six cities (Table 7 in Annex IX). The states and union territories having metropolitan areas are 19 in number. Despite a very large number of metropolitan areas in different states, implementation of provisions of the Metropolitan Planning Committee—yet another mandatory provision of the Constitution—is not very different, rather the response of the state governments and the union territories has been the least.

According to the information given by the Union Minister of Urban Development and Housing and Urban Poverty Alleviation (Table 2, Annex IX), only six states have so far constituted the Metropolitan Planning Committee (MPC). These states are Karnataka, Maharashtra, Punjab, Rajasthan, Tamil Nadu and West Bengal. Such information again, however, does not indicate if the MPCs created in these states are constituted according to the provisions of the 74th CAA and if they are functioning according to constitutional provisions. Some of the other states such as Madhya Pradesh, Bihar, Kerala, Andhra Pradesh, Telangana, Gujarat, and Haryana have enacted laws for MPC. No initiative has yet been taken to constitute MPC in the two union territories of Chandigarh and Delhi.

Of the six states that have constituted MPC, the state of West Bengal was the first to have done so towards the end of 2000. The Kolkata Metropolitan Development Authority had been already functioning in the state even before the enactment of the 74th CAA. After enactment of 74th CAA, it was designated as the technical secretariat of the newly created MPC. According to Article 243ZE, MPCs are required to prepare draft development plan having regard to (i) the plans prepared by the Municipalities and the Panchayats in the Metropolitan area; and (ii) matters of common interest between the Municipalities and the Panchayats, including coordinated spatial planning of the area, sharing of water and other physical and natural resources, and the integrated development of infrastructure and environmental conservation. There is no evidence to show that such a process is followed by the MPC in preparation of plan for the metropolitan area. As almost all the leading metropolitan cities such as Kolkata, Mumbai, Chennai, Hyderabad and others have urban/regional development authorities; creation of MPC has not made any dent on putting in place a system of metropolitan planning envisaged in the Constitution. The metropolitan development authorities have continued to be the prime movers of planning and development irrespective of constitutional provisions in this regard. MPCs have been created only to indicate mechanical compliance to the constitutional provisions so that the states could give justification to the MoUD that they have implemented the state level mandatory reforms under the Jn-NURM of which constituting MPC formed a part. Another aberration found in the discharge of responsibilities by the MPCs is a project based approach adopted by the MPCs rather than formulation of plan according to the provisions of Article 243ZE of the Constitution (Sivaramakrishnan 2011).

Creation of DPC and MPC and the fate of urban development authorities is yet another issue that is not yet settled. The state of Bihar provides a monumental example of a rhetoric of 'strengthening of urban local self-government' especially in the context of a metropolitan city and the actual consequence of such an endeavour. Merging of PRDA with the Patna Municipal Corporation after the enactment of the 74th CAA, was said to be quite a bold and progressive step for empowerment of the Patna Municipal Corporation (PMC). PMC was supposed to have been empowered after this to perform also urban and regional planning functions. After about a little more than two decades of this 'bold step', the erstwhile Patna Regional Development Authority has not only gone into oblivion, but has died its natural death largely through attrition of its staff bringing the PMC back to square one. The state government of Bihar as well did not assign any new urban and regional planning and development role to the PMC after the merged PRDA became ineffective. The state government of Bihar could not sustain this landmark merger by putting in place the required systems and mechanisms for enabling the PMC to continue playing urban planning and development role. There is now a fresh thinking in the state of Bihar to revive and rejuvenate urban development authorities not only in the state capital but to also to create such structures in other cities as well. The newly enacted Bihar Urban Planning and Development Act, 2012 has quite ambivalent provisions for creation of Planning Authorities for every Planning Area that will prepare urban development plans and implemented by 'developers'. The Act has provisions, though, that a Local Authority (municipal government) may as well could be designated as a Planning Authority.

Constituting DPC and MPC and ensuring that they function successfully in various states is inevitably contingent on preparation of plans by the local governments. The fact, however, remains that most of the ULSGs even in most of the metropolitan cities do not possess institutional capacity for preparation of urban development plans let alone the ULSGs existing in India's secondary cities. Despite enactment of 74th CAA, the state governments have not yet cared to provide planners to the urban local self-governments. Existing organizational structure as well as the recruitments rules in several states do not provide for urban planning as one of the sections/cells in the organizational structure of a Municipality and recruitment of urban planners. Even the state of West Bengal where the ULSGs are required to prepare Draft Development Plans under the Municipal Act, barring the local bodies within the Kolkata Metropolitan Area (KMA), the ULSGs in other parts of the state do not have the capability to prepare local plans because they do not have planners on their staff. Even the ULSGs located within KMA got planners under a project called Kolkata Urban Service for the Poor (KUSP) supported by the Department for International Development (DFID), Government of UK. As an option for institutionalization of urban planning in the Municipalities, the state governments could make available services of their

State Town Planning Departments for preparation of plans for the urban local self-governments through a sustained process of consultation with the ULSGs and in accordance with priorities and needs expressed by the respective ULSGs so that the plans prepared by planners are not just thrust on the ULSGs. This as well has not happened in any state. This demonstrates, in a way, reluctance and lack of political will in the states for compliance to the constitutional provision.

OVERALL IMPLEMENTATION OF 74TH CAA

Analysis of provisions of the 74th CAA presented above brings a quite discouraging account of implementation of constitutional provisions. This also brings in sharp focus gaps in strengthening and empowerment of urban local self-government and its institutions. Not less a person than the Union Minister of Urban Development himself observed thus in the Rajya Sabha during the course of answering a question:

> Most of the states have not met the requirements of the Constitution (74th Amendment) Act 1992 in respect of devolution of powers and responsibilities to municipal bodies. . . . Most municipal bodies in the country are financially constrained and lack capacity to discharge functions as per the 74th Constitution. . . . The implementation of the 74th Amendment to the Constitution empowers municipal bodies with transfer of funds, functions and functionaries for effective local governance.[3]

The Minister obviously refered to inadequate devolution of powers and responsibilities to the urban local self-governments by the state governments by transferring funds, functions and functionaries. Such a state of fragile institutional capacity has continued despite constitutional provisions contained in the 74th CAA in general and in Article 243W of the Indian Constitution in particular. This is explained by gaps observed at several levels in conceptualizing and implementing the constitutional provisions. At the first level, there are gaps in the provisions of the 74th CAA itself that have been discussed in greater detail in Chapters 3 and 5. At the second level, there is gap between constitutional provisions and the conformity legislations discussed in Chapter 4. At the third level, there are conspicuous and even glaring gaps in implementation. With these gaps, strengthening and empowerment of urban local self-governments have been substantially diluted. As a result, the big-bang decentralization has not made much difference in empowering them except that they can no longer be superseded for an indefinite period as was the case before the enactment of the new constitutional provisions. Fresh elections are now required to be conducted within six months of supersession.

Why, after all, the much applauded amendment to the Constitution could not make much of an impact in strengthening and empowering the urban local self-governments? Besides the inherent deficiencies in the Constitution (74th Amendment) Act, 1992 that have been discussed in detail in the preceding chapters, there are other reasons that explain not-so-effective implementation of the constitutional provisions. These are discussed below:

Lack of Will at the State Level

Urban development and governance being part of List II of the Constitution, the onus of effective implementation of 74th CAA vests with the state governments. The state governments have, however, betrayed a lack of political will for empowerment of urban self-governing institutions. Lack of will could be due to general apprehension amongst the state level political functionaries towards empowerment of urban local self-governments. An empowered and strengthened urban local self-government, they could be apprehending, may jeopardize their very political interests. It could be, therefore, a part of the psyche of the state level political leaders not to enable the grass-root local self-governments to take roots. Sivaramakrishnan as well mentions this apprehension that was expressed during the discussion on the Constitution Amendment Bill in the Parliament especially with respect to the provisions for constituting District Planning Committees in each district. Some of the members had expressed a view that DPC, if constituted according to the provisions of the Bill, could become politically too strong to be amenable to the influence of the members of the

Parliament (Sivaramakrishnan 2000). A Primer prepared by MoUD on Implementation of the 74th Constitution Amendment and Integration of City Planning and Delivery of Functions for Jn-NURM observes that the state governments 'found it difficult to implement its provisions in totality. The main problem is that functional devolution to ULBs has not been supported by adequate transfer of revenue sources. It also alludes to lack of financial autonomy of urban local self-governments that requires them to seek state government approval even for enhancement of tax rates and user charges beyond the limits mentioned in municipal laws (Ministry of Urban Development jnnurm.nic.in/primers.html). Lukewarm attitude of state governments is reinforced also by the attitude of state level bureaucracy that lacks an interest and is found even diffident in empowering and strengthening of urban local self-government.[4]

A view is also expressed in some of the states that decentralization initiative through the 74th CAA was introduced rather too early; the urban local self-governments are probably not prepared for this. This, according such view, is constraining giving autonomy to them through effective implementation of constitutional provisions. Such views are based on a circular argument that goes like this: urban local governments are not empowered because they are not yet prepared for this, since they are not yet prepared, an initiative for their empowerment will be counterproductive and hence empowerment must wait till the ULSGS are prepared for this. The Commission for Review of the Working of the Constitution, for example, did not favour creation of a separate list of sources of revenue for local government in the Constitution because it felt that the time is not yet ripe, for this even though it was quite 'relevant' during the British rule under the Government of India Act of 1919 that had provided for a separate list of local revenues. It needs to be appreciated that strengthening of an institution whether at the national, regional or local level, does not happen overnight. It takes a long time for establishing sound practices and conventions for institutional strengthening and for such initiatives to be institutionalized and take roots. 'Learning by doing' applies equally well with respect to strengthening of local governments whether rural or urban. There are myriad examples of very long time required for institution building. It took centuries for the British Parliament, for example, to become a 'Westminster Model' of parliamentary democracy and democratic governance. It is a long drawn process that must be put to trial and nourished through handholding and stewardship.

Inability to Ensure the Consistency of Laws with the 74th Amendment

Implementation of the Constitution (74th Amendment) Act, 1992 required to revisit the myriad laws enacted during the colonial rule and after Independence that impinge on the constitutional provisions of the 74th CAA and suitably modify them so that the provisions in these laws are made consistent with the new constitutional provisions. Article 243ZF especially mandates to review the laws relating to Municipalities that were in force before the commencement of the 74th CAA and repeal or amend the provisions that are not consistent with the new constitutional provisions. This had to be done within a year of the commencement of the new constitutional provisions contained in Part IXA of the Constitution. Article 243N similarly provided to review and modify provisions in laws relating to the Panchayati Raj Institutions for removing inconsistencies in them. Even though these two Articles have mandatory provisions, review and modification of the existing laws impinging especially on the Municipalities could not be done. This indicates disregard for even the mandatory provisions of the Constitution of India. Barring the State of Kerala, in other states, the conformity legislations simply incorporated the provisions that were simple in nature that did not involve hard political decisions and political risks. Conducting of local elections, composition of municipalities, reservation of seats for weaker sections, types of local governments to be constituted, and local government structure including the intra-city structures are the examples. On the other hand, provisions requiring devolution to the municipalities in functional and financial spheres involves hard political decisions and hence these were simply copied verbatim from the Constitution and provided for in the conformity legislations as a simple excercise of 'cut and paste'. An exception to this is the state of Kerala where the state government especially constituted an Expert Group that reviewed the existing laws that had an interface with urban governance and suggested suitable changes to make them conform to the constitutional provisions. Absence of such a process of review and fine-tuning of provisions in such laws in other states could not make the conformity laws meaningful. This once again reflects lack of political will in the states for empowerment of urban local self-governments.

The provisions in Articles 243N and 243ZF give an impression that continuance of the laws or the provisions therein that were not modified, will be null and void. Such an impressionistic view is not supported by legal pronouncements by the High Courts and even the Supreme Court. Sivaramakrishnan cites interesting legal pronouncements by these courts. The courts have held that a law that is inconsistent with the constitutional provisions would need to be specifically challenged (Sivaramakrishnan 2011). Provisions in the above mentioned couple of Articles cannot just make these laws null and void. Continuance of such laws that could not be modified within the stipulated time provided for in the two Articles mentioned above, thus pose additional problems for effective implementation of the constitutional provisions contained in the 74th CAA.

Role of the Ministry of Urban Development

The Ministry of Urban Development (MoUD) now the Ministry of Housing and Urban Affairs has quite a pivotal role to play in strengthening and empowerment of urban local self-governments. For this, it should have organized and conducted a series of policy support, strategic thinking for cajoling and convincing the state governments for empowerment of local self-government. It was required to review and monitor implementation processes of policies for empowerment and leverage financial assistance for urban governance reforms. This requires a process of dialogue with state governments on a sustained basis. Earlier in this chapter, an analysis of implementation of constitutional provisions that are common to both urban and rural local governments has revealed quite a pro-active role played by the nascent Ministry of Panchayati Raj (MoPR) that came much later in 2004 as compared to the MoUD that has been there for long. The role of MoUD in working with the state governments for effective implementation of constitutional provisions, on the other hand, has at most been subdued. The MoPR, on the other hand, convened a series of Round Tables with the counterpart state government departments and also with Chief Secretaries of the states for enabling and even persuading the state governments to implement constitutional provisions. Even though implementation of 74th CAA was part of the reform under Jn-NURM and the MoUD had the knowledge about gaps in its implementation, it should have a dialogue with the state government on its effective implementation.

Such initiatives have been conspicuously lacking in the MoUD. The initiative of MoUD was limited to putting implementation of the 74th constitutional provisions as one of the conditions for accessing financial assistance provided for under the Jn-NURM. Though it was a welcome initiative for leveraging urban reforms through financial assistance, the ministry neither had a dialogue on implementation with the counterpart state government departments on a regular and sustained basis nor could it verify the veracity of information provided by the various state governments on actual implementation of the 74th CAA provisions according to constitutional provisions. It simply went by the affirmation of the state governments on implementation of various constitutional provisions. Rigorous, objective and qualitative monitoring and review could not be adopted by the MoUD at any stage after the enactment of the 74th CAA and especially during the implementation of Jn-NURM.

Even in implementing the provisions in Article 243N for ensuring compliance of the existing laws relating to the Panchayati Raj Institutions with the constitutional provisions, MoPR has scored over MoUD. The MoPR, on its own, reviewed some of the central and state laws and brought the inconsistent provisions in them to the notice of the state governments. No such initiative was taken by the MoUD despite the fact that it launched a massive project (Jn-NURM) for augmenting urban infrastructure with an agenda of 'full implementation of the 74th amendment' and provided for financial assistance as an incentive for its implementation. The modalities for accomplishment of this agenda could, however, not be firmed up. At present, implementation of the 74th CAA and the initiatives for strengthening of urban local self-governments no longer forms part of the new agenda of reforms for the new Missions launched by the MoHUA except the initiative for creation of municipal cadre in states that, however, does not form part of the 74th CAA. This gives an impression that implementation of 74th CAA is no longer a serious agenda for the MoHUA. Implementation of constitutional provisions for empowerment of urban local self-governments has disappeared altogether in midst of the new zeal for launching and implementing newer Missions without thinking that implementation of these Missions inevitably requires empowerment and streng-thening of urban local self-government.

It is worth mentioning that unlike MoUD, MoPR also looked into some of the gaps in the 74th CAA and took initiative to address these gaps. It proposed bold amendments to Article 243. The proposed amendments included to delete the provision for including the members of the Parliament and the State Legislatures as members of the elected councils of the local self-governments—both rural and urban. Another important amendment proposed was to totally eliminate the traditional practice of a separate constituency for teachers and graduates for election to the State Legislative Councils in the states that have this Council. It proposed that two-thirds of the total members of the State Legislative Councils should be elected by local governments and that only one-sixth of the total members of this Council should be elected by the members of the State Legislative Assembly. This proposal is to some extent, a replica of the suggestions given also by the Second Administrative Reforms Commission for enhancing the voice of local government (discussed earlier in Chapter 5). Yet another proposal that largely conforms to the suggestions given by SARC, was to constitute District Councils as unified elected district governments in the districts having jurisdiction on both rural and urban areas of the district. Its proposed functions including performance by Local Self-Governments of all the functions listed in the 11th and the 12th Schedule of the Constitution. Thus, the proposed amendments to Article 243 were of far reaching importance. MoPR circulated the proposal in 2010 to all the Chief Secretaries of the states for obtaining their views. It has been lying there since then. It is reported that most of the states are in favour of the proposals of the MoPR. These, by far the most progressive thoughts for empowerment of local government, it seems, have become non-issues. Sivaramakrishnan (2011) is justifiably quite vocal on the need to revisit the provisions of the 73rd and the 74th CAAs by saying thus: 'On a consideration of the various factors involved, it may be preferable to make an attempt to get the Constitutional provisions of the 73rd and 74th Amendments suitably altered rather than endure a series of provisions which have become mere exhortations rather than enforceable prescriptions.'

Lack of Institutional Memory

Lack of institutional memory within MoHUA about mechanisms, process and practices set forth in the past within the MoUD itself is yet another reason behind absence of a pro-active role of this Ministry to spruce up urban governance in the country. Reference has already been made in Chapter 3 to the Central Council of Local Government and Urban Development that has become dormant for long. It used to provide a high power forum and valuable opportunity for reviewing, along with the state ministers of local government and urban development, the process of empowerment of urban local governments and for addressing the obstacles and bottlenecks in this regard. The last time the Council met was during the tenure of the Atal Behari Vajpayee government at the centre during 1998-2004. The ministry is yet to take any initiative to revive this valuable institutional mechanism for strengthening urban governance. It does not seem to have an institutional memory of the existence of this Council in the past and significance of this forum. MoUD also got a Model Municipal Law drafted that contains altogether newer ways of looking at the municipal functional domain and also a number of progressive provisions for modernizing urban governance through legislative enactments. The ministry could not sell the idea for replication of the Model Law or for incorporating its progressive aspects in the state municipal laws. It could not even effectively monitor if the Model law has in fact been adopted or enacted by the state governments. In the mean time, as the model municipal law was enacted long back, some of its provisions are either not relevant in the present circumstances or have gaps. This requires revisiting the model laws itself for a review and further fine tuning of provisions relating to governance and financial management. Like the Panchayati Raj Ministry, MoUD as well was expected to have sustained dialogue with the relevant state government departments to persuade them for its replication.

Though there is a Local Self-Government (LSG) Department within MoHUA that is expected to take initiatives for strengthening of urban local self-government on a sustained basis, it nevertheless happens to be quite weak. Its fragile capacity for strengthening of urban local self-governments gets exacerbated by lack of coordination of the other units of the MoHUA that work on conceptualization, policy formulation, launching and review of urban development initiatives either in a Mission Mode or as its policy initiatives from time to time. There is hardly any dialogue of these units with the LSG department for visioning strategies for strengthening and empowerment of urban local self-governments and provide for this as an important component in the Missions and policies launched by the ministry. Nor does the LSD take any initiative on its own to have dialogue and brain storming about the need to impower and strengthen ULSGs with other departments and sections of the MoHUA. The result is obvious. One hardly comes across any component on strengthening of urban governance in the four Missions launched by the MoUD such as AMRUT (Atal Mission for Rejuvenation and Urban Transformation), HRIDAY (Heritage City Development and Augmentation Yojana), Swachha Bharat and Smart City. The sole initiative taken by the MoUD in this regard for creation of municipal cadre in the states stands as an exception. Effective implementation of the four Missions essentially requires putting urban governance reforms at the fore front. Effective implementation of the Missions is unlikely to be accomplished in a vacuum; it requires effective urban governance structure, systems and mechanisms in place in the states. No wonder, therefore, that a serious commentator on urban governance laments the farewell to basic urban governance reforms in the MoHUA and calls it a 'clerical approach to reform' (Mathur 2015). Effectuation of the objectives of Smart City Mission especially requires smart urban governments along with other key components such as smart economy, smart environment, smart living, smart people, and smart mobility (Cohen 2012). There is hardly any mention of the modalities to put in place smart governance in the four Missions in general and in the guidelines for Smart City Mission in particular. On the contrary, the Guidelines for Smart City has favoured creation of Special Purpose Vehicle (SPV) for implementation of Smart City projects. This is a step that keeps the ULSGs at a distance and precludes their capacity development. This, in away, is recognition to the weak organizational capacity of ULSGs.

Issues in empowerment and strengthening of urban local self-governments are quite wide ranging. It embraces fine tuning of the 74th CAA itself in the context of (i) evaluation of the 74th CAA provisions and implementation of these provisions contained especially in Chapter 3 and (ii) observations of the Commission to Review the Working of the Constitution and the SARC and a critical evaluation of these observations in Chapter 5 of this volume. This requires prevalence of political will in ample measure at the state level, and a pro-active role to be played by the bureaucracy both at the centre and in the state. A lackadaisical approach to strengthening of urban local self-government will perpetuate their existing weak organizational capacity. Their contemporary static and weak organizational framework is likely to be overwhelmed by the dynamics of urbanization and urban growth. It needs to be appreciated that with increase in urban population effective urban governance requires rebust organizational capacity.

NOTES

1. CBUD Project with a tenure of five years (2011-12 to 2015-16), was focused on capacity building of ULSGs. However, its focus changed to providing technical and secretarial assistance to the MoUD on the four new Missions that were launched after the new government came to power in 2014. The information for RBA studies was collected in 2012-13. The RBA Reports for the project cities are available on http://jnnurm.nic.in/rapid-baseline-assessment-of-cbud-city.html.
2. Table 2, which is the part of the answer given to a Rajya Sabha question by the Union Minister of Housing and Urban Affairs mentions only 14 states because the states of Chhattisgarh, Jammu & Kashmir and Kerala, though have metropolitan cities, are mistakenly omitted from this Table. Also the two union territories of Chandigarh and Delhi do not form part of Table 2 in Annex IX.
3. http://metrovaartha.com/en/2014/07/31/municipal-bodies-not-empowered-enough-says-naidu/
4. This is based on author's experience of working in a number of states in the country where during interaction with the state bureaucracy on introducing liberal provisions in the municipal laws and granting further autonomy to the ULSGs in the basic spheres of governance and financial management, he came across such rigid attitudes.

REFERENCES

Bhattacharya, Mohit, 1978, 'Machinery for Metropolitan Planning and Development', in Abhijit Datta (ed.), *Urban Planning and Development Authorities*, New Delhi: Indian Institute of Public Administration.

Cohen, Boyd, 'What Exactly is a Smart City?', 2012, retrieved in March 2016 from http://www.ubmfuturecities.com. See also Boyd Cohen, 'Smart City Wheel', 2013, retrieved in March 2016 from https://www.smart-circle.org/smartcity/blog/boyd-cohen-the-smart-city-wheel

Datta, Abhijit, 1999, 'Institutional Aspects of Urban Governance in India', in S.N. Jha and P.C. Mathur (eds.), *Decentralisation and Local Politics*, New Delhi: Sage.

Datta, Abhijit and Bappaditya Chakravarty, 1981, *Organising Metropolitan Development*, New Delhi: Indian Institute of Public Administration.

Government of India, 2002, *Review of the Working of the Constitution, Report of the National Commission to Review the Working of the Constitution,* vol. 1, New Delhi: Government of India Press.

——, 2007, *Sixth Report of the Second Administrative Reform Commission, Local Governance: An Inspiring Journey into the Future,* New Delhi: Ministry of Personnel, Public Grievances and Pensions, Department of Administrative Reform and Public Grievances.

——, 2010, *Progress Review Report,* New Delhi: Ministry of Urban Development.

——, 2014, Reply of Minister of Urban Development to a question in Rajya Sabha, http://metrovaartha.com/en/2014/07/31/municipal-bodies-not-empowered-enough-says-naidu/

—— (bears no date), *Implementation of the 74th Constitutional Amendment and Integration of City Planning and Delivery Functions.* jnnurm.nic.in/primers.html)

——, *Rapid Baseline Assessment Reports,* 2014, CBUD Project, http://jnnurm.nic.in/rapid-baseline-assessment-of-cbud-city.html

Jha, Gangadhar and Chetan Vaidya, 2011, 'Role of Urban Local Bodies in Service Provision and Urban Economic Development: Issues in Strengthening Their Institutional Capabilities', *Nagarlok,* XLIII (3).

Mathur, Om, 2015, 'Smart City is a Work in Progress', *Financial Express,* 20 July.

PRIA, 2009, *Status and Functioning of District Planning Committees in India.* New Delhi: Participatory Research in Asia.

Shah, Anwar and Sana Shah, 2006, 'New Vision of Local Governance and the Evolving Roles of Local Governments', in Anwar Shah (ed.), *Local Governance in Developing Countries,* Public Sector Governance and Accountability Series, Washington, D.C.: The World Bank.

Shivaramakrishnan, K.C. and Leslie Green, 1986, *Metropolitan Management, The Asian Experience,* Oxford: EDI, The World Bank.

Sivaramakrishnan, K.C., 2011, *Revisioning Indian Cities: The Urban Renewal Mission.* New Delhi: Sage.

TERI, 2010, *Enhancing Public Participation through Effective Functioning of Ward Committees,* Final Report, Project Report No. 2010, UDo4, Delhi: TERI.

CHAPTER 7

Empowerment of Urban Local Self-Government: The Options

Enactment of the Constitution (74th Amendent) Act (74th CAA), 1992 has not made much of difference in functioning of the urban local self-governments. High expectations created at the time of introducing the big bang decentralization through this Constitution amendment could not be actualized. It has belied the hopes of ushering in of an era of empowered, strong and efficient urban local self-government. This is evident from deficiencies in provision of basic urban services and urban infrastructure across the various size categories of cities and towns, deprivation of a large section of urban population from these services, poor quality of municipal services and its unreliability, fragmented municipal functional domain, unplanned urban growth, weak fiscal strength, and fragile organizational capacity of urban local self-governments. It has not succeeded in bringing about a turnaround in the functioning of the urban local self-governments. These lags in urban governance are largely explained by gaps in the decentralization initiative itself. Some of these gaps are quite conspicuous. This is revealed by analysis of nature and contents of the 74th CAA and evaluation of various provisions of the 74th CAA in Chapter 3 as well as from observations of a couple of official Commissions on its various aspects that have been discussed in detail in Chapter 5. Its efficacy in empowering urban local self-governments is further diluted by gaps in the conformity legislations that were enacted in different states. These gaps are exacerbated by conspicuous lags in implementation of the constitutional provisions.

Where do we go from here? Should the 74th CAA, 1992 be revisited for plugging the holes in it or should it be treated as a *fait accompli*? Unquestionably, it has not to be treated as a *fait accompli*. Empowerment of urban local self-governments—the prime institutions for urban governance and management of delivery of basic urban services in cities and towns—is in the nature of an imperative for enhancing the national economic growth, enriching the quality of urban life and making cities and towns livable. This is so because of a number of reasons discussed below. These, by all means, indicate that empowerment and strengthening of urban local self-governments has acquired the nature of an imperative.

First, the level and the scale of urbanization in India is gathering momentum. Urban population of the country increased from about 217 millions in 2001 to about 377 millions in 2011. The urban population of India is more than the total population of many counties individually. The level of urbanization has, consequently, increased from 27.81 per cent in 2001 to 31.2 per cent in 2011 denoting thereby that almost one-third of the total population of the country is already living in urban areas. The 2011 Census results have also revealed that for the first time since Independence, the absolute increase in population was more in urban areas than in the rural areas. A United Nations backed Report on economy and climate change asserts that India is on the 'brink of urban revolution'. According to this Report, the urban population of 377 millions in 2011 is estimated to increase to about 600 millions in 2031. About 40 per cent of Indian's population will be living in urban settlements in 2031 (The Global Commission on the Economy and Climate 2014). Even now, in some of the states in India the urban population is almost 50 per cent of the total population of these states. In Goa, for example, it is more than 62 per cent. Other states where the urban population is close to 50 per cent are (i) Tamil Nadu (48.45 per cent), (ii) Kerala (47.72 per cent). (iii) Maharashtra (45.23 per cent), (iv) and Gujarat (42.58 per cent). These numbers indicate that 'India lives in villages' is gradually becoming a myth.

Increase in the pace of urbanization generates additional demand for urban services and infrastructure. This has important implications for empowerment of urban local self-governments and strengthening their organizational capabilities for effective urban governance and management of effective, inclusive and responsive service delivery for the increasing urban population. Even at the existing level of urban population, the urban local self-governments are not in a position to discharge their mandated functions. Further increase in urban population will additionally constrain their organizational capabilities for governance and service delivery if they are not empowered and strengthened. The United Nations Report mentioned above estimates that the gap in urban infrastructure investment in urban India is to the tune of US $387 billion for the next twenty years. Another official Committee constituted by the Ministry of Urban Development estimated an investment requirement of Rs. 30.98 lakh crore (at 2009-10 prices) for 20 year period (2012-13 to 2131-2) for water supply, solid waste management, sewerage, storm water drain, urban roads, mass transit, street lighting, and traffic support-infrastructure. When the costs of renewal, redevelopment, and capacity building of urban local self-governments are also included in the cost, the requirement of financial resources worked out to Rs. 39.2 lakh crore (GoI 2011). Yet another Report by the World Bank Group states that urbanization in the entire South Asia of which India is a part, has been messy and hidden because its towns and cities have been 'struggling to deal with the pressures of population on their infrastructure, basic services, land, and housing, not to mention the environment'. It points to three fundamental urban governance deficits—(i) a local government empowerment deficit, (ii) a resource deficit, and (iii) an accountability deficit (World Bank Group 2015).

Second, significant economic role of cities requires that the cities need to be made livable. The World Bank Group Report mentioned above refers to the Livability Index which is the most respected scheme worked out by the Economist Intelligence Unit (EIU) for ranking of cities. It observes that even India's largest cities which have the most well-developed infrastructure networks, best access to basic urban services, and the highest standards of living, have performed poorly on the basis of this Index. Out of 140 cities across the world for which the Livability Index was worked out by EIU, New Delhi was ranked 110. Mumbai got a rank of 115.[1] The average ranking of the six South Asian countries falls below the averages for both all the non-South Asian developing country cities and all the developing country cities in the East Asia and Pacific region. The Report further affirms that the urban local self-governments in India are typically characterized by 'weak administrative capacity, service delivery breakdowns, outdated registers, rigid and ambiguous laws, limited private sector involvement, and complex governance setups and political economies'. If not empowered and strengthened, increased pace of urbanization will further overwhelm weak institutional capacity of urban local self-governments. This will substantially restrain the cities to be livable and will adversely affect the cities to act as 'engines of economic growth'.

Third, with changes in times and urban situations, the urban local self-governments are now required to perform altogether new functions that were not even remotely thought to be the functions of the local government in urban settlements either during the British rule or when India became independent. Municipal functional domain has visibly expanded further. It now includes quite many altogether unconventional functions that are now required to be discharged by them. Urban poverty alleviation, local economic development, urban planning, urban environmental protection, use of information and communication technology for efficient performance of various local functions, and e-governance are examples of emerging functions that the ULSGs are now called upon to perform. The new initiative for development of smart cities further requires that the cities and towns must have 'smart government' which is one of the pre-requisites for developing smart cities. These new developments require empowerment of ULSGs and strengthening of their organizational and administrative capability. Newer ways of accrual based municipal accounting system and performance of finance functions are other examples that as well require empowerment and strengthening of the ULSGs and recruitment of municipal staff with altogether different skills.

Fourth, globalization has contributed to unprecedented economic, financial, technological and information flows that are already impacting urban local self-governments especially in mega cities and is expected to throw even more bigger challenges for them in the near future. A White Paper released by Alliance (an NGO) prepared under the aegis of the International City Managers' Association (ICMA) foretells that big economic, technological and social mega-forces are so challenging and complex that these are expected to threaten the viability of local governments across the nations. The traditional direct service model of local government is now severely under threat (Figom et al. no date). Globalization is leading to global economic integration resulting in dense network of interchanging investments, information, goods and people as well as centres of innovation and knowledge management. This is fundamentally altering the role of cities as generators of economic momentum and growth. Cities being the centres of economic, financial activities, and technological innovations, have to bear the brunt of global crises. The recent global financial crisis of 2008 made the cities vulnerable around the world to the destructive as also beneficial effects of international markets including social and political repercussions. A recent state of art document released by the UN-HABITAT on prosperity of cities places the role of cities (hence the role of city governments) at the centre stage in mitigating global crises (UN-HABITAT 2012).

Altogether newer ways, skills, local political acumen and leadership are required to enable the urban local self-governments to deal with complexities of local governance in the globalized world. Making the cities livable through effective, efficient and responsive urban infrastructure and services has acquired the centre stage for attracting direct investments. Politicians manning local government require acquisition of new insights and vision for turning the cities and towns in to engines of economic growth (Pricewaterhouse-Coopers no date). Demand for new services, governance implications of global warming and climate change, requirements for transforming local government into an enterprising business-like organization are expected to dramatically overwhelm the existing local government structure and capabilities. The urban local self-governments are required to have skills and abilities to negotiate participatory approaches for partnerships with the civil society groups and, above all, should have skilled and motivated workforce to face the emerging challenges.

Fifth, Emerging new information and communication technology (ICT) has ushered in unprecedented scope for planning, management and delivery of urban services with transparency and accountability. A new paradigm of governance has emerged in the form of e-governance. The new technology is in the process of its further enriching, strengthening and consolidation for making the cities smart. This has already been creating several new possibilities in the public sector. Access to high-speed information has revolutionized global culture. The new technology has far-reaching implications for the delivery of all existing services including administration, education, healthcare, communication, transportation and many more. In future we may also see greater application of the science of robotics in the public sector. Construction of intelligent houses for taking care of the elderly citizens is one among many examples.

Sixth, increase in urban economic activities in urban areas has been contributing to climate change especially as some of these activities contribute to greenhouse gas emissions that results in dangerous climate changes. Cities have become vulnerable to risks of climate change. Climate change impacts will manifest in increased stress on public health, livelihoods, urban utilities including water supply and infrastructure, exacerbating of urban heat islands, increase in frequency of extreme events such as flooding, precipitation, rise in temperature and civic unrest. In future, climate change is expected to exacerbate urban situation further that will have serious repercussions on the lives of the urban population, urban living and governance capabilities of the urban local self-governments. In view of this they will be required to shoulder the responsibility of mitigating and adapting to climate change effects. Mitigation strategies will require action for low carbon development for reducing carbon. Adaptation measures will be required to shield urban areas from worst climate change impacts. They would, therefore, need to enhance their vision, management capabilities and skills for adopting urban cooling strategies and environmental design. They would be also required to use Geographic Information System for linking water logging, flooding, and water quality because of possibilities of contamination of underground water. Adverse impacts of climate change requires them to possess capabilities to explore carbon finance incentives for reducing carbon emission and earn carbon credits, develop guidelines for carbon emission criteria and devise green energy projects, and enterprises to ensure low carbon prosperity. Yet another challenge of governance emanates from the need to be effectively engaged with natural calamities and disaster management. Skills, management capabilities and motivation for devising mitigation, and adaptation strategy are enormous especially in the existing context of weak institutional capacity of the ULSGs.

The reasons for existence and working of strong as well as effective urban governance are thus critically too important to ignore the imperatives for empowerment of urban local self-governments and strengthening of their capabilities. It needs to be emphasized that the reasons discussed above require both (i) empowerment, and (ii) strengthening of urban local self-governments. Empowerment implies devolving of power and authority to them with clarity in local functional domain including urban planning and zoning regulations and matching sources of revenue for dealing with urban situations. Strengthening, on the other hand, involves injecting catalytic elements in local government organizations that could be instrumental in enhancing their administrative capability to effectively perform the functions devolved to them. Devolving power and authority to them basically entails addressing the gaps in the scheme of decentralization introduced through the 74th CAA. However, this seems to be quite complex. The complexity involved in their empowerment, therefore, requires looking at the possible options for empowerment and a pre-meditated evaluation of these options for empowerment and strengthening. Before looking into these complexities, it would be desirable to first look at the prime objective of the 74th CAA. Clarity in objective is an important precursor for strategizing an intervention.

Was it really an objective of the 74th CAA to empower and strengthen the urban local self-governments? Answering this question is not as complex. The answer is embedded in the very objective of decentralization initiative. A careful reading of the 'Statement of Objects and Reasons' for the enactment of the 74th CAA indicates that it has not used any expression for either 'empowering' or 'strengthening' of ULSGs. Enactment of the 74th CAA was conceived for:

> (i) putting on a firmer footing the relationship between the State Government and the Urban Local Bodies with respect to (a) the functions and taxation powers; and (b) arrangements for revenue sharing; (ii) Ensuring regular conduct of elections; (iii) ensuring timely elections in the case of supersession; and (iv) providing adequate representation for the weaker sections like Scheduled Castes, Scheduled Tribes and women.

A close look at the above quoted passage and an evaluation of the decentralization initiative and its implementation indicate that of all the above mentioned objectives, the 74th CAA could not explicitly address by far the most important Constitutional issue, i.e. 'putting on a firmer footing the relationship between the State Government and the Urban Local Bodies' especially with respect to 'functions and taxation powers'. It is also obvious from a reading of the segment of the 74th CAA quoted above that placing 'functions and taxation powers' on a 'firmer footing' largely impinges on 'empowerment'. However, it is reflected from the nature and contents of the Constitution (74th Amendment) Act that it has neither clarified the local functional domain nor the taxing powers of the urban local self-governments—the two important aspects of empowerment. Functional domain of the ULSGs under Article 243W including the functions contained in the newly appended 12th Schedule continues to be unsettled. These, in order to be devolved to them, still depend on the will of the state governments. Hence, this Schedule serves merely as an illustrative list of local functions, not as a local list of functions that could have constitutional sanctity about it.

As regards taxing powers of urban local self-government—yet another objective of the 74th Constitution Amendment Act cited above—these powers have not been explicitly delineated in any Article in Part IX A of the Constitution that was newly inserted in it through the 74th CAA. Article 243X has provisions that could be said to be the nearest in addressing the taxing powers. It provides that the Legislature of a State may, by law, 'authorise a Municipality to levy, collect and appropriate such taxes, duties, tolls and fees in accordance with such procedure and subject to such limits'. The laws enacted even before the enactment of the 74th CAA by the various State Legislatures already have provisions for delegated powers of taxation for the ULSGs and since it is a delegated power, there hardly exists any element of autonomy for urban local self-government. Functions and tax authority are not yet devolved to the urban local self-governments in true sense of the term and in accordance with the conceptual groundings of 'devolution' per se. Neither the 74th CAA nor the newly enacted conformity legislations in different states have provisions for new sources of revenue. These legislations have neither given autonomy to the urban local self-governments in using the delegated sources of local revenue without previous approval of the state governments nor the authority for setting the rates of various local taxes.

Silence of the 74th CAA on the nature of executive system is yet an additional aspect of empowerment for urban governance that is not yet placed on a 'firmer footing'. Lack of concern observed in the constitutional provisions with respect to empowerment of politically elected heads of urban local self-governments has left one of the most important aspects of governance at the local level unaddressed completely. Ceremonial nature of elected heads coupled with brief tenure of the office of Mayors in Municipal Corporations that happen to be relatively stronger form of local government constituted especially in large cities, has also diluted the empowerment of urban local self-governments and weakened them substantially. As the 74th CAA is silent on the nature of executive system in them, the conformity legislations as well have conveniently ignored this important issue. The 74th CAA has at most ensured only (i) conducting of regular local government election, (ii) provided for new structure of local government and (iii) has rationalized transfer system through provisions with respect to the State Finance Commissions. But creating merely new structures that as well have flaws as discussed in Chapters 3 and 5, ensuring timely elections, and empowering weaker sections of the society, do not go far to empower the ULSGs. It has not and cannot contribute to real decentralization of power. In so far as Constitutional position of the ULBs is concerned, the 74th CAA has only granted to the urban local self-governments a constitutional right to exist as they can no longer be superseded *ad infinitum* in the post-74th CAA regime. But the blessings of the Constitution to them to have a long life do not carry much meaning without empowerment through devolution of functions, matching sources of local revenue, and a political executive system.

It is worth mentioning that the 'Statement of Objects and Reasons' for enactment of the 74th CAA also makes a mention of the context for the enactment of the 74th CAA. The context for enactment is reproduced below.

> In many States local bodies have become weak and ineffective on account of a variety of reasons, including the failure to hold regular elections, prolonged supersessions and inadequate devolution of powers and functions. As a result, Urban Local Bodies are not able to perform effectively as vibrant democratic units of self-government.

Such a realistic observation of the context for the enactment of the 74th CAA should have resulted in explicit provisions in the Constitution for going beyond the mere granting of constitutional right to exist. Though it mentions 'inadequate devolution of powers and functions', it is silent on three very important aspects of urban local governance—(i) empowerment of the elected heads of the ULSGs—Mayors and Chairpersons of urban local self-governments, (ii) devolving independent sources of revenue that could be used by the local government without approval of the state governments and (iii) Clarity on the local functional domain. Enactment of the 74th CAA notwithstanding, empowerment of the ULSGs is thus still unsettled. Going by the existing provisions of the Indian Constitution, it would be erroneous to call ULSGs as the 'third stratum of government' an expression used by many quite frequently. Constitutionally, the ULSGs cannot be said to be the third level of government because Article 1 provides thus: 'India, that is Bharat, shall be a Union of States'. It does not mention India as a union of local governments also. The First Schedule of the Constitution as well defines the territory of India comprising of territories of states and the union territories. Constitutionally, therefore, the ULSGs are even now 'creatures' of the state governments and they need to be created by the state governments and have to operate within the ambit of supervision and control of the state governments.

The existing constitutional position of the institutions of urban local self-governments all the more adds to the complexities of their empowerment as autonomous entities. The way, the 74th CAA is drafted amply reflects that any constitutional provision for strengthening the ULSGs needs to be conceived within the existing constitutional parameters of state autonomy provided for in the Constitution of India. Article 243P defines municipalities as 'institutions of self-government'. Article 243W envisages making them 'function as institutions of self-government'. But conceiving another tier of self-government at the local level within the existing walls of autonomy of state governments seems to be inconsistent and dichotomous. This constitutes the most complicated issue in empowerment of urban local self-governments. How do we re-invent an empowered local self-government for urban governance within the existing basic structure of the Constitution that grants autonomy to the States?

EMPOWERING OF LOCAL SELF-GOVERNMENT: THE OPTIONS

Going beyond granting to the urban local self-governments of a mere constitutional right to exist is thus beset with the present constitutional provisions that envisages semblance of a federal structure of autonomous states. The existing constitutional provisions wherein local governments happen to be the creatures of state governments seem to be too complex to find a way out for empowerment of the local government. The directive of the highest court of the land not to alter the basic structure of the Constitution of India adds additional complexity that seems to further elude any alternative intervention for empowerment of local government through radical constitutional refroms. As discussed in Chapter 5, the Second Administrative Reforms Commission (SARC) also alludes to this complexity much more explicitly. It mentions difficulties in empowerment of local government as autonomous entities within the existing framework of the Constitution which provides for constitutionally autonomous states. It also observes that the states wish 'minimum local empowerment' even though there is need for 'strong constitutional provision (for) mandating effective empowerment of local governments' (GoI 2007). Indifference of the state governments towards empowerment of urban local self-governments is expected to create serious dissent and protest from the former in case the latter are empowered by taking them out from List II of the Constitution. The National Commission to Review the Working of the Constitution (NCRWC) as well thought that existing constitutional provision 'does not guarantee assignment of a set of exclusive functions' to the local governments and performance of their role 'in governance depends on the regime that controls the government of a State' (GoI 2002). These complexities are too perplexing to permit empowerment of ULSGs through constitutional reforms. Any attempt to empower local government whether urban or rural, therefore, would need to be conceived within the existing constitutional framework. This offers limited options for local government empowerment. These options are discussed below.

Option I: Empowerment within the Existing Constitutional Framework

The National Commission to Review the Working of the Constitution (NCRWC) as well as the Second Administrative Reforms Commission was quite conscious of the existing constitutional constraints to provide for an empowered and autonomous local government for urban or the rural areas. Therefore, both the two Commissions that looked into the working of the local government and its existing constitutional status have suggested simplistic solutions to the empowerment of urban local self-governments within the existing constitutional framework only. NCRWC recommended declaring local governments as 'institutions of self-government'. This is presently constrained by Article 243W which provides discretion to the state governments in devolving of power and authority to the local governments. To recapitulate, Article 243W provides that Legislature of a State may endow 'the Municipalities with such powers and authority as may be necessary to enable them to function as institutions of self-government . . .'. The states have taken shelter under the expression 'may' that seems to be giving them discretion in devolving powers to the local governments. NCRWC, therefore, suggested amending the discretionary provision as mentioned below:

Subject to the provisions of this Constitution, the Legislature of a State *shall*, by law, vest the Municipalities with such powers and authority as are necessary to enable them to function as institutions of self-government and such law *shall* contain provisions for the devolution of powers and responsibilities upon the Municipalities, subject to such conditions as *shall* be specified therein, with respect to:

(a) preparation of plans for economic development and social justice;
(b) the implementation of schemes for economic development and social justice as *shall* be entrusted to them including those in relation to the matters listed in the Twelfth Schedule' (the proposed changes are depicted by words written in italics).

SARC, on the other hand, has suggested further improvement over the recommendation of the NCRWC cited above. It has added dimensions of subsidiarity in devolving of functions to local self-governments. Accordingly, it has suggested that devolving of functions need not be limited only to preparation and implementation of plans for economic development, social justice and the functions listed in the 12th Schedule. Devolving of powers, authority and functions to the ULSGs, according to SARC, must be 'in respect of all functions which can be performed at the local level including the functions in respect of the matters listed in the Twelfth Schedule'. As compared to the suggestions given by NCRWC, the amendment suggested by SARC is much more comprehensive.[2] The suggested amendment will thus completely alter the provisions contained in Article 243W. Obviously, unlike the existing discretionary nature of Article 243W, the amended Article 243W will have provisions that would be mandatory for the state governments. Whereas NCRWC recommended making it mandatory by only replacing the word 'may' by 'shall', SARC has suggested completely rephrasing the existing provisions in this Article. Such changes, if incorporated in the Constitution of India, are expected to contribute to the empowerment of local government in so far as the functional domain of the municipalities is concerned. There are, however, a couple of caveats with respect to giving an operational form to this suggestion. First, the central government would need to be receptive to this suggestion and get Article 243W amended by the Parliament along with other required amendments in the existing constitutional provisions introduced through the 74th CAA. Second, which is extremely important, the state governments would need to comply with this amendment by taking appropriate legislative action for devolving power and authority to the local self-governments.

Option II: Enactment of a Framework Legislation by the Parliament

The suggestions discussed above for making Article 243W mandatory seems to be quite sensible in the existing federal framework provided for in the Constitution. But such a simplistic solution notwithstanding, on a closer look, suggestions of both NCRWC and SARC discussed above, seem to be too much optimistic about disposition and will of the state governments in empowerment of the ULSGs. It needs to be mentioned that even if Article 243W is made mandatory by amending it in the manner suggested above, it is unlikely to work for empowerment of local government unless the state governments are favourably disposed to implement the amended provisions. Going by the attitude of the state governments in implementing the provisions of the 74th CAA in the past, the state governments are unlikely to comply with such a mandatory provision as well. This is based on the experience gained about half-hearted implementation of the provisions of the 74th CAA in the last more than a couple of decades of its enactment. As is discussed in Chapter 6 in greater length, even some of the important mandatory provisions of the 74th CAA (provisions with respect to DPC and MPC, for example) are not yet implemented by the state governments even after more than a couple of decades of enactment of the 74th CAA. SARC as well apprehended indifferent attitude of the state governments in empowering of local governments. In such a situation, what is then the option for empowerment of ULSGs?

As a possible option for empowerment of the urban local self-government, SARC rightly argues for much larger stake of the central government in empowerment of urban local self-government. In order to support this argument, it refers to a number of centre sector projects under the erstwhile Jawaharlal Nehru National Urban Renewal Mission (Jn-NURM) that involved huge financial investments[3] for augmentation of urban services in various states. As many as four Missions of the Central Government have succeeded JN-NURM (discussed in Chapter 6). These Missions as well have huge financial allocations for the states as an incentive for them for implementation of these Missions. SARC, therefore, strongly believed that huge financial allocation for urban sector by the central government justifies an enhanced stake of the central government in empowerment and strengthening of the urban local self-governments. An empowered and strengthened urban local self-government would ensure effective implementation of centrally assisted urban sector programmes and projects. SARC, therefore, rightly argues that the central government needs to play a much bigger role in urban sector reforms and empowerment of urban local self-government. Urban local self-governments, therefore, need to be empowered for effective implementation of these Missions.

The case for empowerment and strengthening of ULSGs is reinforced also by observations of official Committees and Working Groups constituted in the recent years. These expert bodies have especially referred to weak institutional capacity of the ULSGs which adversely affected effective and efficient use of JN-NURM funds (GoI 2010; 2011a; 2011b; 2012). Increasing rate of urbanization discussed earlier in this chapter is yet another factor that has led to emergence of new functions to be performed by the ULSGs. Effective performance of these functions at the local level positively impacts the national economic growth and the nation as a whole.

ULSGs, therefore, need to be empowered. But the question of bigger import is: how to go about it with the existing constitutional barriers and the imperatives for local government empowerment discussed above? SARC has tried to get over this constitutional barrier by exploring altogether a new alternative route for empowerment of local self-governments. In order to comprehend this option, we need to recapitulate suggestions of SARC, which examined the following constitutional options for empowerment of local government:

- To place in the Concurrent List (List III) Item 5 of List II (local governments) along with functions that are with the union, or with the states, but which are directly relevant to all three tiers of government. It would then facilitate appropriate, hierarchical and framework legislation by the union or the state. This would also shift 'functions' to 'subjects' with regard to local bodies and will enable the Parliament to legislate on the subject 'local governments' and thus the union could mandate the states the devolution of powers, functions and responsibilities to the local governments.
- To create List IV in the Constitution containing local functions as well as devolving certain legislative powers to the local government.
- To put in place a single legally binding legislative framework providing functional space to both state and local governments as in South Africa.[4]

Although SARC considered these options for empowerment of ULSGs, but as discussed in Chapter 5, it did not favour either creating List IV in the Constitution or transferring Local Government (Item 5) from List II to the List III. It finally suggested yet another simplistic way out—enactment of a framework legislation by the Parliament under Article 252 of the Constitution.[5] This Article empowers the Parliament to legislate for two or more states provided that all the legislatures of these states adopt a resolution to this effect. It also provides that the law passed by the Parliament in such a manner shall apply to any other state if a resolution is passed by other states for adopting this law. The suggestion given by SARC seemingly sounds appealing. However, the big question is: will it really work? Will the states adopt such framework legislation and also implement provisions incorporated in this legislation? Based again on the attitude of a very large number of states in the past, it is felt that adoption of such an Act by Parliament is unlikely to be adopted and implemented by the state governments especially for two important reasons:

1. Diverse political parties ruling in different states and an aggressive contemporary politics that has come to the fore in states in recent years. In such an environment, the states are unlikely to be amenable to adopt and implement a framework legislation enacted by the Parliament.[6] In such a political environment, it is also equally doubtful if the states will agree to pass a resolution for enactment of a framework legislation by the Parliament.
2. As mentioned before, even the mandatory provisions of the Constitution have remained unimplemented in the last more than a couple of decades, there is all the more reason to believe that state governments may not be receptive to provisions of the framework legislation as well and hence may not comply with the provisions of this legislation.

Option III: Creating List IV in the Constitution

In view of the above, creating a local list in the Constitution seems to be the only workable option for empowerment of the ULSGs. But this happens to be too radical a step in the existing aggressive politics observed in different states. Also such a radical step is unlikely to sustain legal scrutiny by the courts, especially with the directive of the highest court of the land not to alter the basic structure of the Constitution. This is also unlikely to help in arriving at a political consensus amongst the various state governments for local government empowerment. Besides, it involves tremendous political risks of not only in arriving at a consensus amongst the state governments but also for ensuring functioning of an empowered local government having constitutional autonomy. The state governments are most likely to abhor functioning of such an empowered local self-government. The situation is likely to be exacerbated by absence of trust amongst most of the state governments for the institutions of local self-governments with larger extent of empowerment and autonomy.

OPTION IV: CREATING POLITICAL CONSENSUS FOR EMPOWERMENT WITHIN THE EXISTING CONSTITUTIONAL FRAMEWORK

The previous three options discussed above seem to have limitations that are unlikely to work. These options also seem to be susceptible to the possible risk of indifference of the state governments towards empowerment of local self-government. If these options are unlikely to be workable in the existing political environment, a possible remedy for empowerment of local government then lies in creating a consensus and better appreciation amongst the state governments for putting in place an empowered, strong and strengthened local government that could have robust institutional capacity for urban governance and effective, efficient, inclusive and responsive delivery of urban services. The state of Kerala is an example of this where local government is qualitatively different from other states. In the state of Kerala, elected Mayors/Chairpersons are the real political executives using effectively the sources of revenue devolved to the urban local self-governments. The Municipal Commissioner in the state is designated as Secretary who is accountable to the Mayor and the elected Council. An attempt has been made in this state to replicate façade of a state government at the local level where the political executive, like the Chief Minister in a state, is in perfect command of local governance and service delivery. The State Government has willingly transferred 165 functions to the urban local self-governments by clustering them into 29 groups and has simultaneously transferred funds and functionaries to the urban local self-governments. Fiscal impact of decentralization in the State is reflected in 45 times increase in the total receipts of ULSGs from just Rs. 247 crore in 1993-4 when the 74th CAA came into being to Rs. 10,980 crore in 2013-14. This constitutes 2.4 per cent of the Gross State Domestic Product. The state government devolved 35-40 per cent of State Plan Fund during 9th Five Year Plan to the local self-government (Oomen 2017). Kerala also has robust participatory mechanisms and processes in the form of Community Development Society and People's Campaign for Planning that positively help in manifestation of aspirations of the local communities in governance and service delivery. Also, it has largely enhanced local government accountability and transparency in urban governance.

There could be several ways of creating consensus for empowerment and strengthening of urban local self-governments. Amongst them, reviving the moribund Central Council of Local Government and Urban Development Ministers discussed in Chapter 2, seems to be a proper way to do it. This could be used as a forum for creating a national consensus in the states for empowerment of urban local self-governments by getting motivation from the Kerala experience. In addition to using this forum for creating political consensus amongst the state governments, the central government would also need to have policy dialogues with the state governments through series of structured consultations with Chief Ministers of various states for identifying the aspects of local governance that need the required legislative changes for empowerment and strengthening. It requires not merely reviving the Central Council of Urban Development and Urban Development Ministers but also a persistent drive by the central government for creating national consensus about empowerment and strengthening of urban local self-governments.

Once a consensus is created amongst the state governments, it will facilitate a review of the existing municipal laws by constituting expert groups/committees for identification of areas that need legislative support and changes for empowerment and strengthening of urban local self-governments. These steps are in the nature of imperatives given the existing indifference of the state governments that acts as an obstacle in strengthening urban local self-government. This would require the Ministry of Urban Development of the central government now renamed as the Ministry of Housing and Urban Affairs (MoHUA) to be much more pro-active for creating the much needed political consensus for empowerment. Need for persistent dialogue with the state governments entails that the capacity of the MoHUA itself would need to be developed for engaging with the states on a sustained basis. This option thus very well fits into the emerging greater stake of the central government in empowerment and strengthening of urban local self-governments. These steps would essentially need to be taken on the demand side of decentralization and its strengthening. On the supply side of decentralization, focused attention shall have to be given to devise appropriate strategy especially for strengthening of urban local self-government organizations and staffing. Deliberate and conscious attempts are required even now for developing their organizational capacity that could enable them to discharge the functions mandated to them. The contemporary literature offers useful modalities of how to go about it. These are discussed in Chapter 8.

In the consensus-based scheme of decentralization and empowerment of urban local self-governments as suggested above, the state governments would need to look into their existing municipal laws and provide for mechanisms, systems and procedures for an empowered and strengthened local government. An empowered local self-government would also require creation of participatory structures, adopting mechanisms and process for popular mobilization for enhancing local government transparency and accountability. This would need to be accompanied by efforts for inculcating a culture of participation amongst the citizens. In the states of Kerala, Gujarat, and Karnataka, the quality of local self-governance is a bit different also because of prevalence and even a long tradition of participatory processes and existence of a culture of cooperation in these states. Much would be desired, therefore, to inculcate participatory culture in other states as well. It is worth mentioning here that a case study of participatory planning in a West Bengal district has recently brought to light limitations of empowered Panchayati Raj institutions in this State in enabling the villagers especially the disadvantaged classes in improving their socio-economic status. The state of West Bengal, it needs to be mentioned, created altogether refurbished, representative, participatory and empowered Panchayati Raj institutions with substantial devolved powers to them in the state along with participatory structures and processes for ushering in the required socio-economic changes. These grassroot institutions were also empowered that provided opportunities especially to the disadvantaged classes to wield power and exploit economic opportunities through a process of participatory self-governance. Yet the process of participatory planning, an important ingredient of empowered rural local self-government in the state, could not yield the desired result largely because of absence of a culture of participation in the state (Sen 2014).

In any scheme of empowerment and strengthening of local self-government—whether urban or rural—it is essential that the state governments have to be at the centre stage for implementation of Article 234W. Municipal services are highly localized in nature and the local self-governments are the best form of self-government for effective discharge of local functions and for managing the cities and towns as the third tier of government. A primer prepared by the Ministry of Urban Development very aptly flags the issues in this regard. It alludes to constraints in implementing the provisions of the 74th CAA in its totality largely because the devolution of functions to the urban local self-governments have not been accompanied by adequate transfer of sources of local revenue, their financial autonomy is undermined by the practice of state government approval of enhancements in the rates of taxes and user charges, and they have limited powers to institute new taxes.[7] The state governments would, therefore, need to devolve powers to the urban local self-governments for their empowerment as institutions of self-government. This, as discussed above, has to be preceded by insistent stance on part of the central government for creating a consensus amongst the state governments about the need for effective urban governance and putting parameters of effective urban governance that could be replicated by the states. Once there is a consensus about it, the means to effectuate the consensus either through new constitutional provisions or through revisiting the existing municipal laws by the state governments could follow. Improvements in the framework of governance and laws could be brought about by providing for the agreed upon parameters including mechanisms for participatory governance contained in the central government's Nagar Raj Bill that provides semblance to direct democracy.

Evaluation of various provisions of the 74th CAA in Chapter 3 and observations as well as suggestions of (i) the National Commission to Review the Working of the Constitution and (ii) the Second Administrative Reforms Commission discussed in Chapter 5 offer valuable suggestions for refurbishing the urban local self-governments. In any scheme of their empowerment or revisiting the Constitution (74th Amendment) Act, 1992, these suggestions would need to be taken into account. The 74th CAA has gaps. The 'conformity legislations' do not really 'conform' to the constitutional provisions of the 74th CAA that itself have quite many gaps. Empowerment has been additionally impacted by half hearted implementation by the state governments. These aberrations need to be addressed for enabling the urban local self-governments to be in total command of urban governance and service delivery. They must be enabled to work and perform as local government in true sense of the term.

Besides empowerment and strengthening, it is also an imperative that the urban local self-governments would need to be much more accountable. Even within the existing legal framework, the ULSGs have not effectively discharged their responsibility for effective exploitation of sources of revenue and performing the functions devolved to them. This is reflected in poor coverage of all lands and buildings located within the local government areas by their Property Tax net that constitutes by far the single most important source of local revenue, poor collection efficiency of taxes and user charges, and deficiencies in accounting and audit of funds raised by them. Even within the existing legislative framework and despite serious fiscal stress faced by them, most of the ULSGs have not yet used all the local tax instruments devolved to them. Their unwillingness to charge is quite conspicuous even though there is a willingness to pay amongst the users of municipal services provided the service delivery is effective, reliable and responsive. Functionaries manning urban governance need to appreciate that good economics is not a bad politics; effective, inclusive and responsive service delivery motivates the users of municipal services to pay. The State Finance Commissions as well need to be responsive to the terms of reference given to them. The Terms of Reference of the State Finance Commissions, for example, include suggesting ways and means of strengthening municipal finance system. They would, therefore, need to factor in their analysis the additional scope for generation of additional financial resources from the existing sources as a target for the ULSGs and a workable strategy for achieving the set target for generation of additional revenue, identify the gap between the expenditure required to be incurred by them according to normative service standards and the own source of revenue along with fiscal transfers from the higher levels of government and then suggests a scheme of transfers. Effective use of own sources of revenue would be thus built into the framework of transfers. It will go a long way in making the ULSGs financially prudent and accountable which they are not at the moment.

The state governments, on their part, need to have trust in institutions of urban local self-governments. This has recently been emphasized by the 14th Finance Commission. The Commission recognized that there is a need to trust and have respect for local bodies as 'institutions of local self-government'. The implicit distrust on part of the state governments, therefore, needs to give way to trust in institutions of local self-government through devolving of functions, devolution of buoyant sources of revenue, deepening of democracy at the local level and stewardship of local government by the state governments as has actualized in Kerala. The pace of urbanization, challenges posed by it for effective urban governance, vital significance of responsive and inclusive service delivery and the catalytic role of cities and towns in enhancing national economic growth are too critically important to be ignored. Even the existing agenda of the central government for creating one hundred smart cities, for its success is ineluctably dependent on the extent to which the municipal entities are transformed into smart urban local self-government. It calls for altogether different quality of urban governance wherein all the urban services are brought under the single umbrella of urban self-government and the elected Chairperson is empowered to be in full command of governance and service delivery. It is worth quoting the statement of one of the former mayors of Philadelphia. Mayor Nutter considered his city government of Philadelphia as a 'business enterprise', treated the 17-member City Council as the Board of Directors, regarded the taxpayers of his local government as the shareholders; and deemed the residents of the city of Philadelphia as 1.5 million customers. He contemplated thus: 'I'm fighting for market share every day, and if I don't deliver my product more efficiently and effectively and cheaply, my customer base will find somebody else' (IBM 2013). Obviously, managing the city government of Philadelphia was a passion for him. Besides empowerment, therefore, the Mayors/Chairperson of ULSGs in the country would as well need to develop such a passion for urban governance. They would need to strive that strengthening of urban governance would need to have a strategy that must include all the parameters of strengthening, all the elements of institutional capacity development discussed in Chapter 8. The state governments would need to play a supportive role in such an endeavour. This will enable ULSGs to use even the existing sources of revenue to the optimum; devolving of additional sources of revenue that have buoyancy will further add to the fiscal health of urban local self-governments.

Strengthening and empowerment of ULSGs, as discussed above, entails addressing both demand and supply side of decentralization. It calls for blending of elements of (i) empowerment, (ii) local government accountability and transparency, and (iii) local government organisational capacity development (discussed in the next chapter). Isolated intervention by focusing only on one of these elements of empowerment is unlikely to achieve the desired result.

NOTES

1. Liveability Index assesses cities on their performance across five dimensions of a 'liveable city'—stability, health care, culture and the environment, education, and infrastructure.
2. After the proposed amendment by SARC, Article 243W will read as: 'Subject to the provisions of this Constitution, the Legislature of a State shall, by law, vest the Municipalities with such powers and authority as are necessary to enable them to function as institutions of self-government in respect of all functions which can be performed at the local level including the functions in respect of the matters listed in the Twelfth Schedule'.

3. Jn-NURM was launched in 2005, and now (in 2015) the new government has lunched Atal Mission for Rejuvenation of Urban Transformation (AMRUT), Smart City, Heritage City Development and Augmentation Yojna (HRIDAY), and Swachh Bharat in mission mode.
4. Article 40 of the South Africa Constitution provides that in the Republic of South Africa, government is constituted of national, provincial and local spheres of government which are distinctive, interdependent and interrelated. The Constitution also provides that all spheres of government must observe and adhere to the principles in this chapter and must conduct their activities within the parameters that the chapter provides. It enshrines yet another important Principle that envisages that all spheres of government and all organs of state within each sphere must
   - respect the constitutional status, institutions, powers and functions of government in the other spheres;
   - not assume any power or function except those conferred on them in terms of the Constitution;
   - exercise their powers and perform their functions in a manner that does not encroach on the geographical, functional or institutional integrity of government in another sphere; and cooperate with one another in mutual trust and good faith (emphasis added).
5. Article 252 of the Indian Constitution provides thus: (1) If it appears to the Legislatures of two or more States to be desirable that any of the matters with respect to which Parliament has no power to make laws for the states except as provided in articles 249 and 250 should be regulated in such States by Parliament by law, and if resolutions to that effect are passed by all the Houses of the Legislatures of those States , it shall be lawful for Parliament to pass an Act for regulating that matter accordingly, and any Act so passed shall apply to such states and to any other state by which it is adopted afterwards by resolution passed in that behalf by the House or, where there are two Houses, by each of the Houses of the Legislature of that state. (2) Any Act so passed by Parliament may be amended or repealed by an Act of Parliament passed or adopted in like manner but shall not, as respects any State to which it applies, be amended or repealed by an Act of the Legislature of that State.
6. Intense opposition by the political parties and the state governments to the enactment of strong Lokayukta for states, proposal of the central government in the recent past for creation of a national security outfit at the national level for fighting terrorism testify the difficulties in arriving at a political consensus about enactment of a framework legislation on local government by the Parliament.

7. *Implementation of the 74th Constitutional Amendment and Integrated City Planning and Delivery Functions*, Ministry of Urban Development, jnnurm.nic.in/wp-content/uploads/2011/01

REFERENCES

Figom, Debra, Kim Walesh, Mark Danaj, and Dr. Frank Benest (no date), 'What's the Future of Local Government?', An Alliance White Paper Intended to Provoke a Needed Conversation, WWW. icma.org/en/icma/knowledge.

Government of India, 2007, *Sixth Report of the Second Administrative Reform Commission, Local Govenance: An Inspiring Journey into the Future.* New Delhi: Ministry of Personnel, Public Grievances and Pensions, Department of Administrative Reform and Public Grievances.

——, 2010, *Mid-term Appraisal of the Eleventh Five Year Plan*, New Delhi: Planning Commission.

—— (High Powered Expert Committee for Estimating the Investment Requirements for Urban Infrastructure and Services), 2011a, *Report on Indian Infrastructure and Services.* New Delhi: Ministry of Urban Development.

——, 2011b, *Urban Development Management for the Formulation of the Twelfth Five Year Plan (2012-2017), Report of the Working Group on Capacity Building*, New Delhi: Planning Commission.

—— (Steering Committee on Urbanization), 2012. Report of the Steering Committee on Urbanization, Twelfth Fiver Year Plan (2012-17), New Delhi: Planning Commission.

IBM, *'How to Re-invent a City: Mayors' Lesson from Smart City Challenge,'* IBM Smart Cities White Paper, 2013, http://smartercitieschallenge.org/scc/executive_reports/IBM-SCC-How-to-Reinvent-a-City-Jan-2013-v2.pdf

Oommen, M.A., 2017, 'Understanding Decentralised Governance and Making it a Viable Component of Democracy and Development in Kerala', *Nagarlok*, pp. 56-74.

Price, Waterhouse Coopers, 'Cities of the Future: Global Competition, Local Leadership', http://www.pwc.com/gx/en/government-public-services/issues-trends/index.jhtml

Sen, Payel, 2014, 'Participatory Planning in Rural West Bengal: A Study of Birbhum District', Ph.D thesis (unpublished), Kolkata: University of Calcutta.

The Global Commission on the Economy and Climate, 2014, *Better Growth, Better Climate: The New Climatae Economy Report*, Washington, DC: The World Resources Institute.

UN-HABITAT, 2012, *State of the World's Cities, 2012-2013, Prosperity of Cities*, Nairobi: United Nations Human Settlements Programme.

World Bank Group, 2015, *Leveraging Urbanization in South Asia: Managing Spatial Transformation for Prosperity and Livability*, http://www.worldbank.org./en/region/publication.

CHAPTER 8

Strengthening Urban Local Self-Government: Organizational Capacity Development

The initiative taken for decentralization through enactment of the Constitution (74th Amendment) Act, 1992 for empowerment of urban local self-government, the gaps in it and the possible options for addressing these gaps by revisiting the scheme of decentralization have been extensively discussed in the earlier chapters. It needs to be mentioned, however, that decentralization through devolution of power and authority, on its own, is unlikely to enable them to discharge their functions efficiently. Undoubtedly, if decentralization is conceived and implemented properly, it will definitely empower them. It is, however, unlikely to strengthen their administrative capability. Analysis of constitutional provisions and also the existing legal framework in major states have indicated that empowerment of urban local self-governments require a fresh look. Empowerment without strengthening organizational capability will hardly enable the urban local self-governments in efficient performance of functions required to be discharged by them. For this, the urban local self-governments need to have robust organizational capacity for making cities and towns livable, enhancing the quality of urban life and attracting investments for economic growth through good governance and service delivery. Presently, they lack the required organizational capacity for discharge of their functions and performance of their role. Most of them, especially those constituted in small and medium towns which are the largest in number, are not able to discharge even their basic functions of keeping urban settlements clean and wholesome. Effective, efficient, inclusive and responsive governance and service delivery essentially requires that they should also have the needed organizational capability to perform their mandated functions. Empowerment, therefore, needs to be accompanied by appropriate strategy for strengthening their organizational capacity. This chapter, therefore, discusses the strategy for strengthening their organizational capacity. It first demystifies the connotation of 'capacity'. Subsequently, it conceptualizes a framework of capacity development[1] and the ways in which organizational capacity of the urban local self-governments could be enhanced so that they could be enabled to perform their functions effectively and in responsive and equitable manner.

CAPACITY DEVELOPMENT: THE CONCEPT

In simple terms, 'capacity' means the ability to perform the entrusted functions. The 'ability to perform' is equally important in relation to an individual, a group of individuals, an organization or a society. This is so because a group is formed of individuals only and a number of groups go to form an organization. Hence 'capacity' means capacity of an individual, or a group or an organization and even of a society to perform the functions entrusted to them. *The Oxford Dictionary* defines 'capacity' as 'the ability or power to do something'. The definition of capacity thus connotes that an individual, a group or an organization or a society should have enough capacity to effectively discharge functions that are expected of them. The literature on capacity building contains a number of formal definitions of capacity. Some of them are contained in Box 1.

The definitions given in Box 1 allude basically to ability, competency and capability to perform. Connolly and Lukas, in order to find an answer to 'what is capacity?' that needs to be developed, after pursuing serious enquiry into this concept, concluded that *capacity* includes capabilities, knowledge, and resources that a non-profit organization needs in order to fulfil its mission through a blend of sound management, strong governance, and a persistent rededication to achieving results (Connolly and Lukas 2002). Capacity building, according to this definition, requires a blending of (i) sound management, (ii) strong governance, and (iii) re-

BOX 1: DEFINITIONS OF CAPACITY DEVELOPMENT/BUILDING

An organization with capacity has the ability to function as resilient, strategic and autonomous entity (Kaplan 1999).

Capacity represents the potential for using resources effectively and maintaining gains in performance with gradually reduced levels of external support (LaFond and Brown 2003).

Capacity is the potential to perform (Horton et al. 2003).

Capacity is the ability of people, organizations and society as a whole to manage their affairs successfully (OECD 2006).

Capacity is that emergent contribution of attributes that enable a human system to create development value (Morgan 2006).

Capacity means the ability of human system to perform, sustain itself and self-renew' (Ubels et al. 2010).

dedication of the staff and the organization in achieving organizational mission. Above all, the work force in an organization, must have skills and competency to perform. This definition con-tains a combination of skills, sound management, strong governance and the motivation of the workforce at all levels in an organ-ization and, therefore, it seems to be quite apt in describing the urban local self-government context that combines a unique blending of governance and management of service delivery.

The definitions given above give a flavour of the concept of capacity and capacity development, its meaning and import as well as its implications. In addition to these definitions, the United Nations Development Programme (UNDP) has defined capacity development most succinctly. It is defined in a manner that also helps in comprehending important aspects of capacity development. According to the UNDP definition, capacity development/building is:

the process by which individuals, groups, organizations, institutions and societies increase their abilities to: (1) perform core functions, solve problems, and define and achieve objectives; and (2) understand and deal with their development needs in a broad context and in a sustainable manner. (UNDP 1997)

Other donor agencies as well have defined capacity development in their own ways. Sustained interest of donor institutions in capacity development has, therefore, led to a variety of definitions. The literature on this subject contains a number of definitions and the ways in which it has been defined. The essence of these definitions points to the need for existence of ability, competence and capability for performance of functions. Individuals and groups in an organization or in a society must have ability, competence and capability to perform. Jan Ubels et al. have added yet another dimension to the concept of capacity by referring to 'ability of human system to perform, sustain itself and self-renew' (Ubels et al. 2010).

A careful reading of the definitions given above suggests a number of attributes of capacity development. These definitions suggest that capacity development is (i) not a static concept; it needs to be developed on a sustained basis with changing times, (ii) it relates to human system that entails different scales or levels in an organization, (iii) it is not limited to devising management tools or training rather points to much broader aspects such as human system's ability to appreciate organizational goals, and (iv) to build and use its resources for accomplishment of that end. It is about performing, sustaining and self renewing. It 'is about creating some form of added value for the members and the outside world (perform), it is about staying alive and active (sustain), it is about adjusting and developing over time (self-renew) on the basis of external pressures and internal drivers' (ibid.). It is generally believed that development of competency and capability of individuals working in an organization will contribute to capacity development of the organization itself. However, Morgan's interpretation distinguishes capacity development of individuals and an organization. For this, he differentiates between the terms 'competency' and 'capability' the two components of capacity. 'Competency', according to him, denotes specific abilities of individuals. 'Capability' indicates specific abilities of organizational sub-systems. A capacity development/ building strategy, therefore, will need to develop competence of the employees as also the abilities of an organization to perform and achieve organizational goals. It needs to be mentioned that development of competence will also need to be accompanied by interventions that will add to the motivation of employees in an organization.

CAPACITY DEVELOPMENT: EVOLUTION OF THE CONCEPT

Capacity development attracted attention especially after the end of the Second World War. A number of national economies were shattered by the Second World War. On a positive side, it also resulted in end of prolonged colonial rule in some of the countries. The war-revaged national economies and the new countries that emerged as sovereign independent nations after the end of colonial rule had to be reconstructed all over again. The concern for reconstruction of national economies destroyed by the war and development of the new independent countries led to devising of a strategy known as the Marshal Plan. The Marshal Plan conceived a scheme of international development cooperation that was based on the premise that achieving development goals required a two-pronged approach of (i) financial assistance, and (ii) technical assistance. An interest was shown in development of capacity of the countries that received funds under this scheme so that they could effectively use the funds for development. Whereas financial assistance was given to address resource and financial constraints confronting the countries, technical assistance was given to them for filling the skill gaps and for capacity development. This was done by making available foreign expertise to the countries that were given financial assistance under international development cooperation. Technical cooperation involved capacity development through technical training and was subsequently included in the lending programme of almost all the international financial agencies like World Bank, United Nations and its affiliates, and non-government organizations. Conceived in the context of international development cooperation, the concept of capacity development subsequently was applied to both profit and not-for-profit organizations for effective accomplishment of their organizational missions. Although capacity development originated after the Second World War in the context of reconstruction and development of national economies, it took considerably long period of time for its application as a strategy in enhancing organizational capability of urban local self-governments that generally have weak organizational capacity. However, considerably long time taken in extending it in the case of urban local self-governments also helped in substantial sharpening of capacity development as a strategy for strengthening organizational efficiency. Used widely by a host of international donor agencies and non-profit organizations, there exist diverse interpretations of capacity and capacity building/development. A simplistic and popular interpretation of capacity building/development happens to be training which it is not; training, as discussed subsequently in this chapter, constitutes only a small part of the total capacity building/development strategy.

CAPACITY DEFICIT IN MUNICIPAL GOVERNMENTS

Having surveyed various definitions of capacity development and clarified it as a concept, the next question is: do the urban local self-governments really need to adopt it as a strategy for effective governance and service delivery? Answer to this question is to be found by looking at the status of their existing organizational capacity. Lack of organizational capacity of urban local self-governments (ULSGs) becomes evident even to a casual visitor to an urban settlement when he comes across piles of garbage stored even by the road side, unclean streets, and open drains emitting offensive odour. Weak organizational capacity is also reflected in the reports of a number of official Committees, Working Groups, and a Commission constituted in the recent past. A sample of the observations of these expert bodies is given below:

The Mid-term Appraisal of the 11th Five Year Plan revealed that central assistance is invariably being given to develop 'hard infrastructure' rather than the 'soft infrastructure' which could substantially contribute to the organizational capacity of the urban local self-governments. It further observed that financial assistance for that central assistance is invariably being given to develop 'hard infrastructure' rather than the 'soft infrastructure' which could substantially contribute to the organizational capacity of the urban local self-governments. It further observed that financial assistance for only the hard infrastructure is invariably given with an ostensible hope that capacity development (the soft infrastructure) will be taken care by the cities on their own (GoI 2010). The Mid-term Appraisal also highlighted inadequate utilization of funds by the urban local self-governments due to lack of their organizational capacity. Weak local government capacity, in particular, also adversely affected implementation of Jn-NURM, a programme with huge financial allocation for augmentation of basic urban services and infrastructure. A Working Group on Capacity Building constituted for management of urban development during the 12th Five Year Plan (2012-17) avers that sub-optimal level of performance of the projects under Jn-NURM—the flagship programme of the central government—was largely because of lack of capacity of urban local self-governments (GoI 2011a). Through a review of schemes, and activities of capacity building undertaken during the 11th Plan, this Working Group concluded that though a wide range of capacity building initiatives have been taken at various levels, the absorptive capacity of the urban local self-governments is limited and is beset with inherent demand side constraints. It highlighted a significant issue, i.e. the inability of states and cities to implement capacity building programmes at a scale and pace that will make a significant difference to the way in which our cities are governed and large scale programmes are implemented. As a result, the cities are not in a position to bring about a quantum shift in the delivery of services. It points out that even though the ambitious Jn-NURM took a holistic view of capacity building, absence of a right eco-system and the deficiencies on the supply side have led to sub-optimal achievement of intended objectives.

Similarly, Report of a reputed global institute has ascribed not-so-successful implementation of the prestigious Jn-NURM to the fact that 'Many states and cities have been unable to leverage available funds or implement reforms because of a lack of local capacity and technical expertise' (McKinsey Global Institute 2010). It further going structural transformation of Indian economy needs synergy from the cities that have assumed the role of engines of economic growth. According to the report of a High Powered Committee on urban infrastructure and services, this requires a concerted effort to strengthen the capacity of institutions and persons who will facilitate this process to deliver faster and more inclusive growth of the economy (GoI 2011b). Yet another official Committee notes that most urban local self-governments 'across the country do not have the required expertise to develop public private partnerships, manage projects and their finances. Consequently, their ability to implement reforms and projects is constrained' (GoI 2012). It notes that 'Insufficient capacity and capability lies at the heart of India's urban challenges'. Views of the Second Administrative Reforms Commission (SARC) are not different. It as well points to 'capacity deficit' in municipal organizations and has noted that 'sustained, well planned enabling exercises need to be undertaken to ensure that the implementing agencies have the capacity and the capability to deal with the challenges in undertaking and implementing these major national programmes apart from being able to fulfil their statutory functions' (GoI 2007).

Weak capacity of ULSGs is supported also by a comprehensive survey conducted by Janaagraha on an annual basis. Annual Survey of India's City Systems (ASICS) conducted by Bangalore based Janaagraha provides yet another insight on weak capacities of our cities. ASICS was launched in 2013 with a modest coverage of 11 cities along with the cities of New York and London as the benchmark cities. The number of cities for ASICS increased to 21 from 2014 onwards. The cities are evaluated on the basis of four city systems such as (i) Urban Planning and Design (Spatial Planning, Urban Design standards), (ii) Urban Capacities and Resources (Municipal Finance, Municipal Staffing, Performance Management and Process efficiencies), (iii) Empowered and Legitimate Political Representation (Powers and functions and legitimacy of city council and elected leaders), and (iv) Transparency, Accountability and Participation (public disclosure of civic data, accountability for service levels and citizen services, citizen participation in neighbourhood decisions). Janaagraha rightly treats these 'city systems' interconnected that throws light on the 'root causes and the systemic nature of our cities, their challenges and solution'. The cities are evaluated by finding answers to 11 principal questions with respect to the four city systems and as many as 83 parameters to get at the root causes of maladies the cities are afflicted with (Janaagrah 2013; 2014; 2015). Thus the Janaagraha Survey is quite comprehensive in diagnosing the capacities of the cities. The cities are evaluated on a scale of 0 to 10 and scores are given to the cities on the basis of where they stand on this scale on the basis of these parameters. The scores obtained by the cities along with the benchmark cities of New York and London are contained in Table 1 (Annex X).

Table 1 (Annex X) depicts two important things. First, even the cities which are India's prime metropolitan cities have been getting low score on all the four city systems. The score varies from 2.2 to 4.2 with respect to urban planning and design against the score of 8.8 to 10 for New York and London. This in case of urban capacities and resources is in the range of 0.9 to 5.3 against the score of 9.9 to 10 for New York and 8.1 to 10 for London. For other city systems as well the range is on a much lower side as compared to the two benchmark cities. Second, the scores given to the four city systems have either been static in the last three years or have only marginally changed. The Janaagraha Survey thus substantiates the observations of the expert bodies discussed above with regard to organizational capabilities.

Observations of official expert groups discussed above thus indicate weak organizational capacity of urban local self-governments. The observations cited above also substantiate absence of required capacity of the urban local self-government institutions. This has been hindering effective, inclusive and responsive governance and service delivery by them. Yet it is perplexing to note that whereas the diagnosis of a weak institutional capacity happens to be quite objective, the prescription for dealing with it is largely out of place. When it comes to suggesting ways for enhancing institutional capacity of the ULSGs, the solution most often is found limited and confined to only training. All the official reports mentioned above largely talk of (i) conducting of short term training courses,

(ii) creation of new resource centres for training, and (iii) conducting of long term courses in urban management. There is only isolated reference to creation of municipal cadre in one of the official reports. As discussed subsequently in this chapter, there are a few exceptions to this general prescription for enhancing urban local self-governments' capacity. SARC, for example, points to the existing 'erroneous notion that capacity relates only to training and imparting new skills to employees'. Capacity development is much more comprehensive a strategy than mere training. SARC rightly suggests that capacity development has two equally important components namely Individual Development and Organizational Development' (GoI 2007). In the contemporary Indian public policy, perception of capacity development is limited to training only which indicates a short sighted view of capacity building/development. Organizational capacity of the urban local self-governments needs to be strengthened through focused and holistic strategy of capacity development, not through training alone.

CONCEPTUAL FRAMEWORK FOR CAPACITY DEVELOPMENT

If capacity development has to be looked upon as a strategy that is much more than mere training, which it must be, it needs to be conceived within a proper conceptual framework. The Working Group on Capacity Development mentioned above also stressed the need for looking at ways and means of capacity building within a formal conceptual framework. It emphasized the need to prepare a framework of capacity building that would guide actual action for capacity development (GoI 2011a). What is important, therefore, is to look for the desired framework for capacity development.

A meaningful capacity building framework should have a coherent set of features, should also have the necessary elements which should help devise a strategy for capacity building. At the same time, the strategy should also be based on established experiential understanding so that it is not reduced to a utopia but has abilities to enhance capacity of work organizations of urban local self-governments. Such a framework will better provide the much needed insight not only for understanding 'capacity' and how to develop it but also for conceptualizing a strategy for capacity development in a real live situation. The literature on capacity development contains quite a few frameworks within which one could conceive and develop a capacity building strategy. A useful framework, in this regard, was developed by Kaplan in 1999 (Kaplan 1999). Kaplan developed this framework in the context of capacity development of an NGO—the Community Development Resource Association (CDRA) in South Africa. The framework developed by Kaplan explains capacity development strategy in terms of seven inter-related elements viz (i) Context and Conceptual Framework, (ii) Vision, (iii) Strategy, (iv) Culture, (v) Structure, (vi) Skills, and (vii) Material Resources.[2] Subsequently in 2008, Baser and Morgan also provided an outline of capacity building framework that as well helps in working out a strategy (Baser and Morgan 2008). Besides these, there are other models of capacity building framework notably Mintzberg's six valid organizational configurations and Seven S of McKinsey.[3] Connolly and Lukas (2002) as well suggest a seven point initiative for capacity development. These are (1) Mission, Vision, and Strategy, (2) Governance and Leadership, (3) Programme Delivery and Impact, (4) Strategic Relationship, (5) Finance, (6) Internal Operations and (7) Management. According to them, mission, vision, and strategy constitute the driving force that gives an organization its direction and purpose. Governance and leadership is like the lubricant that keeps all the parts of governance machine aligned and moving. Programme delivery and impact constitute primary reasons for existence of an organization just as profit is for a business organization. Strategic relationships, finance, and internal operations and management are all necessary mechanisms to achieve an organization's ends. Strategic relationship enables it in maintaining strong relationship with its constituents through communication and partnerships. Finance is of utmost importance in ensuring that its revenues are diversified, stable and sufficient for meeting mission and goals. Internal operations and management suggests that the organization has efficient and effective operations and strong management support systems (Connolly and Lukas 2002). Pellenburg and others, however, look at only three crucially important parameters for capacity development in the context of urban local self-governments. These include (i) institutional and legal framework; (ii) organizational development, and (iii) human resource development (Pellenburg et al. 1998). These three important parameters together contribute to strengthening the capability for additional financial resource mobilization and financial management system and hence drive organizational capacity of the urban local self-governments. Nevertheless, a fourth variable—Fiscal Strength and Financial Management System—needs to be added to it so that municipal capacity to effectively exploit the devolved fiscal tools is developed and strengthened.

The Steering Committee on Urbanization for the 12th Five Year Plan constituted by the erstwhile Planning Commission referred to altogether different elements for capacity development as compared to the ones that form part of Kaplan's framework mentioned above. The elements suggested by the Steering Committee on Urbanization include (i) formal structures, (ii) dedicated cadres, (iii) staffing norms, (iv) organizational procedures, (v) job descriptions, and (vi) pay scales for injecting capacity amongst the urban local self-governments (GoI 2012). Besides these elements, the Steering Committee also suggested commitment of urban local self-governments to common vision and mission, shared norms and values amongst their staff, budgetary support, and communications channels with private sector and civil society that are presently at a low level. It favoured creation of municipal cadres for professionalization of municipal governance and management of service delivery, addressing supply side constraints in the existing training institutions and creating a centre of excellence in each of the important areas of urbanization, viz. housing, planning, water and sanitation, disaster management, urban finance and PPP, e-governance, urban governance related issues and urban poverty alleviation. Stressing the need for focused capacity development initiative on a sustained basis, it suggested creation of a separate division for capacity building in the Union Ministry of Urban Development. The Working Group on Capacity Building referred to other parameters of capacity building such as 'organisational development strategy, a human resource development strategy as well as an institutional and legal framework at the state and ULB level'. It suggested other elements of capacity building such as formal structures, comprehensive cadre and cadre rules, staffing norms, procedures, job descriptions, pay scales, introduction of new technologies, shared norms and values amongst staff, commitment to vision and mission, management styles and budgetary support (GoI 2011a). It observed: '. . . absence of formal structures, comprehensive cadre and cadre rules, staffing norms, procedures, job descriptions, pay scales and introduction of new technologies. shared norms and values amongst staff, commitment to vision and mission, management styles and budgetary support are also low'.

These observations are laudable and allude to other parameters that must as well find place in a capacity building initiative. However, its recommendations at centre, state and local levels in short term, medium term and long term are dominated by steps for creation of municipal cadre, resurrecting the existing system of training, supply side management of training, development of training modules and materials, reorientation of Regional Centres for Training, conducting of long term course, ramping of the National Mission Mode project on e-governance, IT based knowledge platforms and the like. It does suggest evolving a 'comprehensive framework of Capacity Building' for addressing issues such as staffing, training and skill development, institutional issues, and financing. It does not, however, elaborate the nature and contents of such a framework. Its recommendations at the state level include developing a human development strategy for the urban local self-governments comprising staffing norms, and cadre rules which should reflect the service delivery and governance norms to be met by the ULSGs.

Of all the frameworks of capacity development, Fowler and Ubels favour and suggest replication of the framework developed by

Kaplan. They offered three reasons for its replication. First, its foundation lies in reflective and experiential learning across several contexts. Experiential learning gained by Kaplan about capacity development in diverse situations provided him rich insights that helped him develop this framework. Kaplan's framework has, therefore, ingredients of empirical groundings that make this framework much more pragmatic. Second, it is supportive of and contributes to a wider literature on the subject, and third, it is not only prescriptive but is also gainfully used by practitioners (Fowler and Ubels 2010).

As discussed earlier in this chapter, capacity is explained in different ways. These different ways of looking at capacity also explains diverse ways to look at capacity building. It is, therefore, not surprising that there are different ways of accomplishing capacity development and that the strategy for this has different elements that should be included in a focused capacity development strategy. Nevertheless, elements of a capacity building framework mentioned above make it clear that capacity building/development is driven by a set of different parameters that are in the nature of sub-systems in an organization, much so in municipal organizations. It is not necessarily driven by training alone. It is important to mention that not all of them are to be used in devising a strategy for capacity development. Which ones from amongst the set of parameters mentioned above are to be included in a meaningful capacity development strategy that will eventually work, will depend on an assessment of capacity development needs. A Users' Guide for assessment of capacity development needs, therefore, suggests that an assessment of capacity should define (i) the desired future capacities intended to be achieved, (ii) level of future capacities that is intended to be achieved, and (iii) assess existing level of capacity that needs to be enhanced (UNDP 2007). Adopting these three steps for assessment of capacity needs helps in devising a highly customised and tailor-made capacity development strategy in a particular situation. In India, it is important to note that most of the urban local self-governments in different states have fragile organizational capacity as has been discussed in detail earlier in this chapter. The existing state of capacity of the urban local self-government in India, therefore, suggests devising a generic capacity building strategy that could be relevant for all the urban local self-governments across different states.

STRATEGY FOR CAPACITY DEVELOPMENT FOR URBAN LOCAL SELF-GOVERNMENT

A brief account of various frameworks of capacity building and its elements discussed above makes it amply clear that there are certain elements (sub-systems of an organization) that are common to all the frameworks discussed above. These are (i) Vision and Mission statements, (ii) Legal and Regulatory Framework, (iii) Organization Development, (iv) Human Resource Development, and (v) Financial Management including fiscal health of urban local self-governments. A generic capacity building/development strategy for the urban local self-governments in the country, therefore, would need to consist of all these key elements. Concentrating either on one of these or some of these elements only will not ensure success of the adopted initiative except in a situation where the capacity building needs are assessed according to the steps suggested by the UNDP and discussed above. Relying merely on training, for example, is unlikely to enhance institutional capacity of an organization and even of the individual staff if training is supply driven and is divorced from the training needs of each member of the ULSG staff and officials in an actual work situation. It also needs to be mentioned that even if an individual is given training, transfer of learning gained through training in a work organization would be crucially dependent on a host of other factors that are external to the individual such as institutional incentives, prevailing work culture, career development and an enabling environment to work, amongst others.

In view of the discussion above, capacity development of urban local self-governments requires that (i) there has to be a strategy for capacity development and (ii) the strategy must consist of certain key elements or sub-systems of an organization, much so of a municipal organization. The elements that must constitute a generic strategy for capacity development must include the key elements referred to above. These key elements are briefly discussed below.

Vision and Mission

At the local level, a capacity building strategy would need to begin with vision and mission statements by the urban local self-governments so that they could have a sense of direction that will guide them in developing an appropriate strategy for capacity development. A vision statement for promoting local economic development, for example, would require an altogether different strategy for capacity building as compared to the one that is intended to enhance efficiency of service delivery. Clarity in visualizing a sense of direction for urban governance and service delivery through vision and mission statements also provides clarity about the nature of capacity building needs, how to go about it, identification of obstacles in moving towards the charted direction and how to address these obstacles.

Legal and Regulatory Framework

Capacity development strategy involves action both at the state and the local levels. Review of Legal and Regulatory framework would need to be conducted at the state level. The relevant department of the state governments would need to evaluate legal and regulatory framework existing in the state for functioning of urban local self-governments. Legal framework basically denotes the nature of devolution—what the ULSGs are permitted to do, what they are not permitted to do, what are the gaps, if any, that constrain effective governance and service delivery, how they should use the devolved power and authority, and what resources are devolved to them for performance of functions entrusted to them. An evaluation of the existing legal and regulatory framework helps in understanding gaps in it. It also provides useful insights for addressing the gaps that are identified in the legal and regulatory framework for urban governance. A meaningful capacity building strategy requires rationalization of existing legal framework of governance and service delivery, basic institutional framework, and systems and procedures for governance. Such an exercise substantially helps in refurbishing of provisions in municipal statutes with respect to devolving of power and authority to the urban local self-government institutions and strengthening of institutions such as Ward Committee, Area Sabha, Urban Planning System, DPC and MPC. It also involves restructuring of Directorates of Municipal Administration in the states so that the Directorates are transformed from the existing supervision and control that they are mostly engaged with and restructuring of the Directorates on functional lines. Restructuring on functional lines (such as finance, engineering, accounts, planning, e-governance, etc.) will enable the Directorates to have a pool of technical resources for handholding of especially such ULSGs that, owing to resource constraints, are not in a position to afford services of experts in different spheres of governance and management of service delivery from the market. Capacity building initiative at the state level will also require looking into the nature of the existing municipal cadre if there is one in the state, identification of gaps in it, if any, and creation of municipal cadre in case it does not exist for imparting professionalism in governance and management of service delivery. It also requires looking into the existing Recruitment Rules for municipal staffing for ensuring that the Rules have provision for recruitment of staff in all the functional areas of municipal governance and service delivery. Review of Recruitment Rules in the state and modernization of old rules will enable the ULSGs in recruitment of qualified staff in the emerging spheres of governance and service delivery. Simultaneously staffing, HR initiatives, system of skill development of staff and elected representatives as well would need to be reviewed at the state level so that gaps, if any, in these are identified and addressed. A refurbished and enabling regulatory framework for municipal governments and urban institutions, systems and procedures would need to be put in place at the state level for creating a conducive environment for the urban local self-governments for their capacity development. Unless devolution system, instruments and institutions of governance and service delivery are rationalized and refurbished through state level intervention, focusing merely at local level for capacity development will be at most cosmetic in approach and hence unlikely to be sustainable.

Organization Development Initiative

Most of the urban local self-governments have been working with an outdated organizational structure, sagging or rudimentary work culture, unskilled staff and an almost non-existent HRD initiative. Organizational structure, in most of the ULSGs, was conceived and designed more than half a century ago when the nature of municipal function was altogether different and the realm of municipal functions was limited, narrow and traditional. At the time of designing of organizational structure, neither the demographic scale in the urban centres was comparable with the one existing at present nor was the technology available for provision of municipal services comparable to the availability of contemporary technology. Also, some of the functions that are now required to be performed by the urban local self-governments (finance function, poverty alleviation, e-governance, urban planning, accrual based accounting system) were not even remotely thought as relevant municipal functions. At the time of advent of municipal governance, the concept of outsourcing in the form of contracting out/privatization of municipal services was as well not heard of. Absence of emerging areas of municipal functional domain mentioned above, therefore, had a great deal of influence on organizational design and staffing of ULSGs. As a result, a simple organizational structure was designed and put in place. Though, the nature and extent of municipal functions has now become diversified, municipal organizations are still loosely structured with the result that it is neither syncronized with the functions devolved to them nor has clarity in reporting system. As a result, the existing organizational structure does not have any relationship with the devolved functions that are to be performed by them. The ULSGs, at most, have an ad-hoc structure that is guided more by expediency rather than by any rational thinking and approach to the discharging of mandated functions. The persisting old organizational structure has not been reviewed to find flaws in it and bring the same in sync with the municipal functional domain that has now substantially changed. Addition of altogether new functions, emergence of new technologies for management of service delivery, and newer and emerging ways of service delivery have important implications for re-designing altogether a new organizational structure and appropriate staffing for enabling the new structure in efficient, inclusive and responsive delivery of municipal services. Organizational structure and staffing pattern, therefore, needs to be reviewed and restructured. Shortage of sufficient staff has led to multiple responsibilities for an individual staff for which they hardly have the required skills. The shortage of staff has been aggravated by lack of proper skills amongst the staff for performance of functions assigned to them.

In addition to obsolete organizational structure, there is absence of job description, well-defined and unambiguous reporting system, performance management system, and lack of efficient decision-making system. Organization Development (OD) studies conducted by the present author in the urban local self-governments in some of the states also revealed that in quite a number of urban local self-government, the staff is hardly qualified and skilled to perform the job entrusted to them.[4] OD studies also revealed that some of the urban local self-governments especially in small and middle towns were not even aware of the existing organizational structure. Yet others said that they did not have an understanding of responsibilities entrusted especially to the members of the staff that have to perform more than one function due to shortage of staff. This is largely explained by fire fighting system with which most of the urban local self-governments have to be engaged with due to a number of reasons such as shortage of staff, absence of required skills amongst them, multiple jobs most of the members of the staff are required to perform and lack of even rudimentary planning. Presently, staffing is characterized by absence of effective leadership, large number of vacant position against sanctioned strength, freeze on recruitment of new staff, depleting staff position due to attrition, large number of elderly staff, low knowledge base, lack of need-based training, low salaries that are not paid in time and in certain cases, even for months. These have adversely affected staff motivation and morale of the municipal staff.

Inadequate and unskilled staffing notwithstanding, municipal personnel management systems is presently chaotic; there is hardly any rudiment of performance management system that could bring some order and accountability in staff performance. Hardly any state has taken steps to introduce at least a semblance of performance management for the officials and staff of the ULSGs and a structured performance evaluation system either in the municipal laws or through executive order. The Annual Survey of India's City Systems conducted by Janaagraha laments that 'The absence of a legal requirement on Performance Management systems and processes in Municipal Corporation Acts is a significant lacuna across states impacting all cities without exception' (Janaagraha 2014). Interaction of the present author with some of the senior bureaucrats manning urban development and governance in the states and also at the centre, on need for performance management in the city governments was quite frustrating. Most of them looked at it as a utopia and as a fashion to replicate private sector practices that, according to them, are completely out of place in municipal organizations. There is hardly any appreciation that when a simple form of performance management was implemented in the Jabalpur Municipal Corporation under a donor supported project, it proved a great success though it could not be sustained for long. The Janaagraha survey laying a great deal of emphasis on it suggests to legally codifying it to ensure 'data-driven decision-making, accountability, value spending and performance measurement across different levels of the institution and individuals'.

The existing state of municipal staffing discussed above is the result of the antediluvian and antiquated Recruitment Rules that in most of the states were framed decades ago. Some of the states even now do not have Recruitment Rules specifically for the urban local self-governments. Such states use the Recruitment Rules of the State Public Works Department! Moreover, in most of the states, Recruitment Rules were framed more than half-a century ago when the urban situation and the municipal functional domain was entirely different. Therefore, the antiquated Recruitment Rules do not have room for recruitment of qualified staff in crucially important areas of finance, accounts, public health, urban planning, information and communication technology, and poverty alleviation. E-governance being introduced in the urban local self-governments under the central government's e-Governance Mission is an example of how an outdated Recruitment Rule acts as an obstacle in recruitment of information and communication (ICT) staff on a regular basis. E-governance projects in the ULSGs are generally staffed on contractual basis as the existing Recruitment Rules do not permit recruitment of ICT staff on a regular basis. As the ICT staff is appointed on contractual basis only for the project, once the project period is over, sustaining the functioning of e-governance comes to a grinding halt. Recruitment Rules in most of the states being old, the eligibility criteria for recruitment are as well quite traditional. As a result, the municipal staff possess low level of knowledge and skills. Data collected from 26 cities and towns under the purview of a World Bank supported project on Capacity Building for Urban Development (CBUD) in the Ministry of Urban Development that was spread into 22 states reveal that the Recruitment Rules in most of the states pertain to the 1960s and 1970s (Table 8.1). In Rajasthan, the Recruitment Rules were framed in 1963-4. This, in Himachal Pradesh, was done in 1989. In Uttar Pradesh, the Rules were framed in 1959. Absence of Recruitment Rules for the ULSGs mentioned earlier is as well corroborated in Table 8.1 which reveals that some of the states do not yet have Recruitment Rules specifically for the urban local self-governments; municipal staff is recruited under the state civil service Rules or the recruitment Rules of the Public Works Department. The states of Andhra Pradesh, Himachal Pradesh, Uttar Pradesh and Uttarakhand do not have municipal-specific recruitment Rules. Absence of municipal-specific and old Recruitment Rules are not amenable to recruitment according to actual needs of the urban local self-governments in specific areas of governance. Recruitment Rules being old, these are also not conducive to modernization of municipal personnel. As a result, the knowledge base of the employees is low, old and traditional.

Data on the number of positions of officers and staffs sanctioned and actually existing reveal serious staff crunch in the urban local self-governments. Table 2, in Annex X reveals that, on an average, about 28 per cent of the total sanctioned staff in the cities contained in this table is vacant. Out of the 25 cities for which the data are available on staffing, in more than 50 per cent of them

TABLE 8.1: MUNICIPAL RECRUITMENT RULES IN SOME OF THE STATES

State	State Service	Municipal	Year
Rajasthan	–	Rajasthan Municipal Service Rules, 1963	1963
		Rajasthan Municipalities Subordinate & Ministerial Service Rules, 1963	1963
		Rajasthan Municipalities Class IV Service Rules, 1964	1964
Andhra Pradesh	State Government Rules	–	– –
Himachal Pradesh	H.P. Service Rules	–	1989
Uttar Pradesh	–	U.P. Municipal Corporation Act	1959
Chandigarh	–	Punjab Muni. Corporation Employee (Recruitment and Condition of Service) Rules	1978
Odisha	Orissa Civil Service Rules	–	1991
Uttarakhand	Uttarakhand Service Rules, 2004	–	2004
		J&K Urban Local Body Institutions (Management) Service Rules, 2008	2008

Source: RBA Reports, CBUD Project, Ministry of Urban Development, http://jnnurm.nic.in/rapid-baseline-assessment-of-cbud-city.html.

(14 cities), the number of vacant positions is above the average for all the cities. In some of the cities, the number of vacant positions is abnormally high. The percentage of vacant positions in Guntur, for example, is as high as 72 per cent! Of the cities where the proportion of vacant positions is quite high, include Bharuch (50 per cent), Ranchi (47 per cent), Puri (44 per cent), Hubli-Dharwar (43 per cent), and Kurukshetra (42 per cent). The Janaagraha Survey of 2015 reveals that vacant positions in Patna

was at 64 per cent. In Bangalore, it was 52 per cent. This in the cities of Mumbai and Chennai was 21 and 13 per cent respectively (Janaagraha 2015).

Inadequate municipal staffing is further aggravated by a freeze on recruitment of new staff for the last several years in most of the states. Needless to say, municipal staffing happens to be the most neglected subject of municipal governance. It is quite weak and traditional. Yet sophisticated and myriad projects are thrust on the municipal governments that have the weakest foundation due to old, traditional, unqualified, unskilled, and skeletal staff. The result is obvious: programmes and projects are not implemented according to objectives of these programmes and projects. Public policy on urban development at the centre and in the states has hardly taken note of this awful limitation of administrative capacity of the urban local self-governments. Uninhibited and thoughtless focus on training continues unabated as a vehicle for capacity building. Modernizing municipal staff is hardly talked about for effective implementation of centre and state sector programmes and projects for enabling the urban local self-governments in efficient discharge of their functions. One hardly comes across any initiative for modernization of antiquated municipal staffing system in public policy whether at the centre or in the states except Madhya Pradesh, Odisha and to some extent, Bihar. Odisha and Bihar have recently taken initiatives to frame new recruitment rules providing for modernization of municipal staffing.

Capacity building initiative, therefore, needs to have OD as an important element for review and evaluation of organizational structure, staffing, Recruitment Rules and the aspects related with staffing. Review of organizational structure will provide valuable insights into the nature of staffing that is required to perform the various functions devolved to the urban local self-governments. Clarity on the type of municipal staff in the wake of organizational structure review and the insights gained into the particular skills the members of the municipal staff must possess will, in turn, provide an insight for revisiting the Recruitment Rules and hence the legal framework of municipal governance for creation of the required number and types of municipal cadre. Clarity on these will enable the state governments in recruitment of right type of employees with right type of qualification and skills. It needs to be mentioned here that mere creation of state wide municipal services for manning the different functional areas of municipal governance will be useful only if the municipal staffing is modernized. If this does not happen, the functionaries constituting the municipal cadre will be providing professional leadership only to insufficient and unskilled staff. This would hardly make much difference in improving municipal performance.

Human Resource Development

This is another important element of a capacity development startaegy. This points to yet another sub-system of an organization that would need to be looked into for capacity building. Human resource development (HRD) requires a number of things to be taken care of for capacity building. Besides training which is only one of the aspects of HRD, other aspects that would need to be addressed include career development of appointed municipal functionaries, retention of staff, and institutional incentives for enhancing their motivation. Institutional incentives, to begin with, should at least put in place a system of awards for the best performer of the year in each department on the basis of performance evaluation of the staff. The award could be initially given in the form of commendation certificates in an annual function in presence of all the municipal staff. This itself will ignite motivation in other members of the municipal staff for putting their best effort in discharge of their functions. Resources of the urban local self-government permitting, the annual award could be subsequently given in the form of attractive prizes or even monetary benefit like cash award. Exceptionally good performer could also be given advance increment. Practices for giving awards enormously contribute to enhanced motivation of staff.

Training itself has to be need-based so that it could help the staff and officials in enhancing their knowledge and skills in actual work situation. This especially requires training to be informed by a formal training need assessment. Fruitful training would additionally require having a Training officer in each urban local self-government. The Training Officer would assess training needs of officers and staff on a regular basis and arrange need based training for them by out sourcing various training institutions. Training Policy of the Government of India also envisages placement of Training Officer in each department of government. It also suggests providing for a training fund by earmarking a proportion of the budget of each department for funding training on a regular basis (GoI 1996).

Financial Management System

A strong fiscal health is a critical imperative for institutional capacity development. The urban local self-governments are not in a position to effectively utilize the local fiscal tools devolved to them under the municipal Acts. Even in the state of Gujarat that is said to be one of the most progressive states in municipal governance, collection of Property Tax is abysmally low; the urban local self-governments in other states are not exceptions. Municipal corporations constituted even in the national capital of Delhi which has the highest per capita income in the country and constitutes a major trade centre in the entire north and north-east India, find it difficult to pay salaries to their staff on a regular basis due to fragile fiscal health. Resource generating capacity of urban local self-governments from the existing fiscal tools—both tax and non-tax sources—is quite weak across the country because of a number of reasons including poor tax administration and unwillingness to charge. The existing cash based accounting system as well is not in a position to generate the much needed basic information system for improved fiscal health and financial management system. Much is, therefore, desired to effectively use the devolved sources of local revenue and improve internal financial control and accountability of urban local self-governments. Capacity development initiative will also require switching over to new accrual based double entry accounting system and a system of internal and concurrent audit. Generation of additional financial resources requires widening of the local tax base through periodic surveys of land and buildings, use of information and communication technology for harnessing local resources, enhancing collection efficiency, and recruitment of qualified managers for manning finance and accounts. This again brings back the issue of qualified and skilled staffing.

Framework of capacity development discussed above helps in understanding the much needed sub-systems of an organization and bringing about required changes in these sub-systems for enhancing organizational capacity. Such a strategy will substantially contribute to strengthening of urban local self-governments as the strategy is based on experiential learning. A generic strategy for capacity development would need to weave together the sub-systems of a municipal organization discussed above. This is depicted in Figure 8.1. This figure also depicts that initiative for capacity building needs to build on the sub-systems in a holistic

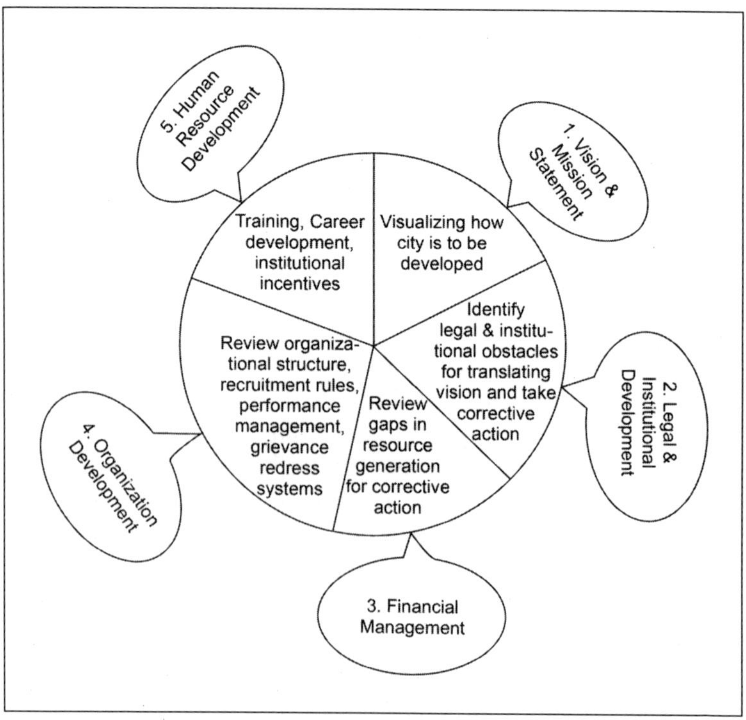

Figure 8.1: Capacity Building Framework

manner. Continued emphasis only on training as the sole means of capacity development will hardly enable the urban local self-governments in effective discharge of their functions and implementation of urban sector programmes. Training as the prescription for capacity building is based on an altogether misplaced diagnosis.

EXISTING PRACTICES FOR CAPACITY DEVELOPMENT

Presently, the initiative for capacity development/building at the centre and in the states consists of a three-pronged action. First is a series of urban sector reforms conceived under the first ever flagship urban sector project of Jn-NURM launched in December 2005. Now urban sector reforms of entirely different nature as compared to the ones under the Jn-NURM are being pursued under the central government's Atal Mission for Rejuvenation and Urban Transformation and other central sector programme launched in a mission mode. Second is the financial and technical assistance given by international financial institutions like World Bank, Asian Development Bank (ADB), Department for International Development DFID, UK), Japan International Cooperation Agency (JICA) and others. Urban sector projects funded by these international funding agencies as well invariably have a set of reform measures which form part of such projects. However, so far neither the reform measures conceived in the centre sector programmes nor the ones contained in the projects funded by the international financial institutions have even peripherally included any reform agenda for improving municipal staffing except the lone project—Kolkata Urban Services for the Poor (KUSP) supported by DFID. Under the KUSP project, the problem of staffing was addressed in a limited manner by making available five qualified staff to each of the urban local self-governments located in the Kolkata Metropolitan Area in the functional areas of (i) urban planning, (ii) finance, (iii) accounts, (iv) engineering, and (v) e-governance. Even this limited reform had positive and visible impact in improving the quality of governance. Third, contemporary method for capacity building is training that is largely driven by supply rather than by demand (need-based training). Besides training courses conducted by the various urban local self-governments on their own, training events also form part of the urban sector projects funded by the central govern-ment and the international financial institutions. Capacity building of urban local self-governments for implementation of reforms which form part of the central government missions and also of the urban sector projects which are funded through financial assistance by the international financial institutions as well is pursued through training—project-based training. Thus presently training happens to be the predominant method of capacity building of urban local self-governments.

Training and Capacity Building

Conceptual groundings of capacity building framework discussed above amply elucidates that it goes much beyond mere training. Of the five essential sub-systems of an organization (vision and mission statements, legal framework, financial management for strengthening fiscal capabilities, organization development and HRD), training forms only a part of one of them—human resource development. Yet entire effort towards capacity building is presently confined to training that has its own limitations for capacity enhancement. Training courses as they are rolled out presently are characterized by several conspicuous shortcomings discussed below:

1. Training is presently driven largely by supply, not by demand for training. Training institutions and agencies generally conduct training courses in the areas in which they have proven expertize and comparative advantage in terms of faculty resources and experience. Therefore, they roll out training courses only in such subject areas in which the training institutions have relatively better expertise. Such a scheme of training does not take into account actual learning needs of the urban local self-government staff and officials both elected and appointed. It is hardly demand driven. Hence it is not instrumental at all in improving competence of the municipal functionaries and the capability of municipal organizations.

2. In a supply driven contemporary training regime, training institutions and agencies become the sole champions and advocates of training. It is they who decide which training the ULSG functionaries need to attend and acquire new learning. The urban local self-governments, because of demand side constraints, keep on nominating their staff and officers to learning events organized and conducted in a manner discussed above. Instances are many when a member of the staff has attended the same training event more than once. Training obviously has become a fad.
3. If the contents of learning events are not informed by a formal Training Needs Assessment (TNA), training courses mounted by the training institutions/agencies become generic in nature. Generic training does not fully contribute to enhancement of knowledge and skills of the municipal functionaries especially in relation to actual learning needs. It does not help them in acquiring knowledge and skills that could help them perform their functions much more effectively. It fails to address their skill gap in actual work situation. Lately, under the Capacity Building for Urban Development project of the MoUD, a TNA was conducted in 2014 to put in place demand-based training in the form of a Strategic Training Plan. Delivery of the need-based training plan, however, requires altogether different state specific institutional arrangement. If not implemented, the Training Plan will be limited to a mere academic exercise.
4. Some of the training courses in the country are driven by projects that are launched by the central government in mission mode from time to time. In such a scheme of training, training itself gets projectized. It needs to be appreciated that even project specific training needs to be informed by an assessment of specific training needs of the project and identification of the staff involved in project implementation at different levels who would require training. Absence of such a system of project related training once again reduces it to a supply driven and generic training with all the limitations of such a system of training discussed above. No effort is made to assess actual training need of the project and of the staff working in the project at various levels.

5. A meaningful training programme needs to be supported by training manual that must define the contours of learning for the participants of the learning event and also help as a guide for the trainer. Contemporary training is hardly supported by meaningful training manual.
6. Municipal personnel system in different states is still traditional as the municipal employees are recruited under the recruitment rules that are quite dated. Old recruitment Rules do not help recruitment of officers and staff in the emerging areas of municipal governance such as information and communication technology, modern accrual based accounting system, urban planning, urban poverty alleviation and the like. Absence of municipal specific and old recruitment rules are not amenable to recruitment according to actual needs of the urban local self-governments. It is also not conducive to modernization of municipal personnel. As a result, the knowledge base of the employees is low, old and traditional. Training, under such a traditional municipal personnel system, becomes largely irrelevant in enhancing of knowledge and skills of municipal officials and staff. Also, it needs to be appreciated that training cannot be a substitute for recruitment of qualified staff in the newly emerging spheres of urban governance mentioned above.

LEGACY OF TRAINING

In view of the above, the existing penchant for training as the only means for capacity building is largely out of place. Capacity building/development is much more than mere training that has pitfalls discussed above. The contemporary predilection for training as a proxy for capacity building is a legacy of the past as discussed below:

1. After Indian achieved Independence, urban sector as compared to other sectors was assigned lower priority both by the state and the central governments largely because of resource constraints. The available resources were required to be allocated to much more critically important priority sectors vis-à-vis the ur-

ban development sector. Since urban sector had a lower priority, capacity development initiative as well took a back seat. The expression municipal/municipality acquired a negative connotation that denoted everything that was inferior. This was reinforced by advent of the World Bank funding in urban sector in the 1970s. The World Bank insisted creation of specific purpose authorities whenever schemes for water supply and sewerage, slum improvement (called slum clearance in those days), urban planning and development were funded by it. The World Bank insisted upon it largely on grounds of 'weak institutional capacity' of ULSGs. Instead of strengthening of urban local self-governments, new organizations were created in several states for accessing financial assistance from the World Bank. This contributed to diminution of municipal functional domain. Parceling out of traditional municipal functions to specific purpose authorities led to further decline of institutional capacity of the ULBs.

2. Diminution in capacity of municipal organizations lately attracted attention of the policy makers to devise mechanisms for their capacity enhancement. Capacity development/building was initially looked at in a very narrow perspective; it invariably meant training. Providing in-service training to the officials and the staff of urban local self-governments was assumed to enhance their organizational capability to a very large extent. This led to the creation of four Centres of Training and Research in Municipal Administration in (i) Indian Institute of Public Administration, New Delhi, (ii) All India Institute of Local Self-Government, Mumbai, (iii) Lucknow University, Lucknow and (iv) Osmania University, Hyderabad by the central government during 1966-7. These centres were given the mandate to plan and implement appropriate academic resource inputs to meet training and research needs relating to urban sector and to conduct in-service training programmes, both of general and specialized nature on a variety of subjects of urban governance. Barring the one at the Indian Institute of Public Administration, New Delhi that is renamed as the Centre for Urban Studies, the other three Centres are renamed as Regional Centre for Urban

and Environmental Studies. These Centres have been engaged in training most of which are supply driven only.

Capacity development/building is thus presently being looked at in a very narrow perspective. The Working Group Report (GoI 2011a) on capacity building as well has pointed to this narrow import of capacity building by observing that 'Capacity Building has been so far accorded very low priority and is largely limited to administrative training'. This legacy of training as the most favoured means for capacity enhancement has continued unabated without realizing its limitations. It is looked at as the panacea for capacity development of the urban local self-governments. As a result, a number of National Resource Centres, Centres of Excellence, and Training Hubs have been identified and created by the MoUD for capacity building largely through training.

TECHNICAL ASSISTANCE BY INTERNATIONAL DONOR AGENCIES AND CAPACITY DEVELOPMENT

Jn-NURM was the first urban infrastructure augmentation project (rather than its official name of 'urban renewal mission' that is altogether a different concept)[5] that tried to leverage urban sector reforms at the state and city levels through financial assistance to the states. Jn-NURM was configured with a package of state and local level reforms which constituted the caveat for accessing the Jn-NURM funds by the states. As discussed in Chapter 6 though implementation of identified reforms was only a qualified success, it, for the first time, brought urban sector reforms at the fore front. The international donor agencies as well have tried to push reforms through technical and financial assistance in different states such as Odisha, Rajasthan, Bihar, Madhya Pradesh, and other states.

Have the reforms through financial and technical assistance by the international financial institutions led to enhancement of institutional capacity and strengthening of urban local self-governments? Certainly these have tried to introduce newer ways of doing things in the spheres of governance, finance and accounting, urban infrastructure provisioning, urban planning (largely through City Development Plans (CDP), and use of ICT for e-governance. But the reforms under the aegis of these initiatives are driven by the consultants. The typical structure devised for urban sector reforms is the usual Project Management and Project Implementation Units that are quite external to the urban local self-governments. Involvement of these governments in reforms is at most marginal even though the onus of implementation rests with the municipal staff. The reforms under the aegis of international donor agencies thus get projectized. After the project is over, sustaining the reforms introduced by the consultants becomes a big question. It proves to be a daunting task for the municipal staff to sustain the reforms introduced under the projects largely because existing knowledge base, skills and motivation of the municipal functionaries become a big constraint. Also, in the event of reforms introduced by agencies that are external to the urban local self-governments, the municipal functionaries hardly get an opportunity to be involved in the process of conceptualization of reforms and their implementation. The existing low level of knowledge and skills of municipal functionaries again raises the endemic issue of modernizing municipal personnel system that is quite antiquated. Instances are many when promising reforms introduced by consultants have withered away soon after institutionalization of reforms in the municipal organizations and the exit of consultants who conceptualized and tried to institutionalize the reforms.

Moreover, there is yet another basic issue in pushing reforms. A reform introduces newer ways of doing things and changing the long established systems and procedures. Altering the status quo is not to the liking of many states and local government actors who have strong vested interest in retaining the status quo. Lack of will and ownership of reforms, therefore, have not led to implementation of valuable ideas characterizing reforms.

To sum up, addressing the long overdue modernization of municipal personnel system is in the nature of an imperative for sustaining urban sector reforms. Reforms in municipal personnel system are long overdue. Review of organizational structure and its fine tuning in view of the 12th Schedule of the Indian Constitution must precede this. A refurbished organization structure provides extremely useful insights into the type of officers and staff needed in terms of their educational qualification and skills. This, in turn, gives equally useful insights for revisiting the recruitment rules and framing of altogether new and modern recruitment rules. The urban reform cell at the state level or the state urban development department will be required to review and evaluate the municipal legal framework for identification of legal hurdles. Training could play a useful role only after organizational structure, work culture, and municipal personnel system are revamped and a capacity development strategy containing its basic elements discussed above in this chapter is developed and implemented. Training and transfer of learning in the existing situation has several limitations for capacity building in true sense of the term. It is time that capacity building initiative is taken out of the training syndrome.

NOTES

1. More often, one comes across the expression 'capacity building' rather than 'capacity development'. The literature on this subject refers to 'capacity development' as more apt and preferable expression and argues that capacity is not 'built'; it is 'developed' because individuals, groups, organizations and society do possess some rudiment of capacity that needs to be developed for accomplishment of their tasks, functions, and mission. Giving an analogy of a car, it argues that in case a car stops on the road, one looks into the important components of the car's engine to find out the fault. Once the problem is identified, the capacity of those components is 'developed' to make the car run again; it is not built (manufactured) all over again.
2. For a detailed elucidation on these elements and their inter-relationships for a meaningful capacity building strategy, see Jha 2013.
3. Mintzberg's framework (earlier called Structures in Five) consists of Simple Structure, Machine Bureaucracy, Professional Bureaucracy, Diversified Form, Advocacy or Innovative Organization, and Missionary Organization (Mintzberg, Henry 1992); McKinsey's Seven S model consists of Strategy, Structure, Systems, Shared Values, Skills, Style and Staff (Pascale and Athos 1992).
4. In one of the states, the Property Tax Department/Section was found headed

by a cleaner of a bus who graduated to this position through promotion and the Accounts department/Section headed by a staff who initially started working in the ULSG as muster roll sweeper.

5. The literature on urban studies defines urban renewal as a strategy for re-development of the traditional urban core that over the years have decayed into squalid and dilapidated areas. The *Chambers 21st Century Dictionary*, for example, defines urban renewal as 'clearing and redevelopment of slums in large cities'. *The Oxford Dictionary* defines it similarly—'redevelopment of slum areas in large cities'. *The Random House Unabridged Dictionary* defines it succinctly as 'the rehabilitation of city areas by renovating or replacing dilapidated buildings with new housing, public buildings, parks, roadways, industrial areas, etc often in accordance with comprehensive plans'. For a discussion on the nomenclature of Jn-NURM, see Jha 2009.

REFERENCES

Baser, H. and P. Morgan, 2008, 'Capacity, Change and Performance: Study Report', *Discussion Paper 59B*, Maastricht: European Centre for Development Policy Management.

Connolly, Paul and Carol Lukas, 2002, *Strengthening Nonprofit Performance: A Funder's Guide to Capacity Building*, Nashville: Fieldstone Alliance, now Turner Publishing.

Fowler, Alan and Jan Ubels, 2010, 'The Multi-faceted Nature of Capacity: Two Leading Models', in Jan Ubels et al. (eds.), *Capacity Development in Practice*, London, D.C.: Earth Scan Publishing for Sustainable Future, pp. 11-24,

Government of India (GOI), 1996, *National Training Policy*, New Delhi: Ministry of Personnel, Public Grievances and Pensions.

——, 2007, *Sixth Report of the Second Administrative Reform Commission, Local Governance: An Inspiring Journey into the Future*, New Delhi: Ministry of Personnel, Public Grievances and Pensions, Department of Administrative Refom and Public Grievances.

——, 2010, *Mid-term Appraisal of the Eleventh Five Year Plan*. New Delhi: Planning Commission.

——, Planning Commission, 2011a, *Urban Development Management for the Formulation of the Twelfth Five Year Plan, 2012-17, Report of the Working Group on Capacity Building*, New Delhi: Planning Commission.

—— (High Powered Expert Committee for Estimating the Investment

Requirements for Urban Infrastructure and Services), 2011b, *Report on Indian Infrastructure and Services.* New Delhi: Ministry of Urban Development.

—— (Steering Committee on Urbanization), 2012, *Report of the Steering Committee on Urbanisation, Twelfth Fiver Year Plan 2012-17,* New Delhi: Planning Commission.

Horton, D. et al., 2003, *Evaluating Capacity Development: Experiences from Research and Development Organizations around the World,* Ottawa: IDRC.

Janaagraha, 2015, *Annual Survey of India's City Systems,* Bangalore: Centre of Citizenship and Democracy.

Jha, Gangadhar, 2009, 'Jawaharlal Nehru National Urban Renewal Mission: Bridging the Missing Gaps for Sustainable Reform', *Urban World,* vol. 2, no. 2.

——, 2013, 'Capacity Development for Effective Urban Governance and Service Delivery: Quest for Precepts, Realities and Realisation', paper presented at the National Seminar on Contemporary Urban Systems: Challenges and Opportunities, organized by the Department of Geography, Banaras Hindu University, Varanasi, 11-13 February 2013.

Kaplan, A., 1999, 'Organisational Capacity: A Different Perspective', *Development Dossier,* no. 10, Non-Governmental Liaison Service, United Nations, Geneva.

LaFond, A. and L. Brown, 2003, *A Guide to Monitoring and Evaluation of Capacity-Building: Interventions in the Health Sector in Developing Countries,* Chapel Hill: MEASURE Evaluation Manual Series, Carolina Population Center, UNC.

McKinsey Global Institute, 2010, *India's Urban Awakening, Building Inclusive Cities, Sustaining Economic Growth.* New Delhi: McKinsey & Company.

Ministry of Urban Development, *Rapid Baseline Assessment Reports,* http://jnnurm.nic.in/rapid-baseline-assessment-of-cbud-city.html.

Morgan, P., 2006, *The Concept of Capacity: Capacity, Change and Performance.* Maastricht: European Centre for Development Policy Management.

OECD, 2006, *The Challenge of Capacity Development: Working Towards Good Practice,* Paris: Organisation for Economic Co-operation and Development.

Pascale, R.T. and Antony George Athos, 1981, *The Art of Japanese Management,* New York: Simon & Schuster.

Pellenburg et al., 1996, 'Building Capacities for Better Cities', *Discussion paper for Habitat II,* Rotterdam: IHS.

UNDP, 1997, *Capacity Development Methodology, User's Guide,* New York: Capacity Development Group, Bureau of Development Policy.

——, 2007, 'Capacity Development', in *Capacity Development Resource Book.* New York: Management Development and Governance Division.

Ubels, Jan et al., 2010, 'A Resource Volume on Capacity Development', in Jan Ubels, Naa-Aku Acquaye-Baddoo and Alan Fowler (eds.), *Capacity Development in Practice,* London: Earth Scan Publishing for Sustainable Future, pp. 2-8.

ANNEXES

ANNEX I

EUROPEAN CHARTER OF LOCAL SELF-GOVERNMENT

Strasbourg, 15.X.1985

European Treaty Series No. 122
COUNCIL OF EUROPE CONSEIL DE L'EUROPE

PREAMBLE

- The member States of the Council of Europe, signatory hereto,
- Considering that the aim of the Council of Europe is to achieve a greater unity between its members for the purpose of safeguarding and realising the ideals and principles which are their common heritage;
- Considering that one of the methods by which this aim is to be achieved is through agreements in the administrative field;
- Considering that the local authorities are one of the main foundations of any democratic regime;
- Considering that the right of citizens to participate in the conduct of public affairs is one of the democratic principles that are shared by all member States of the Council of Europe;
- Considering that it is at local level that this right can be most directly exercised;
- Convinced that the existence of local authorities with real responsibilities can provide an administration which is both effective and close to the citizen;
- Aware that the safeguarding and reinforcement of local self-government in the different European countries is an important contribution to the construction of a Europe based on the principles of democracy and the decentralisation of power;
- Asserting that this entails the existence of local authorities endowed with democratically constituted decision-making bodies and possessing a wide degree of autonomy with regard to their responsibilities, the ways and means by which those responsibilities are exercised and the resources required for their fulfilment,
- Have agreed as follows:

Article 1

The Parties undertake to consider themselves bound by the following articles in the manner and to the extent prescribed in Article 12 of this Charter.

PART I

Article 2: Constitutional and legal foundation for local self-government

The principle of local self-government shall be recognised in domestic legislation, and where practicable in the constitution.

Article 3: Concept of local self-government

1. Local self-government denotes the right and the ability of local authorities, within the limits of the law, to regulate and manage a substantial share of public affairs under their own responsibility and in the interests of the local population.
2. This right shall be exercised by councils or assemblies composed of members freely elected by secret ballot on the basis of direct, equal, universal suffrage, and which may possess executive organs responsible to them. This provision shall in no way affect recourse to assemblies of citizens, referendums or any other form of direct citizen participation where it is permitted by statute.

Article 4: Scope of local self-government

1. The basic powers and responsibilities of local authorities shall be prescribed by the constitution or by statute. However, this provision shall not prevent the attribution to local authorities of powers and responsibilities for specific purposes in accordance with the law.
2. Local authorities shall, within the limits of the law, have full discretion to exercise their initiative with regard to any matter which is not excluded from their competence nor assigned to any other authority.
3. Public responsibilities shall generally be exercised, in preference, by those authorities which are closest to the citizen. Allocation of responsibility to another authority should weigh up the extent and nature of the task and requirements of efficiency and economy.
4. Powers given to local authorities shall normally be full and exclusive. They may not be undermined or limited by another, central or regional, authority except as provided for by the law.
5. Where powers are delegated to them by a central or regional authority, local authorities shall, insofar as possible, be allowed discretion in adapting their exercise to local conditions.

6. Local authorities shall be consulted, insofar as possible, in due time and in an appropriate way in the planning and decision-making processes for all matters which concern them directly.

ARTICLE 5: Protection of local authority boundaries

Changes in local authority boundaries shall not be made without prior consultation of the local communities concerned, possibly by means of a referendum where this is permitted by statute.

ARTICLE 6: Appropriate administrative structures and resources for the tasks of local authorities

1. Without prejudice to more general statutory provisions, local authorities shall be able to determine their own internal administrative structures in order to adapt them to local needs and ensure effective management.
2. The conditions of service of local government employees shall be such as to permit the recruitment of high-quality staff on the basis of merit and competence; to this end adequate training opportunities, remuneration and career prospects shall be provided.

ARTICLE 7: Conditions under which responsibilities at local level are exercised

1. The conditions of office of local elected representatives shall provide for free exercise of their functions.
2. They shall allow for appropriate financial compensation for expenses incurred in the exercise of the office in question as well as, where appropriate, compensation for loss of earnings or remuneration for work done and corresponding social welfare protection.
3. Any functions and activities which are deemed incompatible with the holding of local elective office shall be determined by statute or fundamental legal principles.

ARTICLE 8: Administrative supervision of local authorities' activities

1. Any administrative supervision of local authorities may only be exercised according to such procedures and in such cases as are provided for by the constitution or by statute.
2. Any administrative supervision of the activities of the local authorities shall normally aim only at ensuring compliance with the law and with constitutional principles. Administrative supervision may however be exercised with regard to expediency by higher-level authorities in respect of tasks the execution of which is delegated to local authorities.

3. Administrative supervision of local authorities shall be exercised in such a way as to ensure that the intervention of the controlling authority is kept in proportion to the importance of the interests which it is intended to protect.

ARTICLE 9: Financial resources of local authorities

1. Local authorities shall be entitled, within national economic policy, to adequate financial resources of their own, of which they may dispose freely within the framework of their powers.
2. Local authorities' financial resources shall be commensurate with the responsibilities provided for by the constitution and the law.
3. Part at least of the financial resources of local authorities shall derive from local taxes and charges of which, within the limits of statute, they have the power to determine the rate.
4. The financial systems on which resources available to local authorities are based shall be of a sufficiently diversified and buoyant nature to enable them to keep pace as far as practically possible with the real evolution of the cost of carrying out their tasks.
5. The protection of financially weaker local authorities calls for the institution of financial equalisation procedures or equivalent measures which are designed to correct the effects of the unequal distribution of potential sources of finance and of the financial burden they must support. Such procedures or measures shall not diminish the discretion local authorities may exercise within their own sphere of responsibility.
6. Local authorities shall be consulted, in an appropriate manner, on the way in which redistributed resources are to be allocated to them.
7. As far as possible, grants to local authorities shall not be earmarked for the financing of specific projects. The provision of grants shall not remove the basic freedom of local authorities to exercise policy discretion within their own jurisdiction.
8. For the purpose of borrowing for capital investment, local authorities shall have access to the national capital market within the limits of the law.

ARTICLE 10: Local authorities' right to associate

1. Local authorities shall be entitled, in exercising their powers, to co-operate and, within the framework of the law, to form consortia with other local authorities in order to carry out tasks of common interest.
2. The entitlement of local authorities to belong to an association for the protection and promotion of their common interests and to belong to an

international association of local authorities shall be recognised in each State.

3. Local authorities shall be entitled, under such conditions as may be provided for by the law, to co-operate with their counterparts in other States.

ARTICLE 11: Legal protection of local self-government

Local authorities shall have the right of recourse to a judicial remedy in order to secure free exercise of their powers and respect for such principles of local self-government as are enshrined in the constitution or domestic legislation.

PART II
MISCELLANEOUS PROVISIONS

ARTICLE 12: Undertakings

1. Each Party undertakes to consider itself bound by at least twenty paragraphs of Part I of the Charter, at least ten of which shall be selected from among the following paragraphs:
   - Article 2,
   - Article 3, paragraphs 1 and 2,
   - Article 4, paragraphs 1, 2 and 4,
   - Article 5,
   - Article 7, paragraph 1,
   - Article 8, paragraph 2,
   - Article 9, paragraphs 1, 2 and 3,
   - Article 10, paragraph 1,
   - Article 11.
2. Each Contracting State, when depositing its instrument of ratification, acceptance or approval, shall notify to the Secretary General of the Council of Europe of the paragraphs selected in accordance with the provisions of paragraph 1 of this article.
3. Any Party may, at any later time, notify the Secretary General that it considers itself bound by any paragraphs of this Charter which it has not already accepted under the terms of paragraph 1 of this article. Such undertakings subsequently given shall be deemed to be an integral part of the ratification, acceptance or approval of the Party so notifying, and shall have the same effect as from the first day of the month following the expiration of a period of three months after the date of the receipt of the notification by the Secretary General.

ARTICLE 13: Authorities to which the Charter applies

The principles of local self-government contained in the present Charter apply to all the categories of local authorities existing within the territory of the Party. However, each Party may, when depositing its instrument of ratification, acceptance or approval, specify the categories of local or regional authorities to which it intends to confine the scope of the Charter or which it intends to exclude from its scope. It may also include further categories of local or regional authorities within the scope of the Charter by subsequent notification to the Secretary General of the Council of Europe.

ARTICLE 14: Provision of information

Each Party shall forward to the Secretary General of the Council of Europe all relevant information concerning legislative provisions and other measures taken by it for the purposes of complying with the terms of this Charter.

PART III

ARTICLE 15: Signature, ratification and entry into force

1. This Charter shall be open for signature by the member States of the Council of Europe. It is subject to ratification, acceptance or approval. Instruments of ratification, acceptance or approval shall be deposited with the Secretary General of the Council of Europe.
2. This Charter shall enter into force on the first day of the month following the expiration of a period of three months after the date on which four member States of the Council of Europe have expressed their consent to be bound by the Charter in accordance with the provisions of the preceding paragraph.
3. In respect of any member State which subsequently expresses its consent to be bound by it, the Charter shall enter into force on the first day of the month following the expiration of a period of three months after the date of the deposit of the instrument of ratification, acceptance or approval.

ARTICLE 16: Territorial clause

1. Any State may, at the time of signature or when depositing its instrument of ratification, acceptance, approval or accession, specify the territory or territories to which this Charter shall apply.
2. Any State may at any later date, by a declaration addressed to the Secretary General of the Council of Europe, extend the application of this Charter

to any other territory specified in the declaration. In respect of such territory the Charter shall enter into force on the first day of the month following the expiration of a period of three months after the date of receipt of such declaration by the Secretary General.

3. Any declaration made under the two preceding paragraphs may, in respect of any territory specified in such declaration, be withdrawn by a notification addressed to the Secretary General. The withdrawal shall become effective on the first day of the month following the expiration of a period of six months after the date of receipt of such notification by the Secretary General.

ARTICLE 17: Denunciation

1. Any Party may denounce this Charter at any time after the expiration of a period of five years from the date on which the Charter entered into force for it. Six months' notice shall be given to the Secretary General of the Council of Europe. Such denunciation shall not affect the validity of the Charter in respect of the other Parties provided that at all times there are not less than four such Parties.
2. Any Party may, in accordance with the provisions set out in the preceding paragraph, denounce any paragraph of Part I of the Charter accepted by it provided that the Party remains bound by the number and type of paragraphs stipulated in Article 12, paragraph 1. Any Party which, upon denouncing a paragraph, no longer meets the requirements of Article 12, paragraph 1, shall be considered as also having denounced the Charter itself.

ARTICLE 18: Notifications

The Secretary General of the Council of Europe shall notify the member States of the Council of Europe of:

(a) any signature;
(b) the deposit of any instrument of ratification, acceptance or approval;
(c) any date of entry into force of this Charter in accordance with Article 15;
(d) any notification received in application of the provisions of Article 12, paragraphs 2 and 3;
(e) any notification received in application of the provisions of Article 13;
(f) any other act, notification or communication relating to this Charter.

In witness whereof the undersigned, being duly authorised thereto, have signed this Charter.

Done at Strasbourg, this 15th day of October 1985, in English and French, both texts being equally authentic, in a single copy which shall be deposited in the archives of the Council of Europe. The Secretary General of the Council of Europe shall transmit certified copies to each member State of the Council of Europe.

ANNEX II

MUNICIPAL FUNCTIONS LISTED IN THE TWELFTH SCHEDULE
(Article 243W)

1. Urban planning including town planning.
2. Regulation of land-use and construction of buildings.
3. Planning for economic and social development.
4. Roads and bridges.
5. Water supply for domestic, industrial and commercial purposes.
6. Public health, sanitation conservancy and solid waste management.
7. Fire services.
8. Urban forestry, protection of the environment and promotion of ecological aspects.
9. Safeguarding the interests of weaker sections of society, including the handicapped and mentally retarded.
10. Slum improvement and up-gradation.
11. Urban poverty alleviation.
12. Provision of urban amenities and facilities such as parks, gardens, playgrounds.
13. Promotion of cultural, educational and aesthetic aspects.
14. Burials and burial grounds; cremations, cremation grounds and electric crematoriums.
15. Cattle pounds; prevention of cruelty to animals.
16. Vital statistics including registration of births and deaths.
17. Public amenities including street lighting, parking lots, bus stops and public conveniences.
18. Regulation of slaughter houses and tanneries.

ANNEX III

CRITERIA FOR MUNICIPALIZATION IN SOME OF THE MAJOR STATES

State	Demographic Criteria	Economic Criteria
1. ANDHRA PRADESH: THE ANDHRA PRADESH MUNICIPAL CORPORATIONS ACT, 1994		
Municipal Corporation	In larger urban area with a population of 3 lakh and above	
2. ANDHRA PRADESH MUNICIPALITIES ACT, 1965		
Municipality	Smaller urban area defined as with a population of 40 thousand and above & up to 3 lakh	Municipalities graded on the basis of revenue: *Selection Grade Municipality*: Annual income of more than eight crores of rupees and above *Special Grade Municipality*: Annual income of more than six crores and less than eight crores of rupees; *First Grade Municipality*: Annual income of more than four crores and less than six crores of rupees; Second Grade Municipality: Annual income of more than two crores and less than four crores of rupees *Third Grade Municipality*: Annual income of more than one crore or less than two crores of rupees

State	Demographic Criteria	Economic Criteria
Nagar Panchayat	Transitional area with a population of 20,000 to 40,000	
3. BIHAR: BIHAR MUNICIPAL ACT, 2007		
'larger urban area' (Municipal Corporation)	Population of two lakh or more	'non-agricultural population' 75 per cent or more
'Medium urban area' (Municipal Council)	Population of 40,000 to less than two lakhs	'non-agricultural population' 75 per cent or more
'transitional area' (Nagar Panchayat)	Population from 12,000 to less than 40,000	'non-agricultural population' 75 per cent or more
4. GUJARAT: BOMBAY PROVINCIAL MUNICIPAL CORPORATION ACT, 1949		
Municipal Corporation	In larger urban area State government may notify a city with not less than 3 lakh population as larger urban area	–
5. GUJARAT MUNICIPALITIES ACT, 1963		
Municipal Council	In smaller urban area	–
Nagar Panchayat	In transitional area	–
6. HARYANA: THE HARYANA MUNICIPAL CORPORATION ACT, 1994		
Municipal Corporation	A population of 3 lakh	–
7. HARYANA MUNICIPAL ACT, 1973		
Municipal Council	Smaller urban area with a population exceeding 50,000 but not exceeding 3 lakh	–
Municipal Committee	In transitional area with a population not exceeding 50,000	–
8. KARNATAKA: KARNATAKA MUNICIPAL CORPORATION ACT, 1976		
Municipal Corporation	In larger urban area; Population not less than 3 lakh;	Revenue generated in the last preceding three years not less than

State	Demographic Criteria	Economic Criteria
	Density not less than 3,000 inhabitants per sq km	Rs. 6 crore or an amount calculated at the rate of rupees two hundred per capita per annum, whichever is higher; 50 per cent of the total employment in non-agricultural activities.
9. KARNATAKA: KARNATAKA MUNICIPALITIES ACT, 1964		
Municipal Council	In smaller urban area; Population from 20,000 to 3 lakh; Density 1,500 persons per sq km;	Rs 9 lakh per annum from Tax & Non-Tax sources the in the year of the last preceding census or a sum calculated at the rate of rupees 45 per capita per annum, whichever is higher; 50 per cent of the total employment in non agricultural activities
Town Panchayat	In transitional area; Population from 10,000 to 20,000; Density 1,500 persons per sq km;	Rs. 9 lakh per annum from Tax & Non-Tax sources in the in the year of the last preceding census or a sum calculated at the rate of rupees forty-five per capita per annum, whichever is higher; 50 per cent of the total employment in non-agricultural activities
10. KERALA: KERALA MUNICIPALITY ACT 1994		
Town Panchayat	In transitional area (not defined)	–
Municipal Council	In smaller urban area (not defined)	–
Municipal Corporation	In larger urban are (not defined)	–

State	Demographic Criteria	Economic Criteria
11. MADHYA PRADESH: MADHYA PRADESH MUNICIPAL CORPORATION ACT, 1956		
Municipal Corporation	In larger urban area (not defined in the Act)	–
12. MADHYA PRADESH: MADHYA PRADESH NAGAR PALIKAADHINIYAM, 1964		
Municipal Council	In smaller urban area not defined	–
Nagar Panchayat	In transitional area (not defined)	–
13. MAHARASHTRA: MAHARASHTRA MUNICIPAL COUNCILS NAGAR PANCHAYATS & INDUSTRIAL TOWNSHIPS ACT, 1965		
Municipal Council	In smaller urban area; Population not less than 25,000	Percentage of employment in non-agricultural activities not less than 35 per cent
Nagar Panchayat in Transitional area State Govt can declare any district headquarter or a Taluka headquarter to be transitional area	In transitional area; Population not less than 10,000 not more than 20,000. Is not more than 20 km away from a municipal corporation or a Class A Council	Employment in non-agricultural activities not less than 25 per cent; If located more than 20 km from any municipal corporation or class A Council per cent or such employment not less than 50 per cent
14. ODISHA: THE ORISSA MUNICIPAL CORPORATION ACT, 2003		
Municipal Corporation	Larger urban area: A population of not less than 3 lakh	–
15. ODISHA: ORISSA MUNICIPAL ACT, 1950		
Municipal Council	Smaller urban area: a population of not less than 25,000	–
Notified Area Council	Transitional area; a population of not less than 10,000	–

State	Demographic Criteria	Economic Criteria
16. RAJASTHAN: RAJASTHAN MUNICIPAL ACT, 2009		
Municipal Corporation	In larger urban area not defined	–
Municipal Council	In smaller urban area not defined	–
Municipal Board	In transitional area not defined	–
17. TAMIL NADU: TAMIL NADU LOCAL BODIES ACT, 1998		
Municipal Corporation	Population not less than 5 lakh Density of 750 per sq km; ULBs grouped into ABCDE; E with a population of not less than 35,000 and a above 2.15 lakh	Municipal income from taxation and other sources adequate for discharge of municipal functions; One-half of male population working in non-agricultural activities;
Municipality	Population not less than 30,000 in the last census; Annual income not less than Rs. 50 lakh in last consecutive 3 years	Annual income not less than Rs. 50 lakh in last consecutive 3 years
Town Panchayat	Population not less than 20,000 in last census; revenue.	Annual income not less than 30 lakhs for the last consecutive 3 years (average income of a Panchayat constituted under be Tamil Nadu Panchayat Act, 1994)
18. UTTAR PRADESH: THE UTTAR PRADESH MUNICIPAL CORPORATION ACT, 1959		
Municipal Corporation	In 'larger urban area' a provided for in Art. 243-Q of the Indian Constitution	
19. UTTAR PRADESH: U.P. MUNICIPALITIES ACT, 1916		
Municipal Council	In 'smaller urban area' (not defined in the Act)	

State	Demographic Criteria	Economic Criteria
Nagar Panchayat	In 'transitional area' not (defined in the Act)	
20. WEST BENGAL: WEST BENGAL MUNICIPAL CORPORATION ACT, 2006		
Municipal Corporation	Population not less than 5 lakh; Density of population of three thousand per sq km	Three-fourth of the adult population is engaged in pursuits other than agriculture; The Governor is satisfied that income of the Corporation from taxation and other sources is likely to be adequate for discharge of municipal functions.
21. WEST BENGAL: THE WEST BENGAL MUNICIPAL ACT, 1993		
Constitution of a town as a 'Municipal Area'	Population not less than 30,000; Density of 750 per sq km One-half of male population working in non-agricultural activities; ULSGs are grouped into Group A, B, C, D and E; Group A with a population of above 2 lakh 15 thousand and Group E with a population not exceeding 35,000	Municipal income from taxation and other sources adequate for discharge of municipal functions;
Notified Area Authority: As per Section 41A, Notified Area Authority 'for a notified area means a Nagar Panchayat for a transitional area, that is to say, an area in transition from a rural area to an urban area as defined in Article 243Q of the	(i) To be created in any urbanised area which does not fulfill the conditions for being immediately constituted a municipal area under this Act, or (ii) any area which is (comprised in a newly developing town, or (iii) any area in which	

State	Demographic Criteria	Economic Criteria
Constitution of India;	new industries have been or are being established	

Note: The states of Bihar, Kerala, Rajasthan, and Tamil Nadu have unified municipal Acts that have provisions for all the three types of municipalities such as Municipal Corporation, Municipal Council and Nagar Panchayat.

ANNEX IV

COMPOSITION OF WARDS/WARD COMMITTEE AND AREA SABHA

Committee	No. of Wards	Composition
1. Andhra Pradesh Municipal Corporation Act and Greater Hyderabad Municipal Corporation Act		
Andhra Pradesh Municipalities (Constitution, Conduct of Meetings, Powers and Functions of Ward Committees, Area Sabhas and Ward Sabhas) Rules, 2010.		
Ward Committee	Constituted in each ward	Member representing the ward becomes the Chairperson of the Ward Committee; Not less than four and not more than ten electors from the ward on the basis of population representing the civil society to be nominated by the Corporation/Council; The minimum number of four members, if in a ward the population is ten thousand and less; and one additional member thereafter for every four thousand population subject to a maximum number of ten; Representatives of all Area sabhas within the ward; and Half of the persons so nominated should be women.

Committee	No. of Wards	Composition
Ward Committee	In every Ward of the Municipal Council	As above based on population
Area Sabha (AS)	Population up to 5 lakh: one AS for every 2,000; Above 5 lakh and upto 10 lakh: one AS for every 3,000; Above 10 lakh: One AS for every 5,000 (with 10 per cent variation).	All electors within the jurisdiction of the Area Sabha would be formally constituted within 3 months after Ward Committees are constituted. In the case of Municipalities and Nagar Panchayats, provisions with respect to constitution of Area Sabahs are, almost similar to those for the Municipal Corporations
Ward Sabha	In case of a Municipal Council with less than one lakh population, Ward Sabhas are to be constituted in different wards after the constitution of Ward Committees.	All the voters within the Area Sabha become members The elected Member chairs the Area Sabha.
2. BIHAR: BIHAR MUNICIPAL ACT, 2007		
Wards Committee:	Not less than three wards in cities with more than 3 lakh population	Councillors elected from the wards; Elect one from amongst themselves as Chairperson
Ward Committee	In every ward	Councilor elected from the ward; and All elected Representatives of the Area Sabhas located within the ward
Area Sabha	Constituted in each 'Area' (the body of all persons registered in electoral rolls pertaining to every polling	Area Sabha Representatives elected from the Area within a ward

Committee	No. of Wards	Composition
	booth in an Area in cities with more than 1.5 lakh population).	
3. GUJARAT: BOMBAY PROVINCIAL MUNICIPAL CORPORATION ACT, 1949		
Wards Committee	In cities with more than 3 lakh population; number of Wards Committee varies according to population. It varies from 3 in cities with a population of 3 to 4.5 lakhs to 13 in cities with more than 24 lakh population	Councilors elected from the wards; An officer of the Municipality designated as Officer-in-charge of the territorial area of the WC also a member; Three members nominated by the Councilors elected from the wards from amongst recognized NGO and CBO engaged in social work within the ward.
4. HARYANA: THE HARYANA MUNICIPAL CORPORATION ACT, 1994		
Wards Committee	Left to be provided in Rules	Councilors elected from the wards to be the member
5. KARNATAKA: KARNATAKA MUNICIPAL CORPORATION ACT, 1976		
Ward Committee	Constituted in each ward	Councilor representing the ward, Chairperson; 10 other members nominated by Corporation of whom two to belong to SC & ST, 3 women, & 2 from Residents' Association; An Officer of the Corporation to be designated by the Commissioner, to be the Secretary of ward Committee

Committee	No. of Wards	Composition
Area Sabha	In each 'Area' (polling area of one or more contiguous polling stations in a ward, but in any case not exceeding total area of five such polling stations)	All persons registered as voters in the electoral rolls of the polling stations in an area to be members of that Area Sabha; Area Sabha Representtaive to be nominated by the Councilor of the ward
6. KERALA MUNICIPALITY ACT, 1994		
Ward Committee in every Municipality where population exceeds one lakh	Constituted in each ward	Councilor of the ward who becomes the Chairman; 15 persons elected from among the members of the resident's association of that ward, which are registered in the Municipality; 20 members elected from among the members of the registered neighbourhood groups of that ward which are registered in the Municipality; one person each nominated by every political party having representation in the Municipality; Heads of all recognized educational institutions functioning in that ward; Twenty persons nominated jointly by the Chairperson and the Councillor of the ward, of whom,

Committee	No. of Wards	Composition
		(i) ten from persons representing the cultural organizations, voluntary organizations, educational institutions, industrial-commercial establishments which are functioning in that ward but not necessarily residing in the ward; (ii) five from persons representing those working in that ward as professionals (experts in agriculture, industry, health, education, engineering etc.) not necessarily residing in the ward; and (iii) five from persons in the registered trade unions:
Ward Sabha	In each ward where population does not exceed one lakh	Councilor of the ward to be Convener of Ward Sabha; All persons enrolled as elector in the ward.

7. MADHYA PRADESH: MADHYA PRADESH MUNICIPAL CORPORATION ACT, 1956

Committee	No. of Wards	Composition
Wards Committee	In cities with more than 3 lakh population; The Act also provides for creation of Wards Committee in cities with less than 3 lakh population; The number of Wards Committees to be determined by dividing the total population of the municipal area by 100.	Councilors elected from the wards; Two persons residing within the territorial area of the Wards Committee to be nominated by the Mayor on recommendation of the Chairman of the Wards Committee having knowledge & experience

Committee	No. of Wards	Composition
		in municipal administration and Committee.
Mohalla Committee	In every Municipal Area; Number of Mohalla Committees in a ward to be decided by the State Government	Councilor elected from the ward to be the member of the Mohalla committees in the ward. Number of Members, nature of composition and functions to be provided in the Rules.
8. MADHYA PRADESH; MADHYA PRADESH NAGAR PALIKA ADHINIYAM, 1964		
Wards Committee	If the Municipal Council and Nagar Panchayat so decides, Wards Committees are to be created even in these municipal bodies	Councilors elected from the wards; Two persons residing within the territorial area of the Wards Committee to be nominated by the Mayor on recommendation of the Chairman of the wards having knowledge & experience in municipal administration and Committee.
Mohalla Committee	Created in every municipality notified for this purpose by the State Government	Councilor elected from the ward to be the member of the Mohalla committees in the ward. Number of Members, nature of composition and functions to be provided in the Rules.
9. ODISHA: THE ORISSA MUNICIPAL CORPORATION ACT, 2003		
Wards Committee	In every ward	The Councilor representing the ward becomes President of this Committee;

Committee	No. of Wards	Composition
		An elector of the ward nominated by the Mayor; and Commissioner or any other officer authorized by the Commissioner.
10. RAJASTHAN: RAJASTHAN MUNICIPAL ACT, 2009		
Wards Committee	In Municipalities with more than three lakh population	Councilor elected from the wards; and five persons with more than 25 years of age and with knowledge and experience in municipal administration nominated by the Municipality
11. TAMIL NADU: TAMIL NADU LOCAL BODIES ACT, 1998		
Not provided for in the Act, to be created by the State Government	State Government to decide on number of Wards Committees to be created and the number of wards to be pooled together	Councilors elected from the wards
12. UTTAR PRADESH & UTTARAKHAND: THE UTTAR PRADESH MUNICIPAL CORPORATION ACT, 1959		
Wards Committee	Constituted in Municipal Corporations with more than three lakh population; Each ward to consist of ten wards	Councilors elected from the wards; Five members nominated by the State Government from within the wards having knowledge or experience in municipal administration
13. UTTAR PRADESH & UTTARAKHAND: THE UTTAR PRADESH MUNICIPALITIES ACT, 1916		
Ward Committee	Constituted in each ward	Councilor elected from the ward;

Committee	No. of Wards	Composition
		Ten members nominated by the Municipal Council from within the ward who happen to be office bearers of citizens' welfare societies and representatives of non-government organizations who have special knowledge or experience of municipal administration.

14. West Bengal: West Bengal Municipal Corporation Act, 2006

Committee	No. of Wards	Composition
Borough Committee	For six contiguous wards	Councilors elected from the wards;
Ward Committee	In each ward	17 other members to be nominated by the Councillor and the Municipality from among the residents of the ward; At least three among them nominated from the representatives of CDS, and if there is no CDS then such number of members nominated from among the women members of the BPL families residing in the area. For selection of other members the engineers, doctors, cultural activists, social workers, educationists, etc., from among the residents of the area, are considered.

Committee	No. of Wards	Composition
15. West Bengal: The West Bengal Municipal Act, 1993		
Borough Committee	In every Municipality with a population of 3 lakh and more; Created by grouping the wards of the Municipality into five Boroughs so that each Borough consists of not less than six contiguous wards, and constitute a Borough Committee for each Borough.	Councilors elected from the wards
Ward Committee	In every ward	Councilor elected from the wards; Minimum of 9 and a maximum of 17 other members to be nominated by the Councillor and the Municipality from among the residents of the ward. For a population up to 2,500 such number of other members shall be 9, and thereafter for every 500 additional population, or part thereof, there shall be one additional member subject to a maximum of 17; and If the number of other members varies from 7 to 9 then two, and if the number exceeds 9 then at least three among them nominated from the representatives of CDS. If there is no

Committee	No. of Wards	Composition
		CDS then such number of members shall be nominated from among the women members of the BPL families residing in the area. For selection of other members the engineers, doctors, cultural activists, social workers, educationists, etc., from among the residents of the area, are required to be considered.

Note: The states of Bihar, Kerala, Rajasthan, and Tamil Nadu have unified municipal Acts that have provisions for all the three types of municipalities such as Municipal Corporation, Municipal Council and Nagar Panchayat.

ANNEX V

KERALA MUNICIPALITY (CONSTITUTION OF WARD COMMITTEE AND PROCEDURE FOR MEETING) RULES, 1995

1. *Short title and commencement:* (1) These rules may be called the Kerala Municipality (Constitution of Ward Committee and Procedure for Meeting) Rules, 1995.
   (a) They shall come into force at once.
2. *Definitions:* In these rules unless the context otherwise requires:
   (a) 'Act' means the Kerala Municipality Act, 1994 (20 of 1994);
   (b) 'Form' means a form appended to these rules;
   (c) 'Section' means a Section of the Act;
   (d) Words and expressions used and not defined in these rules, but defined in the Act shall have the meanings respectively assigned to them in the Act.
3. *Constitution of Ward Committees:* The Chairperson shall, as soon as possible, after the general elections for the Constitution of the Municipality and the election to the office of the Chairperson, constitute a Ward Committee for every ward as specified in Section 43.
4. *Meetings of Ward Committees:* The Chairperson concerned shall, convene the meeting of every ward Committee once in every three months and as and when required during the interim period, and give notice intimating the venue, date and time of the meeting to the members at least seven days before the day of the meeting and publish a copy of the notice in the notice board of the Municipality.
5. *Quorum:*
   (a) The quorum of the Ward Committee shall be one-fifth of the total number of its members.
   (b) The Chairman of the meeting shall, if quorum is not obtained within thirty minutes after the time fixed for the meeting is over, postpone the meeting to another day and, as specified under Rule 4, give notice thereof to the members and also publish the same:

   Provided that the meeting so postponed shall be convened again within 15 days.

6. *Register of members:* A register containing the names and details of the members shall be maintained and the members attending the meeting shall mark their attendance in that register.
7. *Subjects to be discussed in the meeting:* The Secretary or the Officer authorised by him in this behalf shall, in consultation with the Chairman of the Ward Committee, prepare the agenda by including the business to be transacted in the Ward Committee and read it over to the members at the beginning of the Ward Committee meeting.
8. *Recording of proceedings of the meeting:*
   (a) The Secretary or an Officer authorised by him in this behalf shall prepare the proceedings of the Ward Committee and the Chairman of the meeting shall put his signature below the Committee decisions. The proceedings of the meeting shall be given to the members within five days after the meeting and its copy shall be published in the notice board of the Municipality.
   (b) The Secretary or the Officer authorised by him in this behalf shall record the minutes, opinions, and general unanimous suggestion of the members and intimate the Chairperson, within fifteen days, the resolutions passed on majority basis.
   (c) The Chairperson shall, as soon as possible, place the suggestions and resolutions of the Ward Committee before the council for its consideration.
9. *Preparation of Development Schemes:* Every Ward Committee shall, in a meeting held three months before the end of every financial year, prepare in accordance with sub-section (1) of Section 51 development schemes for the next financial year along with an expected estimate of the expenditure for each item in the order of priority in the form appended and submit the same to the council through the Chairperson.
10. *Submission of periodical reports:* Every Ward Committees shall, regarding the matters specified in Section 45 submit report to the council through the Chairperson every three months.
11. *Council to consider the resolutions etc. of the Ward Committee:* Council shall give due consideration to the proposals, resolutions, schemes and reports submitted by a Ward Committee under Rules 8, 9 and 10.

APPENDIX FORM

(See Rule 9)

Details of development schemes for the financial year............................passed in the meeting of the...Ward Committee of....................... Municipality held on......................day of.............................

S. No.	Details of development schemes (in order of priority)	Expected estimate cost (Rs.)	Remarks
1	2	3	4

Signature with date
Name of the Chairman of the Ward Committee

ANNEX VI

THE WEST BENGAL MUNICIPAL (WARD COMMITTEE) RULES, 2001

CONTENTS

PART I

PART II

Composition and Constitution of Ward Committee

PART III

Rules of Business of the Ward Committee

PART IV

Powers and Functions

PART V

Creation of Internal Resources

The West Bengal Municipal (Ward Committee) Rules, 2001
(As amended by Notification No. 18/MA/O/C-4/3C-2/2001, dated 8 January 2003)

PART I

1. *Short title, application and commencement:* (1) These rules may be called the West Bengal Municipal (Ward Committee) Rules, 2001.
   (a) They shall apply to all the Municipalities and Notified Area Authorities constituted under the West Bengal Municipal Act, 1993 (West Ben. Act XVII of 1993).
   (b) They shall come into force from the date of their publication in the Official Gazette.
2. *Definitions:*
   (a) In these rules unless the context otherwise requires:
      (i) 'Act' means the West Bengal Municipal Act, 1993 (West Ben. Act XXII of 1993);
      (ii) 'BPL family' means the family below the poverty lines, as determined by the Ministry of Urban Affairs and Employment, Government of India, from time to time, for identification of beneficiaries in poverty alleviation schemes;
   (b) 'Chairman' means the Chairman of the Ward Committee;
   (c) 'Committee' means the Ward Committee constituted under these rules;
   (d) 'CDS' means the Community Development Society constituted in the municipal area for implementation of the Swarna Jayanti Sahari Rojgar Yojana;
   (e) 'Member' means a member of the Committee.
   (f) The Words and expressions used in these rules and not defined shall have the meaning respectively assigned to them in the Act.

PART II

Composition and Constitution of Ward Committee

3. Constitution of Ward Committee:
   (a) The Committee shall be constituted by the Municipality/Notified Area Authority within one month from the date of the first meeting of the Board of Councillors after a general election.
   (b) After constitution of the Committee, the Councillor or the Municipality/Notified Area Authority shall place the names of the members of the Committee, selected by the Councillor as well as the Municipality/Notified Area Authority as per provisions of rule 4, in the next general meeting of the citizens of the ward convened in terms of provisions of rule 8. The proposals, if any, from any general citizen of the ward regarding change of any name proposed by the Municipality of the Councillor, as the case may be, or any other matter relating to constitution of the Committee, shall be considered by the Councillor or the Municipality/Notified Area Authority and if necessary the Councillor or the Municipality/Notified Area Authority, as the case may be, may replace any member of the Committee nominated under rule 4.
   (c) In the case of any casual vacancy occurred in any post of any member, shall be filled up by the Councillor or the Municipality/Notified Area Authority, as the case may be, either in the annual general meeting or a general meeting of the citizens of the ward convened for the purpose, and for filling up any vacant post of any member the manner as prescribed in sub-rule (2) shall be followed.
4. *Composition of Ward Committee*
   (a) The Committee shall consist of the elected Councillor and such other members as may be nominated by the elected Councillor of the ward and the Municipality/ Notified Area Authority from among the residents of the ward.
   (b) The elected Councillor of the ward shall be chairperson of the Committee. He shall preside over the meetings of the Committee. In his absence, the members present shall elect a President from among themselves to preside over the meeting.
   (c) For nominating the members, in a ward where the population is not more than two thousand and five hundred, the number of other members shall be four and, thereafter, there shall be one additional member for every five hundred populations or part thereof, subject to a maximum number of fourteen.

Explanation: In reckoning the number of additional members of the Committee exceeding four, any part of less than two hundred fifty (250) population may be ignored.

(d) The nomination of other members of the Committee shall be made in the following manner:

Category	Total number of other Members of the Ward Committee	To be nominated by the Councillor elected from the Ward	To be nominated by the Municipality
1.	7	5	2
2.	8	5	3
3.	9	6	3
4.	10	7	3
5.	11	8	3
6.	12	9	3
7.	13	10	3
8.	14	11	3
9.	15	11	4
10.	16	12	4
11.	17	13	4

Among the total number of members of the Committee the Councillor shall nominate, in the case of categories 1, 2 and 3 mentioned above, at least two representatives of the CDS, and in the cases of categories 4 to 11 mentioned above, three representatives of the CDS, who are the residents of the concerned ward:

Provided that any member of CDS shall not be nominated in more than one Committee:

Provided further that where the members of CDS are not available, the members as specified in this rule shall be nominated from amongst the women members of the BPL families from the ward concerned:

(e) While nominating the other members of the Committee the aspect of proper representation of engineers, physicians, educationists, social workers, cultural activists, sports-persons, women, persons from economically backward section of society or any other person from among the residents of the ward, shall be made in such manner as may cover all sections of people of the ward as aforesaid.

(f) The elected Councillor of the ward or the Municipality/Notified Area Authority, as the case may be, shall have the right to remove any member nominated by it, if considered necessary.

5. *Tenure of the Committee:*
   (i) Tenure of the Committee shall be the same as that of the Board of Councillors of the Municipality/Notified Area Authority.
   (ii) In case of any casual vacancy in the membership of the Committee caused by the following reasons, it shall be filled up by the Councillor elected from the Ward or by the Municipality/Notified Area Authority, as the case may be, by fresh nomination:
      (a) death,
      (b) resignation, duly accepted by the Councillor elected from the ward or by the Municipality/Notified Area Authority, as the case may be,
      (c) withdrawal of nomination by the Councillor elected from the ward or by the Municipality/Notified Area Authority, as the case may be, or
      (d) shift of residence by any member from the ward to any other ward or elsewhere.

PART III

Rules of Business of the Ward Committee

6. *First meeting of Ward Committee:* The first meeting of the Committee shall be convened by he Chairman of the Committee within fifteen days from the date of constitution of the Committee. Apart from normal business, the Committee shall, at its first meeting, select a Member-Secretary for the Committee from among the members who shall convene the subsequent meetings of the Committee in consultation with the Chairman and shall perform the secretarial functions of the Committee.
7. *Ordinary meetings:*
   (a) The Committee shall meet at least once in every month.
   (b) The Chairman shall fix the date, place and time of the meeting.
   (c) No meeting shall be held unless at least seven clear days before the day of the meeting, notice specifying the date, place and time of such meeting and the business to be transacted there has been given to the members.
8. *Annual General Meetings:*
   1. The Committee shall convene an annual general meeting of the residents of the ward by intimating every resident of the ward and also

by public proclamation intimating the time and venue of the meeting to be held within the 30th June every year to apprise them the activities of the Municipality/Notified Area Authority in general, and the ward in particular, during the preceding year and to assess the popular needs of the ward for the current year.

2. For the annual general meetings, the Municipality/Notified Area Authority shall furnish the following documents to the Committee for public information and deliberation thereon:
   (a) a detailed report about the activities of the Municipality/Notified Area Authority in the ward area during the preceding year;
   (b) a copy of the Annual Administration Report along with the Annual Financial Statement of the Municipality/Notified Area Authority for the preceding year.
3. Annual General Meetings shall be arranged preferably in a public place within the ward.
4. Apart from the meeting as prescribed in sub-rule (1), the Committee shall convene a Half yearly General Meeting of the residents of the ward by intimating every resident of the ward and also by public proclamation intimating the time and venue of the meeting, to be held in the month of October-November each year to apprise them the activities of the Municipality/Notified Area Authority in general, and the ward in particular, during the period from the date of holding of last preceding Annual General Meeting, and to discuss the proposals for preparation of the development plan for the next year.

9. *Minutes:*
   1. Minutes of proceedings of the Ward Committee shall be entered in the 'Minute Book' specifying the names of the members who attended the meeting, the business transacted, the decision of the Committee on each item of business, the date of the meeting and the time of commencement and closing of the meeting.
   2. The minutes shall be written by the Member-Secretary of the Committee and signed by the Chairman, and a copy of the same shall be displayed in some conspicuous place of the concerned ward.

PART IV
Powers and Functions

10. *General Functions:*
   1. The Committee, subject to general supervision of the Borough Committee or the Municipality, as the case may be, shall, within the ward, supervise and monitor:

(a) detection of violation of various provisions of the Act such as unlawful construction, encroachments on municipal and public properties, public nuisance, evasion of taxes, unlicensed activities, and the like;
(b) arresting wasteful uses of various municipal services like tap-water, street hydrant, street light, parks and playgrounds, community centres and libraries, and the like;
(c) collection and removal of garbage;
(d) removal of accumulated water on streets, public places due to rain, and other causes;
(e) health immunisation services;
(f) improvement of slums including its clearance wherever necessary;
(g) redressal of public grievances;
(h) maintenance of essential statistics;
(i) numbering of streets and premises;
(j) execution of various obligatory and discretionary functions and functions transferred by the State Government to the Municipality/Notified Are Authority as per provisions of the Act.

2. The Committee, as per directions of the Borough Committee or the Municipality/Notified Area Authority, as the case may be, shall also monitor and supervise within the ward:
   (a) work of assessment, collection of property tax, other taxes, fees and other sums due to the Municipality/Notified Area Authority;
   (b) maintenance and repair of roads and drains;
   (c) execution of public works;
   (d) maintenance of sanitation and public health;
   (e) the prevention and control of dangerous diseases;
   (f) issue of birth and death certificates;
   (g) all Urban Poverty Alleviation Programmes of the State and the Central Government;
   (h) tree planting in the municipal properties;
   (i) maintenance of parks, tanks, and other municipal properties;
   (j) generation of internal resources; and
   (k) literacy expansion programmes
3. The Committee shall perform other functions as may be entrusted to it by the Municipality or the Borough Committee or the Act or the rules made thereunder and supervise implementation of decisions of the Municipality/Notified Area Authority and the other Committees constituted under the Act in respect of all matters relating to the ward.

11. *Planning:*
    1. Within three months from the date of constitution of the Committee, the Committee shall prepare a list of the schemes for development of the ward during the next five years and also annual priority list of these schemes and submit the same to the Municipality/Notified Area Authority for incorporating them in the Development Plan of the Municipality/Notified Area Authority as per provisions of the Act.
    2. The priority list mentioned in sub-rule (1) shall be prepared after:
       (a) identifying problems of the ward, and
       (b) fixation of priority of problems so identified.
12. *Execution of development schemes:*
    1. When the Municipality/Notified Area Authority executes any development scheme in the ward area, a beneficiary Committee consisting of the citizens of the ward, shall be constituted by the Committee, under it's supervision, for looking after the work and making any suggestion related to the concerned work.
    2. The Committee shall make the work schedule of any development scheme available to the beneficiary Committee constituted under sub-rule (1) for the purpose.
13. *Powers of the Committee:*
    1. The Chairman shall be entitled to:
       (a) call for any information in so far as it relates to any matter within the ward,
       (b) call for any consideration all periodical statements relating to the receipts and disbursements.
    2. Any member may draw attention of the Chairman to any requirement of any locality or to any lapse in execution of the work or to any waste of the Municipal Fund or Municipal Property and may suggest any improvement which he considers desirable.
    3. The Committee may require, with the permission of the Municipality, any officer of the Municipality to attend any meeting of the Committee at which any matter dealt with by such officer in the course of his duties is being discussed. When any officer is thus required to attend any such meeting he may be called upon to make a statement of facts or furnish such information in his possession relating to any matter dealt with by him or produce any document or report as the Committee may require.
14. *Duties of Municipality*
    1. The Municipality shall make available to the Committee the following information:

(a) decisions of the Standing Committee;
(b) decisions or resolutions of the Municipality;
(c) Ward-wise budgetory allocation made by the Municipality;
(d) copy of the ward map;
(e) details of municipal properties ward-wise;
(f) Annual Financial Statement and Annual Administration Report;
(g) demand and collection figures of tax and non-tax revenue of the ward; and
(h) such other information as required by the Committee.

2. The Municipality, on a written requisition from the Chairman of the Committee, shall make available an advance amount required to meet the emergent needs of natural calamity, accident or any other reason, and the Chairman of the Committee, within fifteen days from the date of receipt of such advance, shall submit a report of utilisation of such sum and refund the unspent portion of such advance, if any, to the Municipality/Notified Area Authority.
3. The Municipality shall provide an office for each Committee.

PART V
Creation of Internal Resources

15. *Proposals for creation of internal resources:*
1. The Committee shall consider the opportunities for creation of new sources to augment municipal income by way of,
   (i) using lands vested to the Government or Municipality/Notified Area Authority and any land belonging to any Government department subject to permission of such department for:
      (a) tree plantation on long term and short term basis; or
      (b) constructing market complexes, shops and buildings for commercial use; or
      (c) integrating scattered small-scale industries in industrial complexes; or
      (d) constructing parking spaces for buses, trucks, cars, etc; or
      (e) construction of housing complexes; or
      (f) any other measure the Committee considers feasible;
   (ii) using private, public water bodies for promotion of pisciculture or entertainment purposes;
   (iii) installing unconventional energy sources like solar electricity or bio-gas or any other alternative for commercial distribution;

(iv) using private lands for commercial purpose on joint venture of Municipality/Notified Area Authority and the concerned owner;

(v) running municipal transport system on roadways and waterways for carrying goods and passengers in such routes which are not covered by adequate public system and are financially viable; and

(vi) such other measures which the Committee considers feasible and viable.

2. The Committee, shall submit a detailed proposal for creation of internal resources, as specified in sub-rule (1), to the Municipality/Notified Area Authority:

Provided that if it is felt by the Committee that involvement of other ward/wards is necessary for such creation of new resources, the Committee may interact with the Committee of such other ward/wards for finalisation of the proposal.

3. It shall be obligatory on the part of the Municipality/Notified Area Authority to spend 60 per cent of the income from the newly created internal resources, as per proposal of the Committee, in the ward/wards, where such new internal resources have been created, after deducting the cost for implementation of such project, if any.

16. *Issue of general or special direction:* The State Government may issue such general or special directions, not inconsistent with the provisions of the Act or these rules, as may, in its opinion, be necessary for the purpose of giving effect to these rules or for removing any difficulty in this regard.

ANNEX VII

STATUS OF EXECUTIVE POWER OF MAYOR/ CHAIRPERSON IN MAJOR STATES

Position	Power
1. ANDHRA PRADESH: THE ANDHRA PRADESH MUNICIPAL CORPORATIONS ACT, 1994	
Mayor	Weak
2. BIHAR MUNICIPAL ACT, 2007	
Mayor Chairpersons/Presidents	Strong; Chairs the Empowered Standing Committee (ESC) and all executive power vests with the ESC
3. GUJARAT: BOMBAY PROVINCIAL MUNICIPAL CORPORATION ACT, 1949	
Mayor	Weak; Section 67(3) provides that 'Subject, whenever it is in this Act expressly so directed to the approval or sanction of the Corporation or the Standing Committee and subject also to all other restrictions, limitations and conditions imposed by this Act or by any other law for the time being in force, the entire executive power for the purpose of carrying out the provisions of this Act and of any other Act for the time being in force which imposes any duty or confers any powers on the Corporation vests in the Commissioner. . .'
4. GUJARAT: GUJARAT MUNICIPALITIES ACT, 1963	
President	Weak; Section 44(2) provides that 'the entire executive power of the purpose of carrying out the provisions of this Act vests in the Chief Officer. . .'

Position	Power
5. HARYANA: THE HARYANA MUNICIPAL CORPORATION ACT, 1994	
Mayor	Weak; Section 49 provides that: '. . . the executive power, for the purpose of carrying out the provisions of this Act, and of any other Act for the time being in force which confers any power or impose any duty on the Corporation, shall vest in the Commissioner. . .'
6. KARNATAKA: KARNATAKA MUNICIPAL CORPORATION ACT, 1976	
Mayor	Strong; Section 60(2) provides that 'the Mayor shall have general powers of inspec tion and may give direction to the Commissioner with regard to the implementation of any resolution of the corporation or a standing committee in the discharge of any obligatory and discretionary functions of the corporation, and the Commissioner shall comply with such directions. The Mayor may call any record of the corporation from the Commissioner and the records made available to him shall be returned by him within fifteen days from the date they are made available'.
7. KARNATAKA: KARNATAKA MUNICIPALITIES ACT, 1964	
President	Strong; Section 43 provides that he presides over all meetings of the Municipal Council, watch over the financial and executive administration of the Municipal Council, and issue directions to the Municipal Commissioneror, the Chief Officer to implement the resolutions of the Council or the Standing Committees'.
8. KERALA: KERALA MUNICIPALITY ACT, 1994	
Mayor Chairman	Strong; Section 15(1) provides that 'Subject to the provisions of this Act, the Chair-

Position	Power
	person shall have powers of inspection and may give such directions and orders as he thinks fit with regard to the implementation of any resolution of the Council or Committees in the discharge of any function of a Municipality and the Secretary shall be bound to comply with such direction'.

9. KOLKATA MUNICIPAL CORPORATION ACT, 1980

Position	Power
Mayor	Strong; Section 33 provides that the executive power of the Corporation shall be exercised by the Mayor-in-Council. (Mayor presides over the meetings of the Mayor-in-Council)

10. MADHYA PRADESH: MADHYA PRADESH MUNICIPAL CORPORATION ACT 1956

Position	Power
Mayor	Weak; despite the provision for a Mayor-in-Council form of local government (has quite incongruous and ambivalent legal provisions) that is quite perplexing. Sub-section (3) of Section (69) provides that 'Subject to the approval or sanction of the Corporation or of the Standing Committee, wherever it is in this Act expressly so directed and subject also to all other restrictions, limitations and conditions imposed by this Act, the entire executive power for the purpose of carrying out the provisions of this Act vests in Commissioner. . .' The Act has another provision under Section 25 providing that the mayor 'shall have administrative control over the officers and servants of his office including the Mayor-in-Council and Appeal Committee';

Position	Power
	Section 55 provides that 'The Commissioner shall be the principal Executive Officer of the corporation. . .'
11. Madhya Pradesh Municipality Act, 1961	
President	Weak; Sub-section (1) of Section 50 provides that subject to provisions of this Act and the Rules and regulations made under this Act, administration of the Municipal Council shall be vested in the Council; Sub-section (2) of Section 50 provides that the executive power for implementing the provisions of this Act, shall vest in the Chief Municipal Officer.
Chairman	Strong: Section 51 provides that he supervises financial and Executive Administration of the Municipality and has emergency powers.
12. Maharashtra: Maharashtra Municipal Councils, Nagar Panchayats & Industrial Townships Act, 1965	
President	Strong; Section 58 (1)(b); gives the authority to 'watch over the financial and Executive Administration of the Council; Section 58(1)(d) gives him power to 'exercise supervision and control over the acts and proceedings of Chief Officer of the Council in matters of Executive Administration of and in matters concerning accounts and records of the Council' and Section 58(2) gives him emergency powers for direct execution or stoppage of any work.
13. The Mumbai Municipal Corporation Act, 1888	
Mayor	Weak: Section 64(3) provides that '. . . the entire executive power for the purpose of

Position	Power
	carrying out the provisions of this Act vest in the Commissioner. . . .'
14. Odisha: Orissa Municipal Corporation Act, 2003	
Mayor	Strong: (i) Mayor has emergency powers under Section 34; (ii) Section 28: 'The Commissioner shall be the principal Executive Officer of the Corporation and shall, subject to supervision and control of the Mayor. . . .'
15. Rajasthan: Rajasthan Municipal Act, 2009	
President/Chairman	Strong; Section 48 provides that he presides over the meetings of all the Committees of the Municipality and conducts its business. He is also required to keep an eye on financial and executive administration of the Municipality
16. Tamil Nadu: Tamil Nadu Local Bodies Act, 1998	
Chairperson	Weak; Section (57)(1) provides that 'Subject to the sanction of the council and subject to all other restrictions, limitations and conditions as may be prescribed or as are hereinafter imposed in Act, the executive power for the purpose of carrying out the provisions of this Act shall be vested in the Commissioner'.
17. Uttar Pradesh: The Uttar Pradesh Municipal Corporation Act, 1959	
Mayor	Weak; Sub-section (1) of Section 117 provides that 'the municipal administration of the city shall vest in the Corporation; Sub-section (2) provides that 'Except as otherwise expressly provided in this Act, the Executive Committee shall be vested with, on behalf of the Corporation, with

Position	Power
	the superintendence of the municipal administration of the City'; Section (51)(1)(a) provides that the Mayor 'shall be ex officio Chairman of the Executive Committee'; Nevertheless, it has a strange provision under Section 117 (5) that 'Subject to the general control and direction of the Mayor . . . the executive power of the purposes of carrying out the provisions of this Act shall be vested in the Municipal Commissioner. . . .'
18. UTTAR PRADESH: U.P. MUNICIPALITIES ACT, 1916	
President	Strong; Section 50(bb) gives him power with respect to 'general supervision over all officers and works of the Municipality'; Section 51(b) gives him power 'to watch over the financial and superintend the executive administration of the Municipality'.
19. WEST BENGAL: WEST BENGAL MUNICIPAL CORPORATION ACT, 2006	
Mayor	Strong; He constitutes the Mayor-in-Council, allocates business to the member to the Mayor-in-Council (M-in-C), He presides over the meetings of the M-in-C and Section 44 provides that the 'Commissioner shall be the principal Executive Officer of the Corporation and shall, subject to supervision and control of the Mayor' shall discharge powers and functions given to him under this Act.
20. WEST BENGAL: THE WEST BENGAL MUNICIPAL ACT, 1993	
Chairman	Strong; Section 16(1) provides that 'The Chairman shall be the executive head of the Municipality and the Municipal

Position	Power
	Administration shall be under his control and he shall exercise such powers and functions as conferred on him by or under this Act'.

Note: The states of Bihar, Kerala, Rajasthan, and Tamil Nadu have unified Municipal Acts that have provisions for all the three types of municipalities such as Municipal Corporation, Municipal Council and Nagar Panchayat.

ANNEX VIII

TERM OF OFFICE OF MAYORS/CHAIRPERSONS IN MUNICIPAL GOVERNMENTS IN MAJOR STATES

Reservation	Election	Term of office	Authorities
1. ANDHRA PRADESH: ANDHRA PRADESH MUNICIPAL CORPORATION ACT, 1994			
Chairpersons' seats in the State to be reserved for SC and ST in the same proportion as their population makes the proportion to the total population of the Municipality; One-third of the total number of seats reserved for backward classes; One half of the total number of Chairpersons including one half of seats reserved for SCs, STs and BCs reserved for women	Indirect	One Year	Corporation Standing Committee; Commissioner; and Wards Committee
2. BIHAR: BIHAR MUNICIPAL ACT, 2007			
Municipal Corporation, and other types of ULSGs Not exceeding fifty per cent of the total seats of Chairman in the State reserved for (i) Scheduled Castes; (ii) Scheduled Tribes; and (ii) Backward Classes. For SC & ST, same as in the case of Andhra Pradesh;	Indirect	Five Year	(i) the Municipal Corporation, (ii) the Empowered Standing Committee, (iii) the Mayor, and (iv) the Municipal Commissioner;

Reservation	Election	Term of office	Authorities
Not exceeding twenty per cent of the total seats and within the overall limit of 50 per cent reservation for the Scheduled Castes, the Scheduled Tribes and the Backward Classes; Not exceeding 50 per cent of the total number of seats reserved for SC, ST, & Backward castes reserved for women belonging to the Scheduled Castes, the Scheduled Tribes and the Backward Classes; and As nearly as but not exceeding 50 per cent of the total number of the seats not reserved for Scheduled Castes, Scheduled Tribes and Backward Classes reserved for women.			
3. GUJARAT: BOMBAY PROVINCIAL MUNICIPAL CORPORATION ACT, 1949			
Municipal Corporation: Reservation detailed out in Rules	Indirect	Two & a half year	Corporation; Standing Committee; Wards Committee; and Municipal Commissioner
4. GUJARAT: GUJARAT MUNICIPALITIES ACT, 1963			
Municipal Council Detailed out in Rules	Indirect	Two & a half year	Not provided in the Act; Executive powers for the purpose of carrying out provisions of the Act

Reservation	Election	Term of office	Authorities
			vests in the Chief Officer
5. HARYANA: THE HARYANA MUNICIPAL CORPORATION ACT, 1994			
Municipal Corporation Detailed out in Rules	Indirect	Not provided in the Act, forms part of the Rules	Not provided in the Act, forms part of the Rules
6. HARYANA: HARYANA MUNICIPAL ACT, 1973			
Municipal Committee Detailed out in Rules	Indirect	Not provided in the Act, forms part of the Rules	Not provided in the Act, forms part of the Rules
7. KARNATAKA: KARNATAKA MUNICIPAL CORPORATION ACT, 1976			
Municipal Corporation Seats of Mayor reserved for SC, ST in the same proportion as their population makes to the total population of the City; One-third of the total number of seats for backward castes. But the Act caps the total number of seats to be reserved for these categories at 50 per cent; 50 per cent of the total number of seats from each category mentioned above is reserved for women.	Indirect	One year	1. Corporation; 2. Standing Committees; and 3. Commissioner
8. KARNATAKA: KARNATAKA MUNICIPALITIES ACT, 1964			
As in the case of Municipal Corporation, except that one-third of the total number of seats are reserved for	Indirect	Two and a half year	

Reservation	Election	Term of office	Authorities
9. KERALA MUNICIPALITY ACT, 1994			
Reservation as in Municipal Corporation , Municipal Council and Town Panchayat for SC, ST and women as per usual practice in other states except that the number of seats reserved for women is one-third and there is no reservation for backward caste.	Indirect	Five years	–
10. MADHYA PRADESH: MADHYA PRADESH MUNICIPAL CORPORATION ACT, 1956			
Municipal Corporation Seats of Mayor reserved for SC, ST in the same proportion as their population makes to the total population of the City; One-third of the total number of office of Mayor reserved for women belonging to these castes; 25 per cent for other backward castes; 50 per cent of the total number of seats SC, ST & Backward castes reserved for women; and 50 per cent (including number of seats reserved for women belonging to SC,ST, and Backward castes) of the total number of seats reserved for women.	Direct	Five years	Corporation; Mayor-in Council; Mayor; and Commissioner
11. MADHYA PRADESH: MADHYA PRADESH NAGAR PALIKA ADHINIYAM, 1964			
Municipal Council and Nagar Panchayat Same as in the case of Municipal Corporation	Direct	Five years	–

Reservation	Election	Term of office	Authorities
12. MAHARASHTRA: THE MUMBAI MUNICIPAL CORPORATION ACT, 1888			
Mumbai Municipal Corporation Not provided in the Act, to be prescribed by the State Government	Indirect	One year	Corporation; Standing Committee; Improvements Committee; Greater Mumbai Electric Supply & Transport Committee (BEST); Education Committee; Mayor; Municipal Commissioner; and General Manager, BEST
13. MAHARASHTRA: THE MAHARASHTRA MUNICIPAL COUNCILS NAGAR PANCHAYATS & INDUSTRIAL TOWNSHIPS ACT, 1965			
Municipal Council President (Reservation provided for in Rules)	Indirect	Two & a half years	Council; President; Standing Committee; Subject Committees; Wards Committee; and Chief Officer
14. ODISHA: THE ORISSA MUNICIPAL CORPORATION ACT, 2003			
Municipal Corporation Seats of Chairpersons reserved for SC, ST in the same proportion as their population makes to the total population of the Municipality; One-third of	Indirect	Five years	Corporation; Mayor; Standing Committee; and Commissioner

Reservation	Election	Term of office	Authorities
the total number of office of Mayor reserved for women belonging to these castes; 27 per cent of seats reserved for backward castes; and One-third of the total seats reserved for women (including the reserved seats for women belonging to SC, ST & backward castes			
15. ODISHA: ORISSA MUNICIPAL ACT, 1950			
Municipal Council Notified Area Council Reservation as in case of Municipal Corporation	Indirect	Five years	–
16. RAJASTHAN: RAJASTHAN MUNICIPAL ACT, 2009			
President in Municipal Council Chairman in Municipal Board Reservation provided in Rules	Direct	Five years	Not provide for
17. TAMIL NADU: TAMIL NADU LOCAL BODIES ACT, 1998			
Mayor (a) Seats of Mayor reserved for SC, ST in the same proportion as their population makes to the total population of the City; where no office of Mayor can be reserved for the persons belonging to Scheduled Castes or the Scheduled Tribes based on the total percentage of population of scheduled Castes and the Scheduled Tribes in all the	Direct	Five years	Council; Chairperson Standing Committee and Wards Committee, and Commissioner

Reservation	Election	Term of office	Authorities
Corporations, one of the Mayors of a Corporation having the highest percentage of population of the Scheduled Castes and the Schedued Tribes is reserved for women belonging to the Scheduled Castes or the Scheduled Tribes out of the total number of offices of Mayor reserved for women under (b). (b) One-third of the total number of offices of Mayor reserved for women			
Municipal Council & Municipal Board Seats of Chairpersons reserved for SC, ST in the same proportion as their population makes to the total population of the City; One-third of the seats reserved for backward castes to be reserved for women belonging to these castes; One-third of the total seats reserved for women (including the reserved seats for women belonging to SC, ST & backward castes (no mention of reservation for backward castes).			

18. UTTAR PRADESH & UTTARAKHAND: THE UTTAR PRADESH MUNICIPAL CORPORATION ACT, 1959

Mayor Reservation of seats for	Direct	Five years	Corporation; Ward Committees;

Reservation	Election	Term of office	Authorities
SC, ST, and backward castes in the same proportion as their population is the proportion of the total population of the Municipal Corporation; Reservation for backward castes capped at 27 per cent of the total number of offices of Mayor; One-third of the total number of seats reserved for women belonging to the castes mentioned above; and One-third of the total number of unreserved seats to be reserved for women.			Executive Committee of the Corporation; Mayor; Development Committee of the Corporation; Municipal Commissioner; One or more Additional Municipal Commissioners; and In case the Corporation establishes or acquires electricity supply or public transport undertaking or other public utility services, such other committee(s) with previous approval of the State Government.

19. Uttar Pradesh & Uttarakhand: The Uttar Pradesh Municipalities Act, 1916

Reservation	Election	Term of office	Authorities
President Reservation of seats of President in Municipal Council and Nagar Panchayat the same as in Municipal Corporations.	Direct	Five years	Not provided

Reservation	Election	Term of office	Authorities
20. WEST BENGAL: WEST BENGAL MUNICIPAL CORPORATION ACT, 2006			
Mayor Reservation of seats for SC, ST, and Backward castes in the same proportion as their population is the proportion of the total population of the Municipal Corporation; One-third of the total number of seats reserved for women belonging to the castes mentioned mentioned above; and One-third of the total number of seats including the seats reserved for women belonging to SC & ST castes, reserved for women.	Indirect	Five years	Corporation; Mayor-in-Council; and Mayor
21. WEST BENGAL: WEST BENGAL MUNICIPAL ACT, 1993			
Chairman-in-Council Reservation of seats for SC, ST, and Backward castes in the same proportion as their population is the proportion of the total population of the Municipal Corporation; One-third of the total number of seats reserved for women belonging to the castes mentioned above; and One-third of the total number of seats including the seats reserved for women belonging to SC & ST castes, reserved for women.	Indirect	Five years	Municipality; Chairman-in-Council; and Chairman

ANNEX IX

IMPLEMENTATION OF 74TH CONSTITUTION AMENDMENT ACT

TABLE 1: DEVOLUTION OF FUNCITONS TO THE URBAN LOCAL SELF-GOVERNMENT IN VARIOUS STATES & UNION TERRETORIES

Reforms	Pre-Jn-NURM (Before December 2005)	Post Jn-NURM (After December 2005)	In Progress	Significantly in Progress	Not Done	Applicable/ Not Committed
Transfer of 12th Schedule Functions	08 Chhattisgarh, MP, Gujarat, Kerala, Maharashtra, Bihar, Tripura, West Bengal		14 Chandigarh, Himachal Pradesh, Uttarakhand, Manipur, Nagaland, Jharkhand, Andhra Pradesh, Puducherry, Punjab, Haryana, Sikkim, Arunachal Pradesh, Mizoram, Jammu & Kashmir	06 Tamil Nadu, Karnataka, Orissa, Assam, Rajasthan, Uttar Pradesh		1 Meghalaya
Constitution of DPC	11 Chhattisgarh, West Bengal, Maharashtra, MP, AP, Orissa, Assam, Bihar, HP, Kerala, Rajasthan	03 Tamil Nadu, Karnataka, Gujarat	12 Chandigarh, Uttarakhand, Manipur, Nagaland, Puducherry, Punjab, Haryana, Tripura, Arunachal Pradesh, Mizoram, Jammu & Kashmir	01 Uttar Pradesh	02 Jharkhand, Sikkim	2 Meghalaya

Constitution of MPC	01 West Bengal	2 Maharashtra, Gujarat	8 Chandigarh, Madhya Pradesh, Andhra Pradesh, Tamil Nadu, Karnataka, Rajasthan, Mizoram, Punjab,		3 Jharkhand, Haryana Uttar Pradesh	15 Himachal Pradesh, Uttarakhand, Manipur, Meghalaya, Nagaland, Chhattisgarh, Kerala, Orissa, Arunachal Pradesh, Assam, Jammu & Kashmir, Mizoram, Sikkim, Tripura, Puducherry
Transfer of city planning function	8 Gujarat, Assam, Himachal Pradesh, Chhattisgarh, Madhya Pradesh, Maharashtra,	2 Andhra Pradesh, Karnataka	10 Chandigarh, Uttarakhand, Manipur, Kerala, Puducherry, Sikkim, Tripura,	1 Rajasthan	8 Nagaland, Jharkhand, Punjab, Orissa, Haryana, Mizoram,	

contd.

Table 1 contd.

Reforms	Pre-Jn-NURM (Before December 2005)	Post Jn-NURM (After December 2005)	In Progress	Significantly in Progress	Not Done	Applicable/ Not Committed
	Tamil Nadu, West Bengal		Arunachal Pradesh, Bihar, Jammu & Kashmir		Uttar Pradesh, Delhi	
Transfer of Water Supply and Sanitation	11 Madhya Pradesh, Gujarat, Bihar, Chandigarh, Chhattisgarh, Haryana, Maharashtra Himachal Pradesh, Punjab, Tamil Nadu, West Bengal	1 Uttar Pradesh	12 Uttarakhand, Andhra Pradesh, Kerala, Puducherry, Orisa, Rajasthan, Sikkim, Tripura, Arunachal Pradesh, Assam, Mizoram, Jammu & Kashmir		6 Manipur, Meghalaya, Nagaland, Jharkhand, Karnataka, Delhi	

Notes: 1. 74th CAA is not applicable in Meghalaya.

2. Constitution of MPC is not applicable in Arunachal Pradesh, Assam, Himachal Pradesh, J&K, Manipur, Meghalaya, Mizoram, Nagaland, Orissa, Sikkim, Tripura, Uttarakhand, Puducherry

Source: Grant Thornton, *Appraisal of Jawaharlal Nehru National Urban Renewal Mission (Jn-NURM)*, Final Report, Vol. I, March 2011.

TABLE 2: STATUS OF IMPLEMENTATION OF THE 74TH CONSTITUTION AMENDMENT ACT IN STATES

State	Constitution of Urban Local Bodies and Election	Transfer of Functions under 12th Schedule	Constitution of District Planning Committee	Constitution of Metropolitan Planning Committee
Andhra Pradesh	Yes	No	Yes	No
Arunachal Pradesh	Yes	No	Yes	Not Applicable
Assam	Yes	No	Yes	Not Applicable
Bihar	Yes	No	Yes	No
Chhattisgarh	Yes	Yes	Yes	Not Applicable
Goa	Yes	No	Yes	Not Applicable
Gujarat	Yes	Yes	Yes	No
Haryana	Yes	No	Yes	No
Himachal Pradesh	Yes	Yes	Yes	Not Applicable
Jammu & Kashmir	Yes	Yes	Yes	Not Applicable
Jharkhand	Yes	Yes	Yes	No
Karnataka	Yes	No	Yes	Yes
Kerala	Yes	Yes	Yes	Not Applicable
Madhya Pradesh	Yes	Yes	Yes	No
Maharashtra	Yes	Yes	Yes	Yes
Manipur	Yes	No	Yes	Not Applicable
Meghalaya	Yes	Yes	Yes	Not Applicable
Mizoram	Yes	No	Yes	Not Applicable
Nagaland	Yes	No	Yes	Not Applicable
Orissa	Yes	Yes	Yes	Not Applicable
Punjab	Yes	Yes	Yes	Yes
Rajasthan	Yes	No	Yes	Yes
Sikkim	Yes	No	Yes	Not Applicable
Tamil Nadu	Yes	No	Yes	Yes
Telangana	Yes	No	Yes	No
Tripura	Yes	No	Yes	Not Applicable
Uttar Pradesh	Yes	No	Yes	No
Uttarakhand	Yes	No	Yes	Not Applicable
West Bengal	Yes	No	Yes	Yes

Source: Annexure to the information provided by the Union Minister of Urban Development in the Rajya Sabha on 31 July 2014 in reply to Question Number 2426.

TABLE 3: THE SAMPLE CBUD PROJECT CITIES AND THE STATES/UNION TERRITORY WITHIN WHICH THESE CITIES ARE LOCATED

State/Union Territory	Name of the Cities
Assam	Guwahati
Andhra Pradesh	Guntur, Visakhapatnam
Chhattisgarh	Raipur
Goa	Panaji
Gujarat	Bharuch
Haryana	Kurukshetra, Yamuna Nagar
Himachal Pradesh	Shimla
Jammu & kashmir	Jammu
Jharkhand	Ranchi
Karnataka	Hubli-Dharwar
Kerala	Kollam
Madhya Pradesh	Dewas, Chhindwara
Maharashtra	Sholapur, Nagpur
Odisha	Cuttack, Patna
Rajasthan	Udaipur
Sikkim	Gangtok
Uttarakhand	Dehradun, Haridwar
Uttar Pradesh	Allahabad, Varanasi
West Bengal	Siliguri
Chandigarh	Chandigarh

TABLE 4: DEVOLVING OF TWELFTH SCHEDULE FUNCTIONS TO URBAN LOCAL SELF-GOVERNMENTS IN SOME OF THE STATES

State/Union Territory	Function(s) not Devolved	Agency Presently Performing the Funciton
Assam	Urban planning including town planning	Urban Development Authority
	Regulation of land-use and construction of buildings	Urban Development Authority
	Planning for economic and social development	Urban Development Authority
	Roads and bridges	Public Works Department, ULB, Urban Development Authority
	Water supply-domestic, industrial and commercial	
	Water supply-domestic, industrial and commercial	Jal Board
	Fire services	
Andhra Pradesh	Urban Planning	State Fire Services Preparation of Master Plan: Urban Development Authority; Implementation: ULB & Urban Development Authority
	Fire services	Andhra Pradesh Fire Service Department
	Urban forestry, protection of environment and ecology	State Forest Department
Chhattisgarh	Urban planning including town planning	Preparation of Master Plan: Urban Development Authority and State TCPD
	Water supply-domestic, industrial, and commercial	Public Health Engineering Department
	Urban forestry, protection of environment and ecology	State Forest Department
	Slum improvement and up-gradation	DUDA and RMC
	Urban poverty alleviation	DUDA and RMC
Goa	Urban planning including town planning	North Goa Planning and Development Authority

contd.

Table 4 contd.

State/Union Territory	Function(s) not Devolved	Agency Presently Performing the Funciton
	Regulation of land-use and construction of buildings	(NGPDA) and TC P Department of
	Planning for economic and social development	Government of Goa NGPDA and TCPD
	Water supply-domestic, industrial, and commercial	GoG and NGPDA
	Fire services	PWD Department of Fire and Emergency Services, GoG
	Urban forestry, protection of environment and ecology	
	Slum improvement and up-gradation	Forest Department, GoG CCP
	Urban poverty alleviation	CCP
	Provision of urban amenities and facilities-parks, gardens, and playgrounds	CCP
	Promotion of cultural, educational, and aesthetic aspects	Goa Educational Development Corporation, GoG
	Public amenities including street lighting, parking lots, bus stops, and public conveniences	Goa State Electricity Board, Kadamba Transport Corporation
Gujarat	Urban Planning including town planning	Preparation of Master Plan: Urban Development Authority. Implementation —BMC
Haryana	Urban Planning	State Town Planning Department
	Regulation of land-use and construction of buildings	State Town Planning Department
	Socio-economic planning	Development Board, duly approved by District Planning Committees which have representations from ULBs

contd.

Table 4 contd.

State/Union Territory	Function(s) not Devolved	Agency Presently Performing the Funciton
	Roads and bridges	Public Works Department
	Water supply	Public Health Engineering Department
	Public health, sanitation and SWM	Public Health Engineering Department
	Fire services	Municipal Council
	Urban forestry	Forest Department
Himachal Pradesh	Urban Planning including town planning	Town and Country Planning Department
	Regulation of land-use and construction of buildings	Town and Country Planning Department
	Planning for economic and social development	Town and Country Planning Department
	Water supply-domestic, industrial and commercial	Irrigation and Public Health Department
	Fire services	State Department
	Urban forestry, protection of environment and ecology	State Forest Department
Jammu & Kashmir	Urban Planning including town planning	Urban Development Authority, Town Planning Organisation
	Water supply-domestic, industrial and commercial	Public Health Department
	Fire services	Fire Department
Jharkhand	Urban Planning including town planning	Preparation of Master Plan: by Regional Development Authority (RDA) and ULSG in Corporations (there is no clarity among staff on managing the function)
	Regulation of land-use and construction of buildings	RDA
	Fire services	Jharkhand Fire Department
	Urban forestry, protection of environment and ecology	State Forest Department

contd.

Table 4 contd.

State/Union Territory	Function(s) not Devolved	Agency Presently Performing the Funciton
Karnataka	Urban planning including town planning	Urban Development Authority
	Regulation of land-use and construction of buildings	Urban Development Authority
	Water supply-domestic, industrial, and commercial	Karnataka Urban Water & Sewerage Board
	Urban Planning including town planning	Town and Country Planning Department (TCPD)
Kerala	Urban Planning including town planning	Town and Country Planning Department (TCPD)
	Regulation of land-use and construction of buildings	Regulations are formulated by TCPD and implemented by Municipal Corporation.
	Water supply-domestic, industrial and commercial	Kerala Water Authority
	Fire services	Fire & Rescue Department
	Urban forestry, protection of environment and ecology	Forest & Wild Life Department
Madhya Pradesh	Urban Planning including town planning	Department of Town and Country Planning, GoMP
	Regulation of land-use and construction of buildings	Department of Town and Country Planning, GoMP
Maharashtra	Urban planning including town planning	Preparation of Master Plan: by Improvement Trust, Urban Development Authority, State Town Planning Department—NIT Implementation by ULB, Improvement Trust, Urban Development Authority
	Urban forestry, protection of environment and ecology	ULB and State Forest Department

contd.

Table 4 contd.

State/Union Territory	Function(s) not Devolved	Agency Presently Performing the Funciton
	Slum improvement and up-gradation	ULB and Slum Rehabilitation Authority
Odisha	Urban Planning including town planning	Development Authority
	Regulation of land-use and construction of buildings	Development Authority
	Planning for economic and social development	Development Authority
	Water supply-domestic, industrial and commercial	Public Health Department
	Public health, sanitation, conservancy and SWM	Public Health Department
	Fire services	Home (Civil Defense) Department, GoO
	Urban forestry, protection of environment & ecology	Forest & Environment Department, GoO
Rajasthan	Urban Planning including town planning	Preparation of Master Plan by Town Planning Department Implementation by ULSG & Urban Improvement Trust
Sikkim	Urban Planning including town planning	Urban Development Authority
	Regulation of land-use and construction of buildings	Urban Development Authority
	Planning for economic and social development	Urban Development Authority
	Fire services	Fire Directorate of Department of Home
	Burials and burial grounds, cremations, cremation grounds and electric crematoriums	Primarily by Urban Development & Housing Department (UD&HD)
	Vital statistics including registration of births and deaths	Department of Health Care, Health Services & Family Welfare Department
	Public amenities including	ULSG: Car parking;

contd.

Table 4 contd.

State/Union Territory	Function(s) not Devolved	Agency Presently Performing the Funciton
	street lighting, parking lots, bus stops and public conveniences	Markets UD & HD: Foot-path, Side-walks, Over bridges, Beautification Energy & Power Department: Street Lighting
	Regulation of slaughter houses and tanneries	Department of Animal Husbandry & Veterinary Services
Uttarakhand	Urban Planning including town planning	Dehradun Development Authority
	Regulation of land-use and construction of buildings	Dehradun Development Authority
	Water supply-domestic, industrial and commercial	Uttarakhand Jal Sansthan & Jal Nigam
	Fire services	Police Department
	Urban forestry, protection of environment and ecology	Forest department
Uttar Pradesh	Urban planning including town planning	Urban Development Authority
	Regulation of land-use and construction of buildings	Urban Development Authority
	Planning for economic and social development	Urban Development Authority
	Fire services	Police Department
	Urban forestry, protection of environment and ecology	ULSG in consultation with the State Forest Department
	Safeguarding the interests of weaker sections in the society including the handicapped and mentally retarded	District Urban Development Authority and Municipal Corporation
	Slum improvement and up-gradation	DUDA and ULSG
	Urban poverty alleviation	DUDA and ULSG
	Fire services	Police Department
West Bengal	Urban Planning including	Within KMA by ULSG.

contd.

Table 4 contd.

State/Union Territory	Function(s) not Devolved	Agency Presently Performing the Funciton
	town planning	Outside KMA by State TCPD
	Water supply-domestic, industrial and commercial	PHED-Construction and maintenance City Water Supply Department: Monitoring of services Mechanical Department: Maintenance of the pumps
Chandigarh	Urban Planning including town planning	UT Administration of Chandigarh
	Urban Planning including town planning	UT Administration of Chandigarh
	Urban Planning including town planning	UT Administration of Chandigarh
	Urban Planning including town planning	Union Territory Administration of Chandigarh
	Urban Planning including town planning	Union Territory Administration of Chandigarh
	Urban forestry, protection of environment and ecology	Union Territory Administration of Chandigarh

Source: CBUD Project, Ministry of Urban Development, http://jnnurm.nic.in/rapid-baseline-assessment-of-cbud-city.html

TABLE 5: AVERAGE POPULATION FOR SOME OF THE WARDS COMMITTEES

Name of the ULBs	Population (2011)	Number of Wards Committees	Average population
Delhi	1,10,07,835	12	9,17,320
Pune	31,15,431	13	2,39,649
Greater Mumbai	1,24,78,447	24	5,19,935
Nagpur	24,05,421	10	2,40,542
Kolkata	44,86,679	14	3,20,477
Chennai	46,81,087	10	4,68,109
Bangaluru	84,25,970	24	3,51,082
Bhopal	17,95,648	14	1,28,261
Jabalpur	10,54,336	11	95,849
Lucknow	28,15,601	11	2,55,964
Varanasi	12,01,815	14	85,844
Siliguri	5,09,709	5	1,01,942
Kochi	6,01,574	6	1,00,262
Nashik	14,86,973	6	2,47,829
Kanpur	27,67,031	11	2,51,548

Source: Number of Wards Committees collected from the cities concerned and the population for the cites from the Census of India, 2011.

TABLE 6: STATUS OF CONSTITUTION OF DISTRICT PLANNING COMMITTEE IN STATES AND UNION TERRITORIES

State/Union Territories	Status	Remarks
Andhra Pradesh	Not yet constituted	Law enacted in 2005; guideline issued for functioning of DPCs in 2007
Arunachal Pradesh	Not yet constituted	
Assam	Not yet constituted	DPC constituted, guidelines issued for functioning of DPC in 2007
Bihar	Constituted	DPC constituted but guidelines not issued
Chhattisgarh	Constituted	–
Goa	Constituted	–
Gujarat	Not yet constituted	–
Haryana	Constituted	DPC constituted, guidelines issued by the Urban Local Government Department
Himachal Pradesh	Constituted	DPC constituted; guidelines not issued
Jharkhand	Not yet constituted	–
Karnataka	Constituted	DPC constituted, guidelines issued and DPC functioning. District plan prepared by the Chief Planning Officer, Zila Panchayat, there is separate district budget in Annual Plan of the State. Paucity of staff hindering preparation of perspective plan
Kerala	Constituted	DPC constituted, guidelines issued and DPC functioning. District plan prepared by the Chief Planning Officer, Zila Panchayat, there is separate district budget in Annual Plan of the State. Paucity of staff hindering preparation of perspective plan

contd.

Table 6 contd.

State/Union Territories	Status	Remarks
Madhya Pradesh	Constituted	–
Maharashtra	Constituted	Guardian Minister of the Districts are Ex-officio Chairpersons
Odisha	Constituted	Ministers are Chairpersons
Punjab	Not yet constituted	–
Rajasthan	Constituted	Chairpersons of District Panchayats are the Chairpersons. DPC constituted and District Plans prepared for the 11th Plan and Annual Plans
Sikkim	Constituted	–
Tamil Nadu	Constituted	Chairpersons of District Panchayat are Chairpersons of DPCs
Tripura	Not yet constituted	–
Uttar Pradesh	Not yet constituted	Law for DPC enacted
Uttaranchal	Not yet constituted	Law for DPC enacted
West Bengal	Constituted	–
Andaman & Nicobar	Constituted	–
Chandigarh	Not yet constituted	–
Dadara & Nagar Haveli	Constituted	–
Daman & Diu	Constituted	–
Lakshadweep	Constituted	–
Puducheri	Not yet constituted	–

Source: Collected from various sources including the study conducted by PRIA (2009) and https://en.wikipedia.org/wiki/District_planning_committees_in_India (viewed on 29 August 2015).

TABLE 7: NUMBER OF METROPOLITAN CITIES IN DIFFERENT STATES

State/Union Territorry	Number of Metropolitan Cities	Name of the Metropolitan Cities
Andhra Pradesh	2	Vishakhapatnam, Vijaywada
Bihar	1	Patna
Chandigarh	1	Chandigarh
Chhattisgarh	2	Raipur, Durg-Bhilainagar
Delhi	1	Delhi
Gujarat	4	Ahmedabad, Surat, Vadodara, Rajkot
Haryana	1	Faridabad
Jammu & Kashmir	1	Srinagar
Jharkhand	3	Jamshedpur, Dhanbad, Ranchi
Karnataka	1	Bangaluru
Kerala*	7	Kochi, Kozhikode, Thrissure, Malappuram, Thiruvananthapuram, Kannur, Kollum
Madhya Pradesh	4	Indore, Bhopal, Jabalpur, Gwalior
Maharashtra	6	Mumbai, Pune, Nagpur, Nashik, Vasai-Virar, Aurangabad
Punjab	2	Ludhiana, Amritsar
Rajasthan	3	Jaipur, Jodhpur, Kota
Tamil Nadu	4	Chennai, Coimbatore, Madurai, Tiruchirapalli
Telengana	1	Hyderabad
Uttar Pradesh	7	Kanpur, Lucknow, Ghaziabad, Agra, Varanasi, Meerut, Allahabad
West Bengal	2	Kolkata, Asansol
Total A	53	
B. CITIES THAT MARGINALLY MISSED THE METROPOLITAN STATUS		
Haryana		Gurgaon (9,01,968)
Karnataka		Mysore (9,83,893); Hubli-Dharwar (9,43,857)
Maharashtra		Solapur (9,51,118)
Tamil Nadu		Tirupur (9,62,982); Salem (9,19,150)
Uttar Pradesh		Bareilly (9,79,933); Aligarh (9,09,559)
Total B	8	
Grand Total	61	

Notes: (i) * According to the revised definition of urban agglomeration in Kerala.
(ii) Numbers in parentheses denote population in 2011.

Source: Census of India, 2011.

TABLE 8: SANCTIONED AND VACANT POSITIONS IN SOME OF THE URBAN LOCAL SELF-GOVERNMENTS

City	State	Sanctioned Positions	Existing Positions	Vacant Positions	Vacant Positions as % of Sanctioned Positions
Udaipur	Rajasthan	2,247	1,353	894	60.21
Visakhapatnam	A.P.	3,982	3,140	842	21.15
Shimla	H.P.	1,280	1,174	106	8.28
Hubli-Dharwar	Karnatataka	3,794	2,153	1,641	43.25
Nagpur	Maharashtra	12,507	9,260	3,247	25.96
Chhindwara	M.P.	238	169	69	28.99
Kollum	Kerala	315	278	37	13.31
Yamuna Nagar	Haryana	936	657	279	29.81
Varanasi	U.P.	3,930	2,573	1,357	34.53
Allahabad	U.P.	3,920	3,142	778	19.85
Solapur	Maharashtra	5,385	4,503	882	16.38
Bharuch	Gujarat	526	262	264	50.19
Chandigarh	U.T.	5,204	3,787	1,417	27.23
Cuttak	Odisha	1,705	1,206	499	29.27
Dehradun	Uttarakhand	1,074	993	81	7.54
Haridwar	Uttarakhand	759	528	231	30.43
Dewas	M.P.	794	658	136	17.13
Jabalpur	M.P	4,201	3,420	781	18.59
Jammu	J & K	1,709	1,542	167	9.77
Kurukshetra	Haryana	258	149	109	42.25
Panaji	Goa	413	403	10	2.42
Puri	Odisha	719	403	316	43.95
Ranchi	Jharkhand	1,339	707	632	47.20
Raipur	Jharkhand	3,392	2,123	1,269	37.41
Guntur	A.P	1,677	475	1,202	71.68
Total		62,304	45,058	17,246	27.68

Source: RBA Reports, CBUD Project, Ministry of Urban Development, http://jnnurm.nic.in/rapid-baseline-assessment-of-cbud-city.html

ANNEX X

TABLE 1: CAPACITY INDICATORS OF CITIES

Cities	Urban Planning & Design	Urban Capacities & Resources	Empowerment Legitimate Political Representation	Transparancy, Accountability & Participation
Ahmedabad				
2013	2.5	2.5	3.2	1.5
2014	2.2	3.5	5.2	2.9
2015	2.4	3.2	4.0	2.6
Bangalore				
2013	2.9	0.9	1.9	3.0
2014	2.6	1.4	2.8	4.4
2015	2.7	2.5	2.5	5.4
Chennai				
2013	2.2	2.2	4.1	2.9
2014	2.7	2.1	4.8	3.1
2015	2.9	3.3	5.6	2.8
Delhi				
2013	3.9	2.9	2.2	1.2
2014	2.4	2.2	4.1	2.4
2015	3.7	4.3	3.7	2.9
Hyderabad				
2013	2.9	2.1	2.6	4.4
2014	2.7	1.5	3.3	4.0
2015	2.9	2.4	3.3	5.7
Jaipur				
2013	2.5	2.4	4.5	1.2
2014	2.4	2.3	5.7	2.7
2015	2.6	1.9	4.6	2.2
Kanpur				
2013	2.8	1.8	4.0	3.1
2014	2.4	1.9	4.4	3.9
2015	2.6	2.5	4.3	4.9
Kolkata				
2013	4.2	2.0	4.3	2.9
2014	2.8	3.6	8.9	2.9
2015	3.0	3.3	5.9	4.1

contd.

Table 1 contd.

Cities	Urban Planning & Design	Urban Capacities & Resources	Empowerment Legitimate Political Representation	Transparancy, Accountability & Participation
Mumbai				
2013	2.6	2.7	3.8	3.3
2014	2.4	4.0	4.6	2.9
2015	2.5	5.3	4.6	4.5
Pune				
2013	0.7	2.6	3.8	3.2
2014	1.8	3.3	5.3	3.6
2015	1.9	4.7	5.1	4.6
Surat				
2013	2.5	2.4	3.2	1.4
2014	2.2	3.2	5.2	3.5
2015	2.4	3.5	3.8	2.79.8
New York				
2013	8.8	9.9	9.4	8.9
2014	10.0	10.0	8.3	8.8
2015	9.8	10.0	10.0	8.8
London				
2013	8.8	8.1	9.3	8.1
2014	10.0	10.0	10.0	8.3
2015	9.4	9.9	10.0	8.2

Note: The Survey covered only 11 cities with New York and London as the benchmark cities when the Annual Survey of India's City Systems (ASICS) began in 2013. Though the number of cities increased to 21 in the subsequent Surveys, with an interest in observing changes in the four city systems over time, this Table contains the same cities that were included in ASICS the first time.

Source: Janaagraha Centre for Citizenship and Democracy, Bangalore.

TABLE 2: SANCTIONED AND VACANT POSITIONS IN SOME OF THE URBAN LOCAL SELF-GOVERNMENTS

Name of the ULSG	State	Number of Sanctioned Positions	Number of Vacant Positions	Vacant Positions as % of Sanctioned Positions
Guntur	Andhra Pradesh	1,677	1,202	71.68
Visakhapatnam	Andhra Pradesh	3,982	842	21.15
Raipur	Chhattisgarh	3,392	1,269	37.41
Bharuch	Gujarat	526	264	50.19
Panaji	Goa	413	10	2.42
Yamuna Nagar	Haryana	936	279	29.81
Shimla	Himachal Pradesh	1,280	106	8.28
Kurukshetra	Haryana	258	109	42.25
Ranchi	Jharkhand	3,392	1,269	47.20
Jammu	J & K	258	109	9.77
Hubli-Dharwar	Karnataka	3,794	1,641	43.25
Kollum	Kerala	315	37	11.75
Solapur	Maharashtra	5,385	882	16.38
Nagpur	Maharashtra	12,507	3,247	25.96
Dewas	Madhya Pradesh	794	136	17.13
Chhindwara	Madhya Pradesh	238	69	28.99
Jabalpur	Madhya Pradesh	4,201	781	18.59
Cuttack	Odisha	1,705	499	29.27
Puri	Odisha	719	316	43.95
Udaipur	Rajasthan	2,247	894	39.79
Allahabad	Uttar Pradesh	3,920	778	19.85
Varanasi	Uttar Pradesh	3,930	1,357	34.53
Dehradun	Uttarakhand	1,074	81	7.54
Haridwar	Uttarakhand	759	231	30.43
Chandigarh	Union Territory	5,204	1,417	27.23
Total	–	62,304	17,246	27.68

Source: Ministry of Urban Development, Rapid Baseline Survey Reports, CBUD Project, http://jnnurm.nic.in/rapid-baseline-assessment-of-cbud-city.html.

Index